THE MANNIX ERA

Melbourne Catholic Leadership 1920-1970

Patrick Morgan

Connor Court Publishing

Published in 2018 by Connor Court Publishing Pty Ltd.

Connor Court Publishing Pty Ltd.
PO Box 7257
Redland Bay QLD 4165
sales@connorcourt.com
www.connorcourtpublishing.com.au

National Library of Australia Cataloguing-in-Publication entry.

Author: Morgan, Patrick, 1941-

Title: The Mannix Era: Melbourne Catholic Leadership 1920-1970
/ Patrick Morgan.

ISBN: 9281925826166

Notes: Includes bibliographical references and index.

Subjects: Catholic Church. Archdiocese of Melbourne (Vic.). Archbishop Mannix
(1917-1963).
Catholic Church--Victoria--Melbourne--History.
Catholics--Victoria--Melbourne--History.
Religion and politics--Victoria--Melbourne--History.

Cover Design by Maria Giordano.
Cover illustration: Benediction at Mt St Evin's Hospital, 1934 Eucharistic Congress.

Printed in Australia.

CONTENTS

Abbreviations v

List of Illustrations vii

Preface ix

Between the Wars

1 The Situation in 1920 3

2 The Early 1920s: Ireland Ablaze 27

3 The Late 1920s: Calm Before the Storm 49

4 The Early 1930s: The Campion Society 73

5 The Late 1930s: Catholic Action 95

The War Years

6 The Early 1940s: The Movement 121

The Post-war Years

7 The Late 1940s: Secret Struggles 147

8 The Early 1950s: The Great Split 169

9 The Late 1950s: The Vatican Verdict 191

10 The Early 1960s: The Death of Dr Mannix 215

11 The Later 1960s: The Second Vatican Council 239

12 Epilogue 261

Acknowledgements 279

Bibliography 281

Index 291

ABBREVIATIONS

ACF   Australian Catholic Federation
ACTS   Australian Catholic Truth Society
ACTU   Australian Council of Trade Unions
AIF   Australian Imperial Force
ALP   Australian Labor Party
ANA   Australian Natives Association
ANSCA   Australian National Secretariat for Catholic Action
APM   Australian Paper Manufacturers
ASIO   Australian Security Intelligence Organization
AWOL   Absent Without Official Leave
CA   Catholic Action
CBC   Christian Brothers College
CBD   Central Business District
CIS   Commonwealth Investigation Service
CMC   Catholic Migration Committee
CSIRO   Commonwealth Scientific & Industrial Research
        Organization
CSSM   Catholic Social Studies Movement
CPA   Communist Party of Australia
CWO   Catholic Welfare Organization
CWGV   Catholic Woman's Guild of Victoria
CYMS   Catholic Young Men's Society
DLP   Democratic Labor Party
DSO   Distinguished Service Order
ISO   Institute of Social Order
JOC   Jeunesse Ouvrière Chrĕtienne (Young Catholic Workers)
KC   King's Counsel
MCC   Melbourne Cricket Club
MCG   Melbourne Cricket Ground
MDHC   Melbourne Diocesan Historical Commission

MMBW	Melbourne & Metropolitan Board of Works
Mons.	Monsignor
NLA	National Library of Australia
NCGM	National Catholic Girls Movement
NCRM	National Catholic Rural Movement
NUI	National University of Ireland
NCC	National Civil Council
PM	Prime Minister
QC	Queen's Counsel
RMIT	Royal Melbourne Institute of Technology
RSL	Returned and Servicemen's League of Australia
SJ	Society of Jesus (Jesuits)
THC	Trades Hall Council
UAP	United Australia Party
UCFA	University Catholic Federation of Australia
VC	Victoria Cross
VFA	Victorian Football Association
YCS	Young Catholic Students
YCW	Young Christian Workers

LIST OF ILLUSTRATIONS

1 The Catholic dioceses of Victoria in 1920   x

2 The Italian influence: Pelligrini's showroom in the 1930s   xi

3 Newman College at the University of Melbourne   8

4 Archbishop Mannix, close to the crowd, addresses his flock   10

5 *The Advocate* all-rounder Patrick O'Leary   19

6 The main altar of St Francis' church after it became
a Eucharistic shrine   24

7 Maurice Buckley, back right, with fellow winners of the
Victoria Cross   28

8 Archbishop Mannix, Eamon de Valera and Bishop Foley
of Ballarat   33

9 Corpus Christi College, Werribee, opened in 1923   39

10 T.M. Burke and his wife, left, with Archbishop Mannix   47

11 Archbishop Mannix leads Australian Holy Year pilgrims   50

12 St Patrick's Day procession through Melbourne streets in
1925   55

13 At a garden party at St Mary's Hall in 1928   61

14 The dressing room at St Vincent's Hospital in the 1920s   67

15 James Scullin centre, with Frank Brennan   74

16 Denys Jackson spoke regularly on the 'Catholic Hour'   82

17 Archbishop Mannix's favourite photograph of himself   89

18 The Papal Legate to the Congress, Cardinal MacRory   93

19 Paul McGuire, an early exponent of Catholic Action   98

20 The US folksinger Burl Ives and Rev. Dr Percy Jones   109

21 The staff of *The Advocate* and other Catholic organizations   111

22 The pre-Vatican interior of St Mary's West Melbourne   116

23 Archbishop Kelly of Sydney separates two rivals   130

24 Archbishops Simonds and Mannix give nothing away   131

25 The radiologist Prof. Arthur Schüller   136

26 The army chaplain Fr Alo Morgan celebrates Mass   141

27 Arthur Calwell married Elizabeth Marren 149

28 John Cain senior, Labor Premier of Victoria 153

29 Archbishop Beovich, Bishop Lyons and Bishop Stewart 159

30 The Children's Mass at the Exhibition Building 163

31 Schoolchildren form a living rosary at the MCG 172

32 Title page of a book of Joseph O'Dwyer's poetry 178

33 John Wren, the central figure in *Power Without Glory* 180

34 A dinner in April 1953 to welcome overseas visitors 186

35 Fr Eric D'Arcy and B.A. Santamaria are awarded M.A. degrees 194

36 Dr Mary Glowrey in her early years 202

37 Santamaria and Archbishop Mannix together 203

38 One year's intake of Christian Brothers in Melbourne, 1960 211

39 Dr Andrew Brenan, a link with the hospital's founding 218

40 'Jesus, Mary and Joseph', a bronze plaque by Hans Knorr 225

41 The achievements of senior student George Pell 229

42 Archbishop Simonds meets the Belgian Cardinal Cardijn 233

43 The post-Vatican II interior of St Francis Xavier Church, Prahran 248

44 The medical pioneers Drs Evelyn and John Billings 253

45 Archbishop Knox greets Mother Teresa of Calcutta in Melbourne, 1972 256

46 The Cathedral block in 1929, showing St Patrick's without its spires 260

47 A longevity and dedication to match Mannix's – Fr Henry Johnston, SJ 264

48 The distribution of Catholics 267

PREFACE

1920 was the year Mannix moved on to the international stage. He roused audiences in the United States on Ireland's behalf, he was dramatically arrested at sea by a British destroyer, and was received in Rome by a Pope surprisingly sympathetic to Ireland's plight. Throughout his long career Mannix assessed local affairs from a world perspective. We are blinded by the dust of present controversies; Mannix saw events though the distant mirror of the past, which brings them into clearer focus. He had just witnessed the sudden collapse at the end of the first world war of the Russian, Austro-Hungarian and Ottoman empires, and the humiliation of the recently formed German nation. Like the historians Spengler and Toynbee who were similarly affected by these events, Mannix formed a view of history as a vast panorama of nations successively rising and falling. Ireland's extended travail could more easily be understood, though not excused, from this perspective. This attitude merged in him with the accumulated wisdom the Catholic Church instills in its grandees. The deep religious disposition of *vanitas vanitatum* (the futility of human endeavour), evident in the strain of resignation and remoteness in Mannix's personality, underlay these worldly perspectives.

An earlier work, *Melbourne Before Mannix*, took the story of Melbourne Catholicism up to 1920. Catholic public leadership in the next half century is the focus of the present book, which covers the main actors, organizations, events and issues in the archdiocese from 1920 to 1970. It is as much a social and political history of the archdiocese as an institutional one. The geographical focus in on metropolitan Melbourne, an area smaller than that covered by the archdiocese, which encompasses country regions beyond Melbourne, including Geelong, Bacchus Marsh, Castlemaine, Mansfield, and Westernport. The narrative begins with the activities of those born in the decades before 1900 and therefore reaching old age by 1970, through to the generation born between the wars, which came to maturity in the decades after the Second World War.

THE DIOCESES
OF VICTORIA
C.1900

SOUTH AUSTRALIA

DIOCESE
OF
BALLARAT

DIOCESE
OF
SANDHURST

BENDIGO

ARCHDIOCESE
OF
MELBOURNE

DIOCESE
OF
SALE

BALLARAT

MELBOURNE

BASS   STRAIT

OCEAN

1 The Catholic dioceses of Victoria in 1920. (MDHC)

The Catholic Church in Sydney was led for almost a century, 1884 to 1971, by Cardinal Moran, Archbishop Kelly and Cardinal Gilroy, all of whom spent formative years in Rome before their Sydney appointments. Archbishops Carr and Mannix who ruled in Melbourne for a similar period, from 1887 to 1963, were in contrast trained as leaders at the Maynooth seminary in Ireland. They formed the church in Melbourne more in an Irish than a Roman mould. As a result the style of Catholicism practiced in NSW and Victoria differed markedly. Sydney leaders emphasized personal piety and deference to the views of the hierarchy. In Melbourne, a public-spirited and independently minded lay community was encouraged. The practices of Catholicism were passed on by parents, parish priests and the teaching orders.

The Irish leadership of the Melbourne church was plain for all to see, but it masked another reality: the influence, through the many orders and congregations who ministered here, of continental Catholicism. Famous earlier European orders like the Benedictines, Franciscans, and Dominicans were an important presence with naturally high profiles. By 1940 half the priests in Melbourne were not diocesan clergy but from religious orders, all of whom had their own *esprit de corps* and distinctive forms of piety, which derived

x

from their European origins. Of the fifty religious orders operating in Melbourne, only a small minority were not founded in continental Europe – the Christian Brothers and the Presentation, Brigidine, Mercy and Charity sisters began in Ireland, and the Josephite and Good Samaritan sisters began in Australia.

French and Italian influence was important in Melbourne as well as the overt Irish one. The church in France had to rebuild itself after the devastation of the French Revolution, and the inroads made by secular, often anti-clerical, governments which arose in its wake. The new orders founded in France in the nineteenth century who came to Melbourne included the Salesian, Oblate and Blessed Sacrament orders of priests, the Marist and De La Salle Brothers, the Sacre Coeur, Cluny, Loreto, Poor Clares, FCJ, Our Lady of Sion and Little Sisters of the Poor sisters, and the Society of St Vincent de Paul. They brought among others things Jansenism (disdain for worldly things), and the teaching of French and music in schools. Italian orders included the Capuchin, Pallottine, Redemptorist and Scalabrinian fathers and the Cabrini sisters. Italian influence was evident in Baroque church interiors, plaster statues, religious processions in public, devotions to the Sacred Heart and the Blessed Sacrament, and the wearing of scapulars and medals on ribbons.

2 The Italian influence: Pelligrini's showroom in the 1930s. (MDHC)

Some of these continental orders were established here via their Irish houses, but their religious *forma mentis* was not predominantly Irish – Ireland was one filter through which European Catholicism reached Australia. During its long period of domination by England, Ireland had been sustained by its contact with Europe. Irish aspirants to the priesthood had to secretly proceed to ordination in France, until England allowed seminaries in Ireland at the end of in the 18th century. Even the Irish Jesuits who came here in the 1920s had undergone their higher training on the continent. The Irish influence in the Melbourne church, strong in 1920, declined gradually over the next half century, as Irish immigration slowed to a trickle and home-grown priests replaced Irish ones, and as events in Ireland itself went off the boil. By 2000 few Irish-born priests could still be heard at Sunday sermons; one of them, Fr Jeremiah Coffey, Rector of the seminary at Clayton, was appointed Bishop of Sale in 1989, the last Irish bishop here.

Between the wars English Catholicism had a growing profile, with the Chesterbellocians, plus a string of high profile conversions from Anglicanism, and the influence of thinkers like Fr Martindale SJ, Mons. Ronald Knox, and Fr Martin D'Arcy SJ. Prominent preachers like Bishop Fulton Sheen and Fr Peyton came from the USA. Ireland was no longer playing a leading role; the Irish apparition of the Virgin at Knock could not compete with the continental cults at Lourdes and Fatima. For these reasons Melbourne Catholicism absorbed a much wider dose of European Christian civilization than that provided by Ireland alone. The Catholic Church was multicultural centuries before the recent Canadian invention of the term.

Dr Mannix's public reputation was shaped by his first and last decades in Australia. In the years from 1913 to 1923 he was a leading figure in the pressure group, the Australian Catholic Federation, and in political controversies over the Easter rebellion, conscription, and the Anglo-Irish and Irish civil wars. In the years from 1953 to 1963 he was again a leading figure in political controversies over Communism, the Movement, and the split in the Labor Party and its long aftermath. Both these earlier and later episodes were, unusually in Australian political life, generated by international events.

An enormous amount has been written about both periods, in which Mannix is regarded as pre-eminently a political figure. These issues remain important, but this book includes other times, like the neglected interwar years, important figures other than Mannix, and the church's and Mannix's non-political initiatives.

In both his early and later years in Australia Mannix operated through Catholic Action organizations. These arose because the Catholic Church in Europe in the 19th century felt itself pushed to the margins of society, a role unfamiliar to it. From the time of the Enlightenment liberal and secular ideas, anathema to the church, held increasing sway. Separation of church and state meant the Catholic hierarchy could not throw its weight around on public issues as it had in the past. With the Papal document the 'Syllabus of Errors' of 1864 the church had set its face firmly against modern ideas. As a result it continued to lose the allegiance of many communities, including much of the industrializing working classes of Europe. The depression of the 1890s caused widespread poverty and misery, and a seeming inability of the structures of Western society to cope. A new comprehensive Catholic approach to these social deformations was called for. Pope Leo XIII attempted to have the church's voice heard again in the public domain with his ground-breaking encyclical *Rerum Novarum* of 1891, which offered an account of the social evils of the time, and a series of possible solutions to them.

Capitalism and Socialism/Communism were in the church's view the twin evils confronting society. The former gave too much power to the business class, and latter too much to the state, which replaced the role of God as all-seeing arbiter. To protect the ordinary citizen from power being centralized, decisions should be taken at the lowest possible level, and private property protected. Capitalism could become as rapacious as Socialism and Communism unless controlled by joint worker-employer bodies, with harmonious rather than antagonistic relations between the two groups the desirable norm. Workers had the right to receive a just wage and to form unions to advance their interests. Early in the 20th century the Vatican formulated these ideas into a program of organized activity which it called Catholic Action (CA), lay bodies under episcopal direction designated to carry out Christianising tasks in society. As the hierarchy was unable, because church and state were now separate, to directly enter the political realm, such Catholic lay organizations could influence the key institutions of society with the Church's message of a more equitable organization of the polity. This activity was called a 'lay apostolate', apostles being those sent out to evangelize others. This was a form of renewal for the Catholic Church in modern times, ending its marginalization in the public square.

This story has four heroes: Dr Mannix, the Archdiocese itself, its weekly newspaper *The Advocate*, and the well organized Catholic community. Over the half century Mannix never surrendered his pre-eminence; when Gerald Lyons interviewed him in his 98th year his faculties remained unimpaired. The Archdiocese and *The Advocate* experienced a golden age in the 1920s and 1930s, but in the decades after the Second World War the leading components of the archdiocese faltered under the pressure of events. Arising out of all the details in this study is a meta-narrative. It is the story of a triumph and a tragedy, the story of a Catholic archdiocese in which initiatives were encouraged, to become under Dr Mannix the most energetic in Australia, a self-aware community with high participation rates. It went further ahead in the 1930s with the ground-breaking Campion Society, which led in turn to the founding of an Australia-wide Catholic Action organization in 1938, but it all, suddenly and unexpectedly, came to a shattering crash with the great Labor split of the mid 1950s, in which Catholic Melbourne blew much of its religious and political capital, forfeiting in the process its leading role.

The split of the 1950s was viewed by the wider world as pre-eminently a political event, but for the Melbourne Catholic community it was just as much a religious and social one. This catastrophe so disoriented Catholics that they had trouble picking up the shattered pieces and facing with equanimity new events such as the Second Vatican Council, the permissive sixties, contraception, and the Vietnam War and other geo-political dislocations. As many of these later developments involved attitudes to Communism and to religion, they tended to be read in the light of allegiances forged by the split, which caused further confusions and misinterpretations. The Labor

Party reorganized as it had further election campaigns to fight, the rest of Australia continued its normal activities, non-Catholic Melbourne did not see the split as a paramount issue, but for Melbourne Catholics, hit front and centre and with no escape, it was an explosive event whose dire effects remained for decades, with family networks fractured, and (apart from the Liberal Party) no winners.

BETWEEN THE WARS

1

THE SITUATION IN 1920

Suburban Layout – Archdiocesan Profile – Tribal Chieftain – State and Federal Politics – Prominent Melbourne Catholics – Patrick O'Leary – Ecclesiastical Suppliers – Religious Practices

Suburban Layout

Melbourne is a flat city situated on a coastal plain bisected by the Yarra and Maribyrnong rivers. Studley Park hill is one of the few elevated spots where one can get a view of the inner city. Formed and enclosed by a winding arm of the Yarra River are Richmond and Collingwood, working-class manufacturing suburbs in the 1920s with a high Irish Catholic component; the Richmond flats near the Chapel Street bridge were in earlier days known as Irishtown. The Jesuit St Ignatius' Church on Richmond hill hovers above the suburb. A Vaucluse Convent was attached to the parish, a Catholic technical school was opened by the Christian Brothers at Abbotsford in 1893, and the De La Salle Brothers took over the parish boys' school in 1926. Irish Catholic families like the Loughnans, O'Connells and Cremeans dominated Richmond local politics; Collingwood was a John Wren fiefdom.

By 1920 Melbourne's Catholics were spread out through the whole city. Their distribution in the various regions of the city can be understood through the Catholic school system. Clustering just north of the central business district and close to the cathedral was a group of old, inner secondary schools: St Patrick's Jesuit College, the Mercy Academy, Catholic Ladies College and Parade CBC. These schools catered for students from the inner suburbs, for those further out in the western and northern suburbs, which had few secondary schools, and for students from the eastern suburbs whose parents couldn't afford the more prestigious Catholics schools in their own region. Students travelled in to these schools each day on

Melbourne's transport system which radiated out from the centre. In addition Christian Brothers' students completing their secondary education travelled from all over the city to St Kevin's College, then situated in the grounds of Parade CBC in Victoria Parade, East Melbourne. In 1920 outstanding Matriculation results were obtained by John X. O'Driscoll, Bernard Stewart and William Aughterson, who later reached the top of their professions as judge, bishop and professor of education respectively.

The north western suburbs, from North Melbourne running out along the spine of Mount Alexander Rd to Essendon and beyond had, with the adjacent Brunswick-Coburg area, the highest concentration of Catholics; North Melbourne's population was one-third Catholic in the 1890s. This had come about because immigrant Irish Catholics had first found employment in the North Melbourne livestock and transport hub: the meat market, the Spencer Street railway station, the Eastern Market, Kirk's Horse bazaar, the Newmarket cattle saleyards, the racecourse and abattoirs of Flemington, the Harbour Trust, and associated industries. Catholics in the north-west area were serviced by St Joseph's CBC and St Aloysius' Convent in North Melbourne, the Sisters of Charity's St Columba's Convent in Essendon, and the Good Samaritan Sisters at Santa Maria in Northcote.

Beyond the escarpment of the Yarra and contrasting with the suburbs below it were a cluster of eastern suburbs, Kew, Hawthorn, Malvern, Toorak and Camberwell, the domain of the middle-class business and professional classes. Here, though Catholic numbers were lower than average, the largest collection of Catholic secondary schools was situated – the Jesuit Xavier College on its prominent rise in Kew and its sister school Genazanno Convent, as well as Kilmaire Convent in Hawthorn, De La Salle College and Kilbreda Convent in Malvern, Mandeville Hall in Toorak, and Sacre Coeur in Glen Iris. Some schools were based on mansions which Catholic teaching orders had the resources to buy up after the crash of the 1890s. The Xavier College chapel, the Sacred Heart Church in Kew and St Dominic's Church in Camberwell are all on high ground and can be seen for miles. Channelling the prejudices of Barry Humphries'

Protestant Camberwell parents, Dame Edna Everage lamented about the Catholics: 'You've got to give it to them – they always get the best positions!'

South of the Yarra, and situated in class terms between the poorer north-western and wealthier eastern suburbs, was a Catholic wedge stretching from CBC St Kilda and Presentation Convent Windsor, through to Star of the Sea Presentation Convent, which serviced the Gardenvale-Brighton area, and further south to Kildare Convent and St Bede's Mentone. Port Melbourne and Middle Park had from early times two Carmelite parishes and a collection of Catholic institutions, including Kilbride College at Albert Park. The Christian Brothers opened their second technical school at South Melbourne in 1925.

Archdiocesan Profile

The archdiocese's basic statistics reveal it was continuing its healthy expansion; any downturn caused by the 1890s depression had been balanced by the movement of people from country to city.[1]

	1890	1900	1910	1920
Parishes	28	46	57	28
Diocesan priests	59	89	113	59
Religious priests	21	33	38	21
Brothers	25	32	54	25
Nuns	233	520	851	233
Primary schools	83	114	107	83
Secondary schools	11	39	36	11
Primary School pupils	n/a	n/a	n/a	n/a
Secondary school pupils	n/a	n/a	5058	n/a
Total pupils	14,781	21,918	25,369	35,438

Unlike other religions, the Catholic Church established a primary school in each parish. Primary schools naturally dominated over secondary schools at this stage. Diocesan priests outnumbered those in orders by three to one; by 1940 the numbers were equal as new

---

[1] Archdiocesan statistics are taken from the relevant yearbooks of the *Australasian Catholic Directory*.

orders arrived in Melbourne. The combined number of male clerics was only a third of that of religious sisters, whose expansion was spectacular, as they operated in schools, hospitals and other charitable institutions. Irish immigrants had a higher proportion of women than other groups; for them the principal vocations apart from marriage were domestic service, nursing, secretarial positions and the church. Catholic charitable institutions included four orphanages, several charity homes, two foundling homes, six homes for the destitute and neglected, and two hospitals.

The Catholic population of Victoria increased over the decade from 1910 to 1920, but its proportion dropped to just over 20% because migration from Ireland had dried up, and conversely immigration from Britain was picking up after the First World War. To counter this fall Mannix in his speeches urged Catholics to marry young – too many married late or not at all, he complained. To achieve this we needed, Mannix argued, less birth control and more immigration. Unused land should be unlocked and we required a much bigger population to fill up the continent. Not enough southern and northern Europeans were being sought, too much preference being given to British Empire types. Mannix did not favour the White Australia policy, and spoke out against capital punishment. Mannix also tried to stimulate Australian national consciousness. We should, he argued, put Australia first, manufacture our own goods, fly our own flag, and be confident of ourselves: 'Australians did not realize that Australia was a nation that fought her way to a place among the nations'. The subtext of this Mannix agenda was that we should not be so beholden to Britain.

Prominent Catholic societies included the Catholic Young Men's Society, the Australian Catholic Truth Society, the Australian Catholic Federation and the Newman Society at the university. The Celtic Club, the Hibernians, the St Patrick's Society and the Irish Ireland League catered for Irish Australians, but were not formally Catholic institutions. The CYMS developed debating and public leadership skills in school leavers, and encouraged its members to participate in civic bodies such as the Australian Natives Association. It also sponsored social and sporting activities, running competitions for cricket, tennis and Australian Rules football teams, the latter sport being particularly strong – no equivalent binding force existed in the Sydney organization. The CYMS formed young Catholics in middle level occupations into a leadership cadre; Federal Labor Ministers such as James Scullin and Frank Brennan received their initial training in it. The Hibernians, a medical and social benefits society, had in earlier times supported Irish nationalist aspirations. In 1911 it had founded the Australian Catholic Federation (ACF), which became the vehicle into which Catholic political energies, mainly on State Aid, were channelled, but the Hibernians themselves became more moderate, avoiding political stances.

Fr Matthew Egan SJ, a pioneering Catholic sociologist who had studied at Louvain, published an ACTS pamphlet outlining Catholic attitudes to society. In 1921, helped by the CYMS President Michael Chamberlin, he founded a Social Studies Club as an offshoot of the CYMS. The designation 'Social Studies' indicated a need to investigate problems before taking action to alleviate them; this was a first step in an endeavour which was to become a preoccupation during the 1930s. To provide a route for Catholics into the professional and business strata of society, St Kevin's College at Matriculation level and Newman College at the University of Melbourne were both founded in 1918. In the same year St Mary's Hall in Parkville, conducted by the Loreto Sisters, began as a women's hostel affiliated to Newman College. (It became St Mary's College, a university college, when established on the Newman College grounds in 1966.) A meeting point for Catholic seeking to further their faith and education was the Catholic Reference (later Central) Library which began in 1924, an idea of the recently arrived Fr William Hackett SJ, himself a student of Catholic ideas about society. The books Hackett selected, and his own stimulating presence, lifted the level of enquiry; the library became a club and a sorting house of ideas, a precursor to the Campion Society of the 1930s. In 1919 Michael Chamberlin had been instrumental in founding a Victorian branch of the Knights of the Southern Cross with the help of Fr Lonergan, the CYMS spiritual director. The Knights' purpose was to assist Catholics in business and employment, and to combat sectarian discrimination.

3 Newman College at the University of Melbourne, founded in 1918 for
tertiary education for Catholic men. (MDHC)

In the early 20th century the large Melbourne Irish Catholic
community was consolidating itself as a self-conscious network.
This process was reinforced by an increased number of available
marriage partners, by the church's dislike of mixed marriages, and
by the flow-on from the successful anti-conscription campaigns.
Between the wars there was a small but constant immigration of
Italian Catholics, some of whom assimilated by marrying into the
Irish Catholic majority; the town of Koo Wee Rup, for example, was
for the most part a mixture of Irish and Italian. A small group of
Maronite Catholic families from Syria/Lebanon, with surnames like
Khyat, Callil, Amad and Fakhry, arrived in the first decade of the
20th century to escape trouble in their homeland. One of the first
to arrive was Peter Callil, who had no money and no English. After
some small jobs he opened a store in Melbourne, and eventually
formed the flourishing textile firm of Latoof and Callill. The Maronite
chaplain was Fr Namaar, born at Mt Lebanon in Syria, who died
in 1920, at a time when his flock was diminishing, as its members
were assimilating and in some cases marrying local Catholics. A
group of Spanish families from Catalonia came to Melbourne in
the late nineteenth century, some settling in the suburb of Surrey
Hills. The most prominent of these was the Parer family. Michael

Parer, born about 1860, arrived in the mid 1870s and became the proprietor of Parer's Crystal Café in Melbourne, and the father of the aviator Raymond Parer, who in 1920 with John McIntosh was the first to fly a single-engine plane from England to Australia. Another member of the family, John Parer, was the father of the famous war photographer Damien Parer.

Tribal Chieftain

Dr Mannix was aware that Australian Catholics, living in a nation formed by Britain, had an inferior place in society and often responded by acting deferentially in public. His actions during the conscription referenda had forcibly asserted the Catholic case and in doing so had drawn Catholics out of their parochial ways and into the public sphere. But the sectarian strife which his actions engendered had on the other hand reinforced in many minds the idea that Catholics were not to be fully trusted as loyal citizens. Mannix continued his own leadership through his many addresses on current issues, particularly on the situation in Ireland, and by encouraging his flock to ignore prejudice against it. Every morning he read the newspapers avidly, and had his speeches, which he delivered without notes, clearly worked out in his mind beforehand. This was shown when on one occasion an *Advocate* reporter missed a Mannix panegyric; when approached next day, Mannix was able to repeat the speech almost word for word. He spoke each week at functions like Communion breakfasts, blessings of new churches, school openings, fetes and bazaars, old boys' gatherimgs, evening meetings of societies, and school speech nights. He was careful to speak on these occasions outside the church building, so he could not be accused of mixing religion and politics. One person who heard Mannix speak praised his style:

> In calm unhurried phrases he spoke with never an attempt at flights of oratory. His clear, cultured, rather resonant voice was itself a pleasure to hear. His language was simple and direct, his reasoning logical, and his conclusions irresistible.[2]

Mannix's religious homilies at 8am Sunday Mass at the cathedral

---

[2] Rev. Walter Ebsworth, *Archbishop Mannix*, p. 286.

were described by a listener as 'gems, quietly and beautifully spoken, and extremely practical', but unlike his public speeches their content went unrecorded.

4 Archbishop Mannix, close to the crowd, addresses his flock. (MDHC)

Mannix regretted that on occasions during his public addresses unfortunate phrases escaped his lips before they had been processed through his mind. His talks, which were usually not on directly religious questions, took on a familiar pattern, opening in a low key with a few gently humorous remarks about the occasion, with his audience gathered densely around him and on side. He would then seamlessly move into the main topic of the day, protesting he was not going to take sides, asking only for tolerance for his views, just as he was tolerant of others. He would then illustrate in a ridiculing manner some of the contradictions in his protagonists' views, then move up a gear into a full-blown, though lightly delivered, demolition of his opposition, where his own views became clear by contrast. He was slyly, in spite of his earlier words, taking sides. He would begin by saying he was not going to talk on politics, then talk at length on it, he would say he would not distinguish between the Free Staters and Republicans in Ireland, and then end up backing de Valera.

The rapturous way Melbourne's Irish Catholics received Mannix's speeches and the way he was in turn energized by their support revealed a close, symbiotic relationship. He did not speak *at* his flock, admonishing them, like some bishops in the past; on the contrary he faced the other way, speaking on their behalf to a wider public, which made them sympathetic to him. Mannix's role was to give public expression to the deep but unformulated grievances of his people. Eamon de Valera was often quoted as saying: 'If I wish to know what the Irish are thinking, I look into my own heart.' Similarly with Mannix, whose insights came as much from his own deep intuitions as from book knowledge.

If Mannix was a tribal chieftain, who precisely was his tribe? The Ireland Australia got was not the whole of Ireland – the Ireland we got was predominantly Munster, the south-west quarter, the province least subdued by London and Dublin governments. A deep Irish civilization was preserved there as a resistance culture, the *Hidden Ireland* of Daniel Corkery. Many of the great Irish nationalists of the 19th century came from Munster: the 'Liberator' Daniel O'Connell, Archbishop Croke, Michael Collins, Eamon de Valera, as well as Mannix himself. Some Melbourne Catholic lawyers had as their favourite recreational reading Maurice Healy's classic *The Old Munster Circuit,* which is based on the difference between officious Dublin lawyers and cunning Munster locals. Mannix used his subtle, deadpan Munster humour to corrode the dignity of the powerful. In Melbourne he felt at home speaking to his Munster own and their descendants, who instinctively understood his idiom – scorn of imperial pretensions was in their DNA.

In the decade 1913 to 1923 Ireland was in a state of continual revolutionary turmoil. Many Melbourne Catholics were deeply affected, as Ireland was the source country to which they looked. In addition they had a leader, the Irish Archbishop Mannix, who was first a partisan and then in 1920 a participant in these events. Instead of giving Ireland the Home Rule it had promised at the end of the war, the British imposed martial law. In response 73 Sinn Fein candidates, elected to Irish seats in the British Parliament in 1918, formed an Irish parliament, known as the Dáil, in Dublin in 1919. Eamon de Valera, a hero in the local Catholic press, was elected President of the first Dáil, which aimed for self-determination for

Ireland. At the same time Irish irregulars began attacking British-controlled barracks around the country, skirmishes which soon degenerated into the Anglo-Irish war (also known as the Black and Tan war, or the war of independence), which ended in the signing of the Treaty in December 1921. Melbourne Catholics, informed by Mannix, followed these momentous events closely, as they held out hope of ending seven centuries of British rule in Ireland.

State and Federal Politics

Mannix encouraged Melbourne Catholics to be active in public life, but here Catholics were at a disadvantage in contrast to Sydney. In supporting the London and Australian strikes of the early 1890s, Cardinal Moran formed a permanent alliance between Catholics and Labor. The Labor vote was strong in regional NSW coal mining areas. By 1920 NSW Labor had been in office for six years, with 45% of its membership Catholics, plus two thirds of its caucus. So many leading Labor figures were Catholics that the conservative Nationalists raised the sectarian bogey by accusing the NSW Catholic Church of being 'officially' behind the Labor Party.

In contrast the Victorian ALP was inhospitable territory for Catholics. The party, strongly influenced by the Victorian Socialist Party, was dominated by a left-secularist faction. In the countryside the gold miners' organization, the Australian Mining Association, was evangelical, mildly anti-Catholic and liberal rather than Labor oriented in its politics. A gerrymander in favour of county seats made it harder for Labor to gain office; the Victorian ALP was much more an urban party. Even after the Hughes Protestant group's walkout of the Labor Party in 1917 over conscription, only about 20% of the Victorian ALP caucus was Catholic. By 1920 the Labor Party in Victoria had never been in power (except for an impotent two week period in 1911). Because its radical views were unacceptable to the electorate at large, not just to Catholics, it had a miserable election record. Its most recent historian, Paul Strangio, has called his book on the Victorian branch *Neither Power Nor Glory*.

The Labor Party was important for Catholics, since it was only through it that they could aspire to political office, the conservative parties not being available to them at this juncture. In the seven decades from 1900 to 1970, the NSW Labor Party was in office for forty years, 57% of the time, a remarkable achievement, with the Queensland ALP's record being even better. Sydney and Brisbane Catholics therefore saw political advancement almost as a birthright. In the same 70 year period Victorian Labor was in office for eight years, 12% of the time, an abysmal performance. This long period of non-Labor state rule afforded little scope for Victorian Catholic political ambitions. As a result an anomalous situation obtained here: Catholics who had been energized by Carr and Mannix to engage in the public realm and trained by the CYMS and ACF to do so, were frustrated. No wonder explosive tensions built up. In February 1920 Mannix said in a speech:

> Those who are ashamed or afraid of association with Catholics are no democrats at all...I do not say this with any desire to injure the Labour Party: quite the reverse. The Labour Party must rid itself of sectarianism, if indeed it be infected with sectarianism. The Labour Party does not belong to non-Catholics any more that it belongs to Catholics. It belongs to all equally.

A letter writer to *The Advocate* in June 1920 lamented:

> As a member of the Labour Party I regret that the Catholics as a body have never made an attempt to cleanse the Party of the undesirable element that has wormed its way into the internal workings of the Party...Once the extreme section of the Party, which is hostile to every church, succeeds in capturing the Party, it will be too late to effect reforms.

These sentiments reveal that both factions, the radical secular socialists and the Catholics, treated the Victorian Labor party with some disrespect, as an object to be taken advantage of, a situation still prevailing in the 1940s and 1950s. As a result of their relative weakness in the Labor movement at the time, Melbourne Catholics were forced, unlike their Sydney and Brisbane counterparts, to devote their main energies to Catholic organizations rather than political ones. The result was a tight-knit Melbourne Catholic family network of extraordinary strength.

The Federal Labor MPs whom Hughes took with him when he walked out of the Labor caucus in November 1916 formed a new conservative coalition, which was naturally enough a mostly Protestant group. This departure meant the relative position of Catholic forces in the Labor movement was stronger in the interwar years. But this advantage did not show up immediately since the Catholic forces in the Victorian Labor movement were still in a minority position. Arthur Calwell and Patrick Kennelly joined the ALP during the first years of the First World War. By the end of that war Catholics were still to some extent on the outer in public opinion. Australia's participation in the First World War was seen as a triumph for the British Empire, a view to which returned servicemen naturally contributed strongly. This social marginalization was compounded by the lack of a Catholic voice in politics. Some discrimination against Catholics in the workplace was evident in the first half of the twentieth century. The prestigious *Age* newspaper for example did not generally employ Catholics till the 1960s, though some slipped through, like the leader writer Benjamin Hoare, a convert, whom the owner David Syme favoured because of Hoare's strong protectionist views.

Billy Hughes and his conservative coalition continued to rule in the Federal parliament. His particular animus to Mannix was on display in his 1918 memorandum to the British Government: 'Had anyone else dared to say the things he has said, he would have been interned or deported long ago'. Britain's Foreign Secretary Arthur Balfour wrote in the same year to the British representative at the Vatican that the Australian Government 'cannot permit his [Mannix's] activities to continue. They will be forced to allow the law to take its course unless the Vatican recall him. He is liable to arrest at any moment'.[3] With Ireland being devastated during the Anglo-Irish War of 1919-1921, the ALP was now looked on more favourably by Catholics, as it backed the Irish striving for freedom, while the Nationalists and other conservative parties didn't. Before Mannix left for his overseas trip in 1920, he was guest of honour at a meeting of the St Joseph's North Melbourne CBC Old Boys. The

---

[3] *The Real Archbishop Mannix From the Sources*, ed. James Franklin et al., p. 18.

toasts to him on that occasion were moved by Arthur Calwell (then 24 years old) and Nicholas McKenna (25). Over four decades later in the 1960s these two were the leaders of the Federal Parliamentary Labor Party in Canberra, but were not so inclined to toast Mannix after the split.

Prominent Melbourne Catholics

In 1899 Fr John Barry had come out from Ireland (he was a Corkman like Mannix), and proved himself able at finance and administration. He was Administrator and Chancellor of the Archdiocese, appointed to these positions in March 1917, in the last months of Archbishop Carr's life. Mannix habitually kept these two posts, plus those of Vicar General and Dean of St Patrick's, in the hands of one or two senior priests. When Fr Barry was appointed Bishop of Goulburn in 1924, Dean Carey was appointed Vicar General. In 1913 Carey had to vacate St Mary's West Melbourne for the incoming coadjutor Mannix. Mannix closed the Catholic monthly magazine of ideas, *Austral Life,* in 1920, partly because he had recently bought the weekly Catholic journal *The Advocate*. In 1920 its managing editor was Fr W.M. Collins, parish priest of Kew; he was replaced by Fr Francis Moynihan in 1925. *The Advocate,* whose office was at that time located behind St Francis' Church in the city, assumed a more important role because, in addition to reporting events, it now, with the demise of *Austral Life*, carried the longer articles produced by Catholic opinion formers. Its wide coverage included labour and industrial matters; country, interstate and overseas news; weekly letters from Rome, Dublin and London; and sections on women's and children's interests edited by the author Marion Miller Knowles, whose novels were serialized in its pages. It covered the main activities in the suffragan dioceses of Sandhurst (Bendigo), Ballarat and Sale.

As well as publishing the paper The Advocate Press handled commercial and social printing orders, produced memoriam cards and published books. *The Advocate's* reputation remained high, as its tone was low key and reasonable. It was considered the best Catholic newspaper in Australia, being widely read in other states, though it had closer clerical control than the earlier *Advocate* and *Austral Light*. As a weekly journal it was both a retailer of news and a clearing house of information – these roles made it the glue which enabled an expanding archdiocese to cohere and converse with itself. Its writers were embedded in the Catholic community, reflecting as well as reporting it. The shorter *Tribune*, with Fr Mangan as managing editor from 1913 to 1924, remained an independently owned Catholic weekly newspaper of record more than comment, directed at the lower middle and working classes. It was more concerned with daily bread-and-butter matters, and workplace concerns like employment, wages and industrial relations, and closer to the Labor movement.

Melbourne Catholics were encouraged to be conscious of their history. Francis Mackle ran a series on the early church in Victoria in *The Advocate* from 1920, eventually published by the Advocate Press in 1924 as *The Footprints of Our Catholic Pioneers*. The centenary of the first priest officially practising in Australia, Fr Therry, was celebrated in 1920, as was the jubilee of St Ignatius' Church Richmond. John Carmody, aged 84 in 1920, was the only participant at Melbourne's first Mass in 1839 still alive. From London James Hogan, originally from Geelong and author of the first history of the Irish in Australia, wrote occasional articles on Australian church history based on his researches in England. In 1920 *The Advocate* published obituaries of two important figures in the Archdiocese's past: the Dublin-born City of Melbourne Councillor George Ievers, who had arrived in goldrush Melbourne as a boy in 1855 and became involved in many public organizations, and Dr Nicholas O'Donnell, Australia's authority on Irish language and literature, and its leading advocate of Irish nationalism. In 1925 Mr T. Landrigan, President of the Irish Foresters, reminisced on the St Patrick's Society, founded in 1842, an organization described as the 'cradle of Irish sentiment in Victoria'. He recalled its pioneers including Edmund Finn ('Garryowen)', the early Premier Sir John O'Shanassy, the stonemason Peter Jageurs, and Joseph Winter, owner-manager of *The Advocate*, who had died in 1915.

Melbourne Catholics were attached to the past and dutiful to its famous dead. They loved celebrating jubilees, centenaries and other anniversaries. With so many organizations, churches, schools, orders and clergy, there always seemed to be a commemoration on the horizon. They were not living in the past, it was simply that for a recent immigrant group the past ensured stability, and provided a perspective on the present and future. This was admirable, but at times the immense weight of Catholic and Irish tradition could become disabling. Tradition and renewal need to go together. Some attitudes that were natural in the 1920s, such as having the parish as the prime focus of one's life, were not as sensible, or even possible, by the 1970s. The long reign of Mannix meant the process of turning over ideas slowed down; as a consequence the *aggiornamento* of Vatican II, announced a year before his death, came as something of a shock.

Many figures from Archbishop Carr's time, including the authors Marion Miller Knowles and Fr J.J. Malone, the organizer Dr Leo Kenny, the activist Dr Gerald Baldwin, William McMahon (a founder of both the ACF and *The Tribune*), the Labor politicians Frank Brennan and James Scullin, and the bookseller William Linehan, continued to be active in the inter-war years, with Scullin rising to be Prime Minister. A typical networker was Edward Adams from North Melbourne, an executive member at various times of the CYMS, the Hibernians, the Catholic Workers Association and the ACF. Three of his children entered the religious life, and he was in addition an uncle of Bishop Arthur Fox, whose own family had many religious. Count Thomas O'Loughlin was a generous donor to charities; his family's fortune derived from his uncle Martin O'Loughlin who had amassed his wealth in nineteenth century Australia.

The inter-war decades witnessed the rise of a new group of Catholic public figures, but only a handful, apart from Mannix himself, were to be prominent for the whole period from 1920 to 1970. Notable among them were Arthur Calwell and Michael Chamberlin, who had first come to public notice together in 1919 as secretary and treasurer of the radical pro-Sinn Fein lobby, the Irish Ireland League of Victoria. But they were to be protagonists on opposite sides of the great Labor split in the 1950s. By 1920 Arthur Calwell (b. 1896) had already been secretary of both the Melbourne branch of the ALP and the State Service Clerical Association. Michael Chamberlin (b. 1891), also a member of the Victorian public service, was seconded in 1918 to the State War Council, and in 1921 was president of the CYMS.

The future priest and musicologist Percy Jones came from a Geelong musical family, his father Percy Jones senior being bandmaster of St Augustine's Geelong and a music teacher. His sister was a prominent singer and his brother Basil a violinist. Young Percy first appeared, with photo, at the age of six in *The Advocate* in 1920 as the youngest Geelong candidate to sit for the Royal Academy of Music exams. His father, who advertised his services as a music teacher in *The Advocate*, kept the paper's readers informed of his son's progress. Percy junior, an outstanding student at CBC Geelong, was precocious, having met Percy Grainger by the age of ten. He learnt from his father not only music, but how to keep himself in the public eye. Fr Henry Johnston SJ (b. 1888), who arrived from Ireland in 1923, was to argue the Catholic case in public in a seemingly endless series of talks and writings over six decades. In contrast to the measured Fr Johnston, the ebullient journalist and polemicist Denys Jackson (b.1899), who arrived from England in 1926, covered world politics with an output which exceeded even that of Fr Johnston. All five figures were still in the public eye in 1970.

Patrick O'Leary

The Advocate staff in the early 1920s included its managing editor Fr Collins and news editor Harry Minogue. In 1920 Patrick Ignatius O'Leary, born in 1888, formerly from South Australia, was appointed to its staff to write on literary topics. O'Leary had worked in the bush as a Labor organizer where he absorbed the mixture of radical unionism and bush mateship nationalism in vogue at the time. Married at Broken Hill to Mary Slattery, with whom he had four children, he had no fixed profession and was selling silver polish at the Victoria market after he first arrived in Melbourne. O'Leary had a love of learning, read extensively, and was a self-taught thinker, with a naturally curious cast of mind and an encyclopaedic memory.

He mixed in Melbourne in artistic and literary circles, being friends with Vance Palmer, Frank Wilmot and C.J. Dennis, and had poems published in the *Bulletin,* and articles in the *Triad* and *Lone Hand* periodicals. O'Leary composed a poem on the legacy of the Easter week martyrs: 'For speed you are still as a stone,/For speech your tongues have no word,/But the flame of your feet runs on,/ And your silent voices are heard.'

5 *The Advocate* all-rounder Patrick O'Leary. (MDHC)

O'Leary soon ran in *The Advocate* a serialized novel *A Glimmer of Gold* by J.M. Walsh, educated at Xavier College and a prolific author (over 50 books) of popular crime and adventure novels, some set in Australia and the South Seas. His father was T.P. Walsh, a frequent contributor on Irish affairs, a Gaelic scholar, and a council member of the ACF. Less understandable was the appearance of O'Leary's friend, the novelist Vance Palmer, to write a weekly column on foreign affairs. Palmer and his wife, Nettie, who did some book reviewing on O'Leary's Literary Page, were prominent in the dominant socialist-left faction in the Labor Party against which the Catholics were battling at the time. They did not last long on *The Advocate*. O'Leary revealed himself no sympathizer with Communism. In reviewing a book on the Russian Revolution by the early Australian Communist leader Robert Ross, he wrote presciently: 'It may be that out of all this welter of warring movements some Napoleonic figure shall emerge to ride the whirlwind and direct the storm and destine the world to a Caesarism, for which history has no parallel', an accurate prophecy of the rise of Stalin.

From 1921 onwards O'Leary put together in each issue of *The Advocate* its Literary Page, as well as providing a miscellany of materials from a wide range of sources. By the later 1920s he was running two literary pages plus book notes, poetry selections and other snippets. His 'Memories and Musings' column was based on browsing through the files of early *Advocate* issues. He wrote thousands of words a week for decades with enviable fluidity, gradually taking over the role of literary editor from Marion Miller Knowles, who moved her material to the Ladies Page. At various stages O'Leary wrote columns under pseudonyms such 'M', 'Historicus' and 'Francis Davitt' – he was the godson of the Irish radical nationalist Michael Davitt, who had agreed to the role during his Australian visit. O'Leary became known colloquially as 'P.I.O'L', the way he signed his articles. He widened his outlook, moving to Irish and European themes as well as Australian ones, and becoming interested in the mystical thought of the French Catholic writers Charles Peguy and Leon Bloy. He was national secretary of the Self Determination for Ireland League in 1921, and later President of the Catholic Dramatic Society. He believed, naturally enough, Australian Catholics should be more interested in literature and art. He had found his metier, and a focus for his wide ranging talents.

Ecclesiastical Suppliers

Though we don't usually look at it this way, the Melbourne archdiocese, as a growing institution, was one of the biggest business organizations in the state, taking up many pages in the Melbourne telephone directory. It had a large number of practising adherents, and as a result attracted many ecclesiastical suppliers. A leading Melbourne advocate for Irish causes was Morgan Jageurs. He and his father Peter Jageurs, from Ireland with remote German ancestry, arrived in Melbourne in 1870. They were monumental stonemasons; their family business, founded in 1875, operated from Sydney Rd, Parkville. Most of the Celtic crosses in the cemetery nearby and elsewhere are their work; they also manufactured church furniture. A similar father-and-son business was Pellegrinis. Umberto Pellegrini migrated from Tuscany, and in 1890 set up a small shop in Melbourne importing the marble and painted plaster-cast statues familiar in many Australian Catholic churches, with Our Lady veiled in blue and white, and St Francis of Assisi in a brown cloak and holding a lily. Umberto's son Ulisse joined him in the enterprise, which expanded into becoming a supplier of vestments (made of lighter material for the Australian climate), and a range of devotional and ecclesiastical goods. Pellegrinis eventually had outlets in most Australian capital cities. Ulisse Pellegrini, who had moved to take charge of the family business in Sydney, received a Papal knighthood in 1947 before his death in 1950. The firm called its Melbourne premises 'The Catholic Depot'; it published the later novels of Marion Miller Knowles.

A rival firm, Louis Gille, based in Sydney, had a Melbourne outlet which called itself the 'Australian Catholic Depot'; to further differentiate itself it advertised that its church and religious accessories were locally made, not imported. There was also the Catholic Art Gallery, which sold reproductions of the great masters, and repaired rosaries. Gaunts the jewellers produced church plate, monstrances for Benediction, religious plaques, gold crosses and objects for private devotion, all made in its own workshops. Buckley & Nunns as clerical outfitters offered priests' coats, cassocks, stoles, surplices and so on. The firm of Nunans supplied church furniture and fittings, including communion rails, *prie dieux*, baptismal fonts, confessionals and pulpits. Lewis & Whitty sold oil for sanctuary lamps, Kitchens provided altar candles, and Craigs supplied altar laces, ribbons, church carpets, and soutanes and surplices for altar boys. The Jesuits from Sevenhill in South Australia produced altar wines for the Australian market. When on a shopping trip in the city a parish priest had plenty of opportunities to kit himself and fit his church out. A number of these businesses, such as *The Advocate, Tribune* and ACTS offices, and Pelligrini's shop, were situated near St Francis' Church, making the area a small Catholic precinct. The Catholic Book Depot in South Yarra sold devotional books. An even bigger market was the school one, with school books (from William Linehan booksellers and others) and school uniforms (from The Leviathan and London Stores).

Religious Practices

Though Melbourne Catholicism was more outgoing than its Sydney counterpart, practices of personal piety were the bedrock of religious belief until the 1970s, when they diminished after the Second Vatican Council. Melbourne was the home of the Jesuit devotional magazines *The Madonna* and *The Messenger of the Sacred Heart*, both edited by Fr Boylan. The church in the nineteenth century had begun a process of internal evangelization, wooing back slack members though a regimen of pious practices. The typical Catholic was familiar with prayer, Benediction, incense in thuribles, retreats, novenas, Redemptorist missions, regular Confession, fasting from midnight, the family rosary, litanies, indulgences, red sanctuary lamps, guardian angels, St Christopher medals, the catechism, prayers for the sick and the deceased, holy pictures and bereavement cards inserted into Missals, manifold devotions to Our Lady, the Sacred Heart and the Eucharist, grace before and after meals, hymns (Faith of Our Fathers, We Stand for God, Salve Regina, Hail Queen of Heaven), liturgical calendars including saints' feast days, holy water, the nativity crib at Christmas, the Angelus recitation at midday, stations of the cross, abstinence from meat on Fridays and fasting in Lent, the Nine First Fridays, and saints for specific needs (for example, St Jude hope of the hopeless, St Christopher for travellers, St Anthony for losses).

Grottoes to the Virgin or to saints were a familiar sight in convent gardens, and in older inner churches like the Sacred Heart in Carlton and St Brigid's North Fitzroy. (Ironically the most prominent Melbourne wayside shrine or cross, common in the Catholic countries in Europe, was erected in 1924 outside the High Anglican church of St Peter opposite the cathedral.) Charitable works involved alms giving, visiting hospitals and cemeteries, donating annually to Peter's Pence, and, for the wealthy, pilgrimages to Rome, Lourdes and Fatima. This network of religious practices combined individual piety and communal worship, and as a result provided the archdiocese with a dense spiritual substratum. Uniting these practices was a distinctive spirituality which, deriving from its Jansenist and Counter Reformation origins, focussed on the last things and produced fervid but troubled souls. In Australia we received an attenuated version of this through Irish Baroque, of which St Francis' was Melbourne's prime example. We were taught to think of ourselves as both sinners and penitents, who constantly fell and were saved from backsliding by a regimen of contrition, Confession, prayers to the saints, and by the imitation of Christ.[4]

The bluestone St Augustine's Church at the western end of Bourke St was important in the immigration decades of the nineteenth century, but declined as North Melbourne became the suburb where Irish Catholics settled; the church has since been used by a small congregation of locals and travellers. Melbourne has two contrasting sites of Catholic worship: St Francis' Church and St Patrick's Cathedral. St Francis' has been a focus of Catholic popular piety since the early days of the colony. Set in the valley of Elizabeth St, the lowest and most frequented part of Melbourne, it is a squat edifice squashed into its narrow block. Its atmosphere is warm, intimate, dark and communal, suiting popular religious sentiment. Associated with no famous priest, the building itself, particularly its Baroque interior, created its own personality. The church of the ordinary Catholic, it is unusual in being always busy, with a succession of daily Masses, with city shoppers 'dropping in' all the time for Confession, Benediction, novenas, rosaries and private devotions. Arthur Calwell and Pat Kennelly naturally gravitated to it when made to feel unwelcome at their own parish churches in the

---

[4] In *A Portrait of the Artist as a Young Man* James Joyce, who had experienced this type of spiritual formation and then detached himself from it, parodied sermons given at missions merely by the act of recalling them.

aftermath of the split. In 1929 the church was handed over to the care of the Blessed Sacrament Fathers, who enhanced its reputation as a centre of piety by the making it a Eucharistic shrine, with frequent Benediction, and perpetual adoration of the Blessed Sacrament. Before this change photographs of the interior of St Francis' reveal it as dark but relatively uncluttered. After it the church's crowded candlelit interior became a fairy tale extravaganza, a larger scale version of Pellegrini's showroom.

6 The main altar of St Francis' church after it became a Eucharistic shrine.
(MDHC)

One does not associate Dr Mannix with St Francis'. St Patrick's Cathedral had a history of delays, with three starts and a long construction period, being opened only in 1897, half a century after St Francis', and even then without its spires, completed in 1939 to mark the centenary of Melbourne's first Mass. The cathedral complex is located in a quiet, spacious setting occupying a whole block, and functions as an administrative centre as well as a church. High up on the Eastern Hill just outside the CBD the cathedral soars above the city, and has few local parishioners. In contrast to St Francis', St Patrick's is Gothic, filled with light, airy, austere, formal, and usually empty. Its ambience has been created by its former long term ruler, whose statue now scrutinizes those entering his domain, more than by any feature of the cathedral itself. One attends it infrequently, for Sunday High Mass, on special occasions such as weddings and funerals, and for Easter week and Christmas midnight services. The contrasting experiences of piety and exultation the two churches offered were still evident in the 1950s, as the student Josie Arnold discovered:

> At Christmas time the high altar [of St Francis'] would be decorated with silver glitter Christmas trees. The mobile congregation was made up of the most extraordinarily heterogeneous group of people. A priest was always available for confession. It was definitely high-camp low-church and I loved it. The late Masses at St Pat's drew me there, too. In that Cathedral I found the mysterium in my soul. The cold tessellated floors, the soaring fluted columns paid for by children's pennies and parishioners' goodwill, and the wonderful stained-glass windows combined with the music to feed my soul.[5]

---

[5] Josie Arnold, *Mother Superior Woman Inferior*, p. 196.

2

THE EARLY 1920S:
IRELAND ABLAZE

The Victoria Cross Controversy – Mannix's Overseas Trip – The Irish Civil War – Jesuits – Women's Organizations – Businessmen

The Victoria Cross Controversy

The Vatican had instructed Mannix to heal divisions in the Victorian community. At the St Patrick's Day march in 1920 Mannix was escorted by a guard of fourteen resplendently dressed Victoria Cross winners, a publicity stunt organized by John Wren, through which both he and Mannix hoped to gain badly needed respectability in mainstream circles. During the war Wren had sponsored sportsmen volunteering together in an endeavour to overcome his dubious reputation. It was just as cheeky for Mannix to seek credibility by posing as the army's friend now that the war was over, as he had made a number of very uncomplimentary remarks about war, militarism and the British Empire in general. Over the preceding four years Mannix had successfully brought Melbourne Catholics around to agree with him on these matters, so to now suddenly drape himself in army finery was confusing to his supporters, and a bridge too far. As Mannix and Wren were still regarded as disreputable operators by the establishment, a predictable frenzy of criticism erupted over their use of the VCs. Newspapers like *The Argus* claimed the VCs had been duped by Mannix, who replied in a speech (*The Advocate*, 15 April, 1920):

> In the mind of this clumsy [*Argus*] writer, these "gallant and distinguished soldiers" have that type of courage that may be found in the zoological gardens, but have not sufficient intelligence to know that, in the St Patrick's Day procession, they were walking after the greatest traitor in Australia. (Laughter) Mind, they had no excuse. My treason was plain

and palpable to even the dullest. (Laughter and applause) The "Argus" found it out long ago, and made no secret of it. (Laughter)

One of the VCs, Maurice Buckley, had a remarkable military career. Buckley, educated at CBC Abbotsford, had enlisted in December 1914. But he caught an infection in Egypt and was returned to the military hospital at Langwarrin, from which he went AWOL and was therefore declared a deserter. But having missed out on the Dardanelles campaign, he was keen to participate in the war, so to get back into the army he enlisted again in mid 1916 as Gerald Sexton (a combination of family names), and was sent to the Western Front in France. In an engagement after the battle of Hamel he repeatedly silenced enemy posts with his machine gun fire and then, out in the open, he sought out and destroyed a hidden gun. For this outstanding bravery he was awarded the Distinguished Conduct Medal. Later, in the attack on Le Verguier, he rushed at and destroyed a number of machine gun positions, capturing a field gun and many prisoners, for which he was awarded the Victoria Cross. As he had received the decoration under a name that did not exist, his award had to be re-gazetted under the deserter's name of Maurice Buckley before he could receive it from King George V at Buckingham Palace.

7 Maurice Buckley, back right, with fellow winners of the Victoria Cross. (MDHC)

After the war John Wren arranged employment for returning VC winners from Victoria. Buckley was allotted a position as supervisor of the gang constructing the Morwell River Road near Boolarra in the south Gippsland hills. One evening in January 1921 on leaving the Boolarra Hotel, perhaps tipsy as he mounted his horse, the war hero was challenged by his fellow drinkers to jump over the nearby railway gates. He fell in the attempt, and being seriously injured was taken to Mount St Evin's Hospital where he died some days later. Buckley had survived the horrors of the Western Front but not the Boolarra pub. Mannix, with much greater issues on his mind in England, found time to cable Wren: 'Convey deep sympathy death brave Australian soldier'. Buckley's VC medal was donated to the Vincentians at Malvern in the 1950s.

In the wake of the Victoria Cross controversy Mannix argued (*The Advocate*, 25 March, 1920):

> There are some in Australia, and possibly some of them are Irish, or of Irish descent, who would persuade you that Australia has her own problems, and that she has no time for the affairs of other countries. And yet these were the very same people who told us that we should give the last conscripted man and the last shilling for the little nations that were fortunate enough not to be Ireland (Laughter)…If your experience is like mine, you will have discovered that the Irishmen or the Irish Australians who love Ireland most, love Australia best (applause) – and that the man who is a traitor and a renegade to Ireland is a very poor Australian.

Many incidents illustrate the inflamed nature of the times. Hugh Mahon, member of Federal Parliament and former Labor foreign affairs minister, was expelled from parliament on the motion of the PM, Billy Hughes, for calling British and Empire rule 'this bloody and accursed despotism'. The renowned Irish tenor John McCormack was interrupted during a concert in Adelaide. As he sang the Irish melody 'Mother Machree' someone made a loud remark about Sinn Fein, then a section of the audience proceeded to sing the national anthem; the rest of the concert had to be cancelled. The Melbourne City Council tried to ban the 1922 St Patrick's Day march. Catholics ignored this and marched anyway. Those who were summonsed for this action took the matter to court, where the eventual ruling was that the Council had exceeded its authority – only the State government could authorize or prevent a march. When the Council retaliated next year by trying to vet the program for the St Patrick's night concert before it occurred, Mannix suggested the Council might need to see the program 'lest some seditious person might render a disloyal number or play treason on the flute'.

Mannix's Overseas Trip

In 1920 Mannix had been in Australia for seven years so his *ad limina* visit to Rome was now due. As he had already been twice reprimanded by the Vatican during the war he was in no hurry to get there. His year long 'detour' to the US and the British Isles was much longer than his brief stay in Rome. Before the trip Mannix called for self-determination for Ireland, a prospect now less likely than it had seemed. In Ireland demobbed British soldiers and other irregulars were committing frightful atrocities outside the rule of law, and the Irish responded with guerrilla attacks on British formations. In a speech on Irish prisoners on hunger strikes Mannix commented (*The Advocate*, 29 April, 1920): 'These men, whose lives were hanging in the balance, were taken to their own homes or to hospitals, to recover or die. England kept her fingers on the pulses of the prisoners, and let out those whose pulses were just about to stop'. When he left a month later, the Administrator Very Rev John Barry was placed in charge of the Archdiocese; the aging Dean Carey remained Vicar General.

The principal purposes of Mannix's trip were to rouse the United States against the British authorities, as he has done so successfully in Australia, and then act as a key player on the Irish stage. This was a crucial time, the height of the Anglo-Irish war, with pointless slayings, which both sides wanted ended. Two influential figures, the English Benedictine head Cardinal Gasquet and Sir Shane Leslie, Churchill's cousin and an MP, suggested Mannix as a sympathetic negotiator between the sides.

Mannix had been exiled to Australia in 1913 just as the

temperature was beginning to rise in Ireland. Maddeningly, as a deep Irish nationalist he had to sit out the tumultuous years 1913 to 1920, which might lead to a defining moment in Irish history, with centuries of external domination lifted. On his first day in Melbourne he spoke in the cathedral of Ireland as 'the mistress – as I hope she soon will be – of her own destiny'. He followed events closely, he supported the Easter Rising (unlike the Irish hierarchy), he effortlessly wiped the floor with a Welsh PM here when his Irish compatriots couldn't lay a glove on another Welsh Prime Minister in England. In Australia he demonstrated the qualities needed in troubled times to lead on the public stage. Ireland lacked such a leader in the messy sequence of events which led up to the Black and Tan War, and the disputed Treaty negotiations, a leader who could operate above the fray, command universal respect, and lead his country out of the chaos into freedom.

There's a well-known phenomenon in history of a person outside the establishment being *called* by the populace, and by his own instincts, in desperate times to lead his or her country, as Joan of Arc did, likewise Churchill and de Gaulle in the Second World War. The paradigm from classical times is Cincinnatus, a Roman who left his farm to enter public life and save the republic. Mannix combined the leadership talents necessary in a national emergency: radical nationalist, prince bishop, tribal leader, tribune of the people, and convincing orator. This is not just a retrospective view – it was recognized at the time. A correspondent to *The Advocate* (9 November 1922) wrote:

> There is no other man in the world today who possesses the confidence of the conflicting parties in Ireland…[his] proved ability and oneness of purpose, as well as in his sacerdotal office and personal character must undoubtedly prevail in a conference of the conflicting parties…Archbishop Mannix is the only living man whose personal intervention would put a stop to the internecine strife that is rending our beloved 'Dark Rosaleen'.

Mannix had a further quality the Irish situation needed. In Ireland one great fault line was over religion. When the Easter

Rising occurred the Irish hierarchy looked askance, thus forfeiting a national leadership role. At the same time many Sinn Feiners were moving away from religious belief as part of their process of personal radicalization. The Catholic Church rightly suspected it now had a rival for the people's affections, since Irish nationalism contained within itself a Celtic religion. Mannix was one of the few public figures in good standing with both Irish groups, and so was uniquely placed to bridge this debilitating gap and to bring about the long-called-for national unity, essential in a crisis.

Because of censorship Mannix couldn't be frank about his views in Australia during the war, but in America he felt freer now that the war was over. But he went too far in his Plattsburg address in New York State when he revealed his deepest convictions:

> England was your enemy. England is your enemy today. England will be your enemy for all time. England is one of the greatest hypocrites in the world. She pretended to be your friend in the war, and now that the war is over she tells you to mind your own business.[6]

The statement was a tremendous mistake for a potential conciliator, as Mannix himself later admitted. This absolutist sentiment played into Lloyd George's hands, as he now had enough damning evidence to move against Mannix. It shows the foresight of the British PM that he recognized the danger that Mannix could successfully rouse Ireland, so he took the extraordinary step of having him arrested at sea by a British warship to prevent him landing there. An *Advocate* editorial at the time confidently claimed that 'even from England's point of view' the arrest was 'the greatest mistake that could have been made'. It was in fact the greatest mistake Mannix ever made, as his banning from Ireland was a fatal obstacle to his true purpose, which was to, like Moses, lead his people out of the wilderness into the promised land. Lloyd George had snookered him. Mannix described himself as 'in cold storage' in England, indicating by contrast his real ambitions. It was this lost chance, this great blow, which had a determining effect on his personality for the rest of his life.

---

[6] Rev. Walter Ebsworth, *Archbishop Mannix*, p. 229.

8 Archbishop Mannix, Eamon de Valera and Mannix's cousin Bishop Foley
of Ballarat, in New York in 1920. (MDHC)

Mannix's arrest and detention in England and his being banned
from Ireland led, as expected, to a huge protest demonstration in
Melbourne, organized by the Irish Ireland League. The Anglo-Irish

war became a dominant issue among Melbourne Catholics and led in March 1921 to the formation of the Self-Determination for Ireland League of Australia. This new body soon eclipsed all others in publicity and importance. Among those prominent in it were Frank Brennan, Dr Gerald Baldwin, T.M. Burke, John Wren, Pierce Cody, Fr Collins of *The Advocate,* as well as a future Victorian Premier Ned Hogan and a future Prime Minister James Scullin.

Mannix lingered on in England, reluctant to go to Rome, and then home. While in Rome Pope Benedict XV surprised Mannix with his solicitude for the Irish people. Impressed by Mannix's account of Ireland's woes the Pope asked him to draft a statement on the matter, which the Pope subsequently issued, with some alterations, in his own name: 'Ireland today is subjected to indignity, devastation and slaughter...not sufficient consideration was given to the desires of nations'. The Pope suggested a conference of the Irish nation to determine a settlement. But for Mannix the Pope's intervention, though welcome, was merely a consolation prize, after missing out on his main Irish mission.

The young seminarian Norman Gilroy, studying in Rome at the time, noted in his diary: '[Mannix] said he loved Ireland above any nation in the world, afterwards adding however that he loved Australia the land of his adoption with Ireland land of his birth.'[7] Gilroy disapproved of Mannix's Irish priority, and wasn't convinced by the qualification. Gilroy was correct: Ireland was foremost in Mannix's mind. Mannix returned to Australia in August 1921, having been away for fifteen months, just as the controversial truce between Ireland and England was being negotiated in London; it was signed in December of that year.

Mannix then supported de Valera in opposing the 1921 Treaty. One possible reason was that de Valera could now carry out the 'save the nation' role, as a surrogate for Mannix missing out that role himself. Mannix and De Valera had swapped places; De Valera in his early years wanted to be a bishop, Mannix now aspired to the role of statesman. Both were tall, aristocratic, and with, in Roy Foster's

---

[7] Brenda Niall, *Mannix*, p. 237.

phrase, an 'aloof charisma'. In both an attitude of superiority led to them positioning themselves above the fray, taking a 'pure', uncompromising, long-term view.

The Irish Civil War

After the Treaty was signed the majority Free State Government, led by Arthur Griffiths and Michael Collins, was opposed by the Republican breakaway faction led by de Valera, who would not accept an oath of allegiance to Britain nor a separate Ulster. In April 1922 a large Pan Irish Conference in Paris produced the headlines: 'Unbounded Enthusiasm and Unbroken Unity: Glorious future of the Gael', all unfortunately the opposite of what was about to transpire. In Ireland internal hostilities broke out in June 1922, followed by Irish-on-Irish guerrilla fighting, terrible cruelties, split families and disbelief that the high hopes for Ireland could have come to this. The civil war ended after a year when de Valera's Republicans surrendered militarily in May 1923.

Melbourne Catholic opinion was now divided on the Irish question. The old guard of moderate Home Rulers, followers of John Redmond, transferred their loyalties to the Treaty and the new Free State government. *The Tribune*, the paper of the silent majority, adopted this stance. Mannix was now back in a minority position. The anti-Treaty de Valera faction was less popular in Melbourne, but noisier, as it had the backing of *The Advocate,* Mannix and a new organization, the Irish Republican Association. Bishop Phelan of Sale was in favour of the Free State, but Mannix maintained: 'I would never have put my signature to the Treaty, which was signed in London under threat of war', so he had 'bowed his head to the Republican colours'. *The Advocate* avoided editorializing on the matter, but its news reports overwhelmingly favoured de Valera. Its letter columns gave space to both sides. T.P. Walsh and Agnes Murphy were the leading pro-Republicans, and Thomas Shorthill and *The Tribune* newspaper the main Free Staters.

In 1923 two de Valera delegates, Sean O'Kelly and Fr Michael O'Flanagan, toured Australia to promote their cause. Mannix in characteristic mode said he was not taking sides, but gave the delegates a good hearing and continued to argue the anti-Treaty case. *The Tribune* had been edited for a decade by Fr Mangan, a chaplain during the war and founder of the Newman Society. His newspaper considered the de Valera delegates 'irregulars', and a disaster for Ireland. *The Tribune* favourably compared the rebels of 1916, who fought the English, with the de Valera rebels of 1922 who were fighting their own countrymen, accusing Fr O'Flanagan of 'blood-stained zeal'.

The issue soon developed into a spat between the two Catholic papers, with *The Advocate* accusing *The Tribune* staff of being 'Castle Catholics'. Sean O'Kelly described Fr Mangan, a man of diminutive stature, as 'a little Papish mosquito' who took the same position as the Orange Lodges and the Protestant Federation. *The Advocate* had to apologize to *The Tribune* for publishing these insulting remarks. *The Tribune's* peculiar status as a Catholic paper, though not owned by the church, was revealed when its long-time editor Fr Mangan resigned from his position at the end of the year. The paper commented that his announcement 'caused some surprise'. A Mannix favourite, Fr Monyihan, soon to be editor of *The Advocate,* replaced Fr Mangan on *The Tribune* staff, and the paper gradually moved to the de Valera position. Mannix had control over what his priests did, and therefore ultimately over *The Tribune*, the editorship of which could only be held by a priest with his approval, which he had most likely withdrawn. Mannix had form on this issue. During the conscription controversies, he contrived to have the pro-conscription editor of *The Advocate*, Tom Brennan, replaced by an anti-conscription one, Thomas Shorthill, even though the paper was not then owned by the church. Both sides had long memories of these events. When Fr Mangan died in 1960 he was buried by Archbishop Simonds, who remarked in his panegyric: 'There were times when his audacity as a writer led him into troubled waters'.

When the Irish civil war broke out old Irish stalwarts like Morgan Jageurs and many Melbourne Irish simply retired from the fray, appalled by the descent into civil war after all their efforts. Mannix vainly tried at intervals to revive passions on Ireland. He gave comfort to the republican delegates' visit in 1923, he stumped the country for de

Valera during his 1925 visit to Ireland, he encouraged Calwell in 1933 to start up the *Irish Review*, he backed the founding of The League for an Undivided Ireland in 1948, but none of these efforts aroused any momentum here. Irish affairs were off the agenda until 1969, after Mannix's death, when the new Northern Irish troubles began.

In 1924 Fr John Lonergan replaced Fr Barry when the latter was elevated to become Bishop of Goulburn. Fr Lonergan was simultaneously appointed to three powerful positions: Administrator of St Patrick's, Chancellor of the Archdiocese, and private secretary to Mannix. Born in 1888 in South Melbourne and educated at St Patrick's College, Fr Lonergan had previously been chaplain to the CYMS and inspector of religious education for the Archdiocese. Like Bishops Phelan and Barry, who had had similar rises under Carr, Fr Lonergan had a likable personality, a multitude of talents and the ability at this stage to juggle a heavy workload. There were hints of some resentment among the clergy at Fr Lonergan's rapid rise, as he had been a priest only thirteen years, in an age when it often took two decades after ordination to become a parish priest. Fr Lonergan's appointment removed some of the daily administrative pressure from Mannix, who now began to station himself above things. This strategy became a pattern, as Monsignors Lyons, Fox and Moran subsequently filled similar multiple roles. By focusing all the crucial administrative positions in one deputy Mannix was free to be a scholar prelate, devoting his energies at Raheen to reading, and musing on the larger issues of the day. Fr Matthew Beovich eventually succeeded Fr Lonergan as education inspector. In addition to his three key posts Fr Lonergan accumulated leadership positions in the Hibernians, the St Vincent's de Paul Society, *The Tribune* newspaper, the ACTS, the marriage tribunal and Catholic insurances, all of which together eventually tired him out. He was further promoted in 1929 to Monsignor, with the rank of domestic prelate, but rarely used the title.

Jesuits

In the 1920s the Jesuits helped Mannix by taking on projects beyond their previous roles in parishes and schools. One of Dr Mannix's special interests in Ireland was higher education, as he had been in charge of Ireland's leading seminary, Maynooth, a post-secondary institution, and had been on the Senate of the National University of Ireland. So it was natural that he began to set up Catholic institutions of higher learning in Melbourne: Newman College at the university, the Catholic Central Library in the city, and the new Corpus Christi seminary at Werribee, all staffed by Jesuit priests. Five influential Irish Jesuits, all highly educated and with a life-long love of learning, came to Melbourne in this period. Fr Albert Power SJ was appointed the first rector of Newman College in 1918. Born in 1870 in Dublin, he completed an MA in Classics at the National University of Ireland (NUI), then travelled to Australia in 1896 for a six year stint as a Jesuit scholastic at Riverview College in Sydney. Like Mannix he was to spend half his life in Ireland and half in Australia. He returned to Europe to complete his studies in Holland and Ireland, and was ordained in 1906. Appointed Rector of the Jesuit Milltown Park seminary in Dublin, he was known to his students there as 'Albertus Magnus' after Master Albert, a famous Dominican theologian of the University of Paris, who taught Aquinas. In 1918 Fr Power returned to Australia as first Rector of Newman College, and was then transferred to be the first Rector of Corpus Christi seminary at Werribee in 1923.

Werribee Park was a Chirnside family mansion and 1000-acre property purchased in 1922. Up till this stage Victorian candidates for the priesthood had been trained at Sydney's Manly seminary. Melbourne having its own seminary was a sign in its own eyes that it now shared equal billing on the Australian Catholic scene with the foundation see of Sydney. The Jesuits encouraged trainee priests at Werribee to take initiatives, to handle ideas, and to be outgoing in their apostolic pursuits. Cluny sisters from France were brought out after the Second World War to help the seminary community. Fr (later Bishop) Arthur Fox was among the first batch of ordinands in 1930. Corpus Christi was to be the great work of Fr Power's life, being Rector there from 1923 to 1930, and then Professor of Scripture and spiritual director until 1945. Over these years he nurtured about two hundred students on their way to ordination. Though he had a great

9 Corpus Christi College, Werribee, opened in 1923. (MDHC)

store of knowledge, he was not a self-seeker; full of energy but short in stature he was nicknamed 'the mighty atom', in the Australian vernacular a greater compliment than being named after a famous theologian. After leaving Werribee he kept up a round of lecturing and writing ACTS pamphlets.

In 1923 Fr Power was succeeded at Newman College by Fr Jeremiah Murphy SJ, who had a long and influential tenure at the college, paralleling that of Fr Power at Werribee. Jeremiah Murphy, born in 1883, was from Kilkenny, as was Fr William Hackett with whom he grew up. Like Fr Power Fr Murphy had an MA in classics from the NUI, with studies in Classics at Oxford. During his long reign at Newman College (1923-1953) his great achievement was to nurture the Catholic professional men who became prominent in the decades before and after the Second World War. He was one of the founders and early speakers on the radio program, the 'Catholic Hour'. Fr Murphy had a significant influence not just at Newman but on Melbourne University life generally. A man with a gentle and witty personality, he was revered by Newman students.

Fr Henry Johnston SJ, born in County Down in 1888, studied like his other two Jesuit colleagues for a Classics degree at NUI, then completed a doctorate in Sacred Theology at the Gregorian University in Rome. In 1925 he was appointed a Professor at Corpus Christi seminary, changing places with Fr Power in 1930 to become Rector, a post he held till 1947. Remarkably, his brother, Fr Thomas Johnston SJ, was rector of the diocesan seminary in Christchurch in NZ. A handsome man with a distinctive shock of wavy white hair and tan skin, Fr Henry Johnston was a fixture on the Catholic lecture circuit for half a century, including the 'Catholic Hour' on radio and the Catholic Evidence Guild on the Yarra bank. A master of apologetics, he filled a role somewhat similar to the Sydney 'radio priest', Dr Rumble, in explaining Catholics doctrine and liturgical practices, and answering queries about the faith in public forums.

Mannix's intense interest in Ireland was aided by the presence in Melbourne of Fr William Hackett SJ. He became Dr Mannix's closest friend and confidant over the next three decades; they had in common being radical Sinn Feiners at a time when the Catholic Church in Ireland and Australia took a more middle-of-the-road position. Both were in a sense exiles from Ireland in Australia. Raised in Kilkenny, Hackett was a contemporary of James Joyce at the Jesuit school Clongowes Wood College, then a scholastic in Holland and France, and was ordained in 1912. He was deeply involved in the Black and Tan War, in which he acted as messenger, agent and partisan for the Irish insurgents, having several narrow escapes. He was in contact with Michael Collins in the days before Collins was ambushed and shot in Cork in 1922, and was a friend of the executed Erskine Childers and of de Valera. Fr Hackett was sent out to Australia in 1922, perhaps because the Jesuit authorities thought he had become too closely involved with figures in the Irish internecine warfare of the time. In Australia he was a stalwart of the Catholic Central Library, and Rector of Xavier College in the later 1930s, though that was an unhappy experience for him. He supported the Catholic Women's Social Guild, helped launch the 'Catholic Hour' on radio 3AW in 1932, and fostered the beginnings of the Campion Society.

Fr Eustace Boylan SJ, born in Dublin in 1869, was a contemporary of Fr Power and studied like the others on the continent and in Ireland. For most of the interwar decades he edited the religious magazines *The Messenger* and *The Madonna,* which had devoted Australia-wide readerships, while holding teaching positions at St Patrick's and Xavier Colleges. He found time during his decade at Xavier to write a popular novel, *The Heart of the School,* based on his stay there; in April 1920 Patrick O'Leary reviewed it favourably in *The Advocate.* The Jesuits were at the forefront of Catholic intellectual life in Melbourne between the wars.

Women's Organizations

The Catholic Women's Social Guild (CWSG) was begun in 1913 with the help of the Jesuit Fr William Lockington. Among other activities the CWSG provided family support, helped homeless children and arranged hospital visitations. Active in inner suburbs like Fitzroy, it grew to be a large Catholic organization in the interwar years, and the pioneer of Catholic social services in the archdiocese. Its founders were a group of impressive women who believed in taking initiatives, in contrast to the then current image of the Catholic woman as a dutiful mother confined to the domestic sphere. The inaugural President (1913-1917) was Dr Mary Glowrey, a medical graduate and Collins St specialist in eye diseases, and a founding member of the Newman Society. Dr Glowrey later devoted her life to setting up medical services for women in India. She was succeeded as CWSG President by Anna Brennan (1918-1920), one of the earliest women lawyers and a doyenne of Catholic organizations during her long career. Julia Flynn, who had gained a BA and Dip. Ed. with interests in maths and science, was also prominent. A leading educationalist, she was appointed Chief Inspector of Secondary Schools in 1924. Flynn became influential in realms few Catholic women ventured into: she eventually became a member of the Lyceum Club, the Board of Convocation of the university, and the Council of the Emily McPherson College of Domestic Economy. She was recognized after her death in 1944 by the Julia Flynn Memorial Prizes for outstanding Matriculation results. (The first recipients in 1949 were

Brenda Niall, later an academic and biographer, and Ian Howells, later a Jesuit priest.)

Another medical graduate influential in the early years of the CWSG was Dr Eileen Fitzgerald, later the Chief Medical Officer of the Victorian Education Department. In 1929 Maude O'Connell, the first secretary of the CWSG and originally a trade union activist, founded the Grey Sisters, a religious community of Catholic women (like the Grail) who did not take vows, and whose mission was to help young mothers in the home. The CWSG founded a boarding house for single working women, the Carmel Hostel. These CWSG professionals were moderate female activists who encouraged Catholic women to participate in welfare and other social organizations, and in the workforce. In 1920 the CWSG decided to affiliate with the National Council of Women (NCW) to give Catholic women a wider voice. This caused a falling out with Mannix. The NCW had been a strong supporter of conscription, and the hierarchy was averse to Catholic bodies which they did not control, especially in areas in which they did not feel comfortable. Fr Lonergan, second in charge of the archdiocese, thought women who mixed with the NCW displayed Bolshevik tendencies. This contretemps split the organization, with a drop in membership, and with prominent members like Brennan and O'Connell resigning. A new committee more acceptable to Mannix was installed.

In August 1917 Agnes Murphy, one of the most active Catholic women in Melbourne at the time, gave a talk to the CWSG on the responsibilities of women in looking after sick, unfortunate and neglected people. She urged women to be less inert, and to get themselves on electoral rolls in order to work effectively for the common good. Agnes Murphy had been secretary to Dame Nellie Melba; she wrote an early biography of her, first serialized in the periodical *The Lone Hand*, and then published in London in book form in 1909. Born in Ireland, Murphy was an assertive Republican supporter of de Valera during the troubles and afterwards. She became, among her many other activities, a theatrical agent, managing the tour of the Sistine Choir during the Victorian leg of its Australian tour. In 1925 she was in London doing publicity work for the Royal Opera Company. Her later career was based in London, with time in the US and on the continent. Agnes Murphy was a confident and versatile woman with strong convictions, at home in the cosmopolitan world of music and the arts.

A musical star was Amy Castles, a soprano originally educated at the Bendigo Convent of Mercy. She came, like Fr Percy Jones, from a large, musically inclined country family, with her two sisters and four brothers noted singers. Amy began singing Gilbert and Sullivan at the Austral Salon in Melbourne, then toured Australia before studying in Europe. She had a successful debut in London, performing with her fellow Victorian singer Ada Crossley. In concerts she would sing excerpts from opera, plus old favourites such as 'Home Sweet Home', 'Ave Maria' and 'Believe me if all those endearing young charms'. Her farewell tour of Australia took place in 1925. About one of her concerts the music critic of *The Argus*, a paper with an anti-Catholic slant, wrote dismissively: 'It was an easily pleased audience'. The music gave 'great pleasure of a somewhat unsophisticated kind... The whole concert was characteristically Italian...There was much artistry of a deliciously instinctive kind...The intellectual strain was reduced to a minimum'.[8] This review displayed the then common prejudice that the Italian and Irish races were too emotional, and less advanced in civilization than the more cerebral English and German ones. The comment was made in the context of objections at the time to southern Europeans settling in Australia. The unstated prejudice against them was that they were Catholic.

Businessmen

Catholics were prominent in social work, but not in business. Coming mainly from backgrounds in rural Ireland they did not have family traditions of commercial enterprise. In Melbourne they were mostly in the lower classes and without capital, and as a result aspired to positions as employees, teachers and public servants. In addition an attitude inimical to business success was induced by Catholic moralists who preached that money was the root of all evil, and that we should not become attached to worldly

---

[8] *The Advocate*, 11 December 1924, p. 20.

valuables. Papal encyclicals denounced capitalism *tout court*. In the early 1920s the Melbourne Catholic author J.M. Walsh published a short story entitled 'If Riches Entice Thee'; sermons with titles like 'The Fetish of Material Progress' were common. In July 1922 a prominent Melbourne priest, Fr. Merner, explained in a lecture: 'Wealth can be in the highest degree detrimental to the soul of its possessor'. As a result many Catholics did not think in economic terms much beyond having a State Savings Bank deposit book. In the nineteenth century some Catholics had made money in the liquor industry, in the construction and building trades, and in insurance companies as an expansion of charitable activities linked to mutual benefit societies such as the Hibernians. A large insurance business, the National Trustees Executors & Agency Company, was centred on the Madden and Fitzgerald families. Walter Madden, brother of the Chief Justice Sir John Madden, was its managing director until his death in 1925.

John Buxton, a Protestant who arrived from England in 1869, eventually took over his uncle's South Melbourne real estate business, which became J.R. Buxton and Sons, still a prominent firm. It had flourished during the land boom, and for many decades had its headquarters in Collins St, with branches stretching down the bayside suburbs. The family, but not John Buxton, became Catholic on his marriage in 1875 to Mary O'Brien, from an Irish small-farm and hotelier family of Nar Nar Goon, much poorer than the wealthy Buxtons. As in many families of mixed marriages, the children were brought up as Catholics, but in this case the sons went mainly to non-Catholic schools, and the daughters mainly to Catholic ones. The Buxtons had nine children; some sons joined the family firm, with Ray Buxton becoming the senior partner in the next generation. His two sons in turn joined the firm, with Frank Buxton the senior partner by the time of his father's death in 1950. One daughter of the original couple, Gertrude, married Henry Pitt, from an Irish Catholic family; Henry rose to be head of the State Treasury Department. They had three children Lorna, John and Kathleen. Another daughter, Kathleen, married Henry's brother Ernest, who rose to become Chief Librarian of the Public (later State) Library. The social life of the extended Buxton clan at the family mansion 'Hughenden' in Middle Park was lovingly recreated by one of the nineteen grandchildren of the original couple, Kathleen Fitzpatrick neé Pitt, in her memoir *Solid Bluestone Foundations* (1983).

Some prominent Catholics had long careers in business. John Wren (born 1871) had become a notorious figure with his illegal Collingwood tote operation and his City Tattersall's Club. He had been engaged in betting coups, and in setting up racing bodies in opposition to established ones, as well as sponsoring boxing and cycling contests. From these activities he made his early fortune. He was disdained by respectable society but became a hero to the inner-city working class. By the 1920s he had diversified his interests, moving into more mainstream business enterprises, some interstate and overseas: theatres, newspapers, real estate, grazing properties, gold mines in Queensland and Fiji, and liquor interests. He was known to have widespread influence in inner suburban councils, and behind the scenes in State and Federal Labor politics. Niall Brennan believed his father, the Federal Attorney General Frank Brennan, had Wren connections. Most of Wren's activities were non-transparent. Like Mannix, who lived near him in Kew but kept his distance, Wren was abstemious, and often walked into town from home. He was by the 1920s less of a social pariah.

Pierce Cody, born in 1867 in Kilkenny, arrived in 1889 and established a grocery business in Richmond, then expanded it, becoming a wine and spirit merchant with his Austral Wine and Spirit Agency in Little Collins St, the main Victorian distributor of the Jesuit's Sevenhill Wines. Cody set up a distillery in Port Melbourne, an enterprise similar to Wren's, with whom he had business connections. Cody, who became a director of the Catholic Church Property Insurance Company of Australia, lived in Kew and had six children. He and his wife Anastasia, also from Kilkenny, both died in 1923; John Wren was a pall bearer at his funeral. The children, particularly Matt and Pat Cody, carried on the family businesses. James Hogan was another Irishman with a wine and spirit business in the city; the Cody and Hogan businesses became connected through the Austral Wine and Spirit Agency. The wealthy

Wren, Cody and Hogan families supported Irish causes, and were generous donors to local Catholic charities.

Who was J.J. Liston? After the Second World War Melbourne sportsgoers had heard the name J.J. Liston, because a horse race, the J.J. Liston Stakes, and the Victorian Football Association's best player award, the J.J. Liston Medal, were named after him, but few remembered the career that lay behind the name, or even what the initials J.J. stood for. Between 1900 and 1940 John James Liston had an extraordinarily varied and successful career which closely paralleled that of John Wren, but in Liston's case was clean. Born in 1872 in Ireland he was in his youth a CYMS member and footballer. He first made his name as the dominant force in Williamstown affairs as hotelier, businessman, racehorse owner, councillor and mayor on numerous occasions, and the main promoter of Williamstown's development, using his position on the Harbour Trust to arrange public works in his area. His many other activities included being the liquor industry's representative opposing the campaign for prohibition. He was also president of the Druids' Benefit Society, president (amazingly) of both the VFA and the Victorian Soccer Association, and a Melbourne City councillor. In 1931 he missed out by one vote on becoming Lord Mayor of Melbourne after a sectarian attack. He was appointed to the MMBW board and the Melbourne Town Planning Commission, and was a trustee of the MCG. When he died in 1944 he left an estate of almost £300,000, exceptional wealth for the time. Mannix was present at his funeral, Scullin and Michael Chamberlin were pallbearers, and Calwell represented the Federal Government.

The real estate agent Thomas (known as T.M.) Burke, born in 1870, became known in the interwar years as a pioneer in selling large subdivided estates. He came from Ararat, and was a member and eventually Victorian president (1902-3) of the Australian Natives Association. This was a body many aspiring Catholics joined, as it was open to their talents, being non-sectarian and non-party political, and with an Australian nationalist rather than British Empire agenda. While working in his early life as a clerk in the railways T.M. Burke was a leader in strike action for better wages.

10 T.M. Burke and his wife, left, with Archbishop Mannix at the blessing of a new chapel at Xavier College's Burke Hall in 1926. (MDHC)

His real estate business expanded rapidly in the 1920s into a very large enterprise, with offices in every state and some overseas. The firm contracted drastically in narrowly surviving the 1930s depression. Burke recognized the need for personal development, was a promoter of co-operatives, a member of the 'Develop Australia League', and an advocate of an Australian manufacturing industry and of technical education. He pointed out that aspiring businessmen were not trained after school for their career, as other professions were. He was one of the first to realize Catholics were not business minded, so he started up through the CYMS a Melbourne Business Institute to equip Catholic young men in business knowledge, and to overcome prejudice against Catholics in business circles. As a result CBC Parade and CBC North Melbourne ran evening courses in accountancy. Like other prominent Catholic businessmen he was a generous donor to charities, and in 1920 presented the mansion Studley Hall, purchased from the state government, to the Jesuits of Xavier College as a preparatory school. Situated opposite Raheen, it is known as Burke Hall. Like Wren and Liston, Burke was a successful racehorse owner. He was the first National President of the Knights of the Southern Cross in 1922, and a substantial donor to the founding of the Corpus Christi seminary at Werribee which opened a year later.

The businessman Michael Chamberlin, born in 1891, from the

generation after Wren, Burke and Liston, became in some ways their successor. Educated at St Augustine's CBC at Geelong, he had a similar start in life to T.M. Burke, firstly joining the railways. Then his belief in self-improvement lead him to advance via examinations into the Victorian public service. He moved up the ranks of the CYMS to become president in 1921, and assisted Burke with his Business Institute. In 1922 Chamberlin began his long career in business by joining Burke's real estate firm, managing its Sydney office during the great depression in the early 1930s. He moved in 1933 to manage the National Trustees Executors & Agency Company. Most Catholics successful in business had no inherited wealth – they were self-made men.

3

THE LATE 1920S:
CALM BEFORE THE STORM

Mannix's 1925 Visit to Ireland – Portents of Trouble – The Conservative 1920s – The Rise of the Catholics – Victorian Politics – Brennan and Scullin – Arthur Calwell – Medicine & Law

Mannix's 1925 Visit to Ireland

Before his 1925 trip to Ireland Mannix claimed that the tide was turning in Ireland; he 'hoped that the real men of Ireland [he meant de Valera and his followers] would govern and control Irish affairs'. (*The Advocate,* 8 January 1925) His campaigning around Ireland in 1925 helped de Valera, at a low point in his career, to gain momentum for his successful bid for leadership of Ireland later on. Mannix had a combination of achievements which gave him clout in Ireland. His previous feats were acknowledged in an address presented to him when he arrived in Dublin, in which he was described as a 'valiant and able advocate of the Irish cause, and to the Irish he stood not only as a great churchman and with the old missionary ardour of the Gaelic race, but also as an unfaltering champion of democracy. His resistance to conscription in Australia it was recalled strengthened a similar resistance here'. (*The Advocate*, 6 August 1925)

Much more attention has been focused on his dramatic 1920 attempt to land in Ireland than on his 1925 visit, which was for him an equally searing experience. Mannix had been nurtured by Ireland and by the Catholic Church. Now as a radical Sinn Fein supporter he was in a minority position in Ireland, and in addition the Irish Catholic hierarchy ostracized him on this trip because of his views. In the evening after a large reception for him in Cork, a lone bishop, who had avoided the reception, paid a visit to his room under the cover of darkness. Mannix's rebuke to him: 'So you have come at last, like Nicodemus in the night', a typically deft putdown, barely

11 Archbishop Mannix leads Australian Holy Year pilgrims in
St Peter's Square, Rome, in 1925. (MHDC)

concealed how bereft he felt. His country and his church were not
providing the maternal comfort they once had. He instinctively
grasped that he was now on his own, with the prospect of a rocky
road ahead. His coadjutor Simonds wrote perceptively of Mannix
after his death:

> I am certain he was hurt again and again, although you
> would never know it by word or attitude…He felt deeply for
> [Cardinal] Newman, who was constantly misunderstood,
> both in and out of the church. Newman's writings are full
> of the unhappiness he felt at this lack of trust. No such
> complaint can be found in any sentence written or spoken
> by Mannix. In the misunderstanding of Newman he saw his
> own, and his greatness never became so inhuman that he
> ceased to feel.[9]

In 1924 Mannix had referred to himself wistfully as 'a sort of
castaway in the southern seas', an admission that he viewed himself
as an exile. His two Ireland visits had failed for different reasons.
For the rest of his life he acted in ways consistent with regret at

[9] Rev. Walter Ebsworth, *Archbishop Mannix*, p. 429.

having missed out on a once-in-a-lifetime chance of determining the destiny of his own country. Mannix returned to Australia, never to visit Ireland again, and for many years nothing matched these Irish events in importance. His withdrawal into a mild melancholy, combined with a certain hauteur deployed as a distancing device, most probably derived from this. He did not now involve himself in local political contests as he had with Hughes. He did not take to Australian life, he barracked for no football team, he did not assimilate. In Ireland in 1925 people remarked that, though he had been in Australia for twelve years, his accent had not changed. He let others run the archdiocese, he travelled less overseas and interstate. He confined himself physically to the triangle of Raheen, the cathedral and speaking functions, after which he often declined to enjoy refreshments with the local priest. He preferred to spend his time alone at Raheen or with Jesuits like Frs Hackett and Murphy, lesser comrades from Ireland of the troubles. In Mannix's personality humour and sadness were inextricably mingled together; his detachment allowed him to describe others with a mordant wit. Many anecdotes of his humour have been recorded, but the more important element, his deep sadness, has been less understood. The many plaudits he received in later life were scant consolation for what he had earlier missed out on.

Portents of Trouble

Irish issues were never in focus again in his lifetime, as other international issues took precedence. Melbourne Catholics had always had a keen interest in overseas events; each weekly issue of *The Advocate* had at least five pages reporting world events, which were discussed by its readers. A kind of Catholic International with a global perspective had grown up to look after the Church's interests. Vatican representatives, the eyes and ears of the church, were accredited to most countries in the world – no other religion had such reach. The British ran a similar system through their empire.

As the 1920s progressed, tremors in various countries presaged the horrors that would rock the world in the 1930s. In Spain the widening gap between establishment and republican forces would lead to civil war a decade later. In *The Advocate* of 17 January 1924 Hitler and Ludendorff's beer hall putsch was reported as a ridiculous anti-climactic event, which had aimed to suppress Catholics, Jews and democracy. A tendency in Germany during the Weimar period to revert to the old pagan worship of Odin and Thor was denounced by the German Cardinal Faulhaber. In 1926 Pope Pius XI condemned the royalist Action Française faction because its leader, Charles Maurras, was a rationalist using the church for his own purposes, which was to put politics above religion. Maurras, who was to support the German-installed Vichy government during the Second World War, had some support among Catholics around the world. These events were all reported in the local Catholic press.

In August 1925 Captain Francis McCullagh, a world-roving journalist attached to the American fleet, gave a talk to the Newman Society entitled 'The Shadow of Japan', on how the Japanese were objecting to European imperial powers expanding into Asia and the Pacific: 'The Japanese had worked themselves into a dangerous state of excitement' over such issues. In addition, because of their own population problems, they thought they should be allowed to settle in countries like Australia. He warned Australians of the dangers of isolationism in the face of a resurgent Japan. No one was listening.

More immediately serious were the situations developing in Mexico, Russia and Italy. For Catholics the rise of the Soviet Union presented a fairly clear-cut case. The church condemned Communism from the start as atheistic, secular and materialistic, and because it conducted campaigns of mass murder, including the killing of priests and believers, and the closing of churches. In the later 1920s the Calles government in Mexico suddenly launched a similarly horrific suppression of the Catholic faith. This was of course widely condemned in the Catholic press. The fall of four hierarchical regimes (the German, Russian, Austrian and Ottoman dynasties) at the end of the First World War had worried the hierarchical Catholic Church. In response to this and to the subsequent rise of secular dictators, the Pope instituted the feast of 'Christ the King' in 1926 to strengthen allegiance to a monarchical authority system which transcended politics. *The Advocate* reported on 14 July 1927, that the Mexican Catholic martyrs issued the cry 'Viva Christo Rey!' as they went to their deaths. This cry became the triumphant slogan of Catholics defending the church during the Spanish Civil War in a famous debate at Melbourne University. It was the earlier Mexican persecutions which occurred during his teens which first motivated Bob Santamaria.

For Catholics in the 1920s however the rise of Mussolini and his Fascist movement in Italy was a complicated case, since it involved not only Catholicism, but also the Italian political system in which the Vatican, as both an Italian institution and as a separate city-state after 1929, was a central player. Mussolini's continuing career was keenly watched in Melbourne Catholic circles. Some praised him wholeheartedly, a few like Arthur Calwell and Patrick O'Leary presciently abhorred him and his works. Much Catholic opinion took a favourable line at this stage; the early Mussolini was seen as sensibly right-wing, praiseworthy for stopping anarchism and Communism, and for restoring order. But he had to be watched, Catholic commentators warned, as he had a tendency to employ violence, to be a one-man band, and to act unconstitutionally. As a non-believing Nietzschean he had an instrumentalist, hot-and-cold attitude to the Catholic Church, like Charles Maurras.

In 1919 the Catholic priest Don Sturzo had founded a political party, the Partito Popolare Italiano (PPI), which had a strong Catholic following. Some of its deputies were ministers in Mussolini's early cabinets, but resigned when Mussolini subverted the democratic system and curtailed civil liberties. Don Sturzo's actions were favourably reported in the Catholic press. Mussolini disbanded the PPI, his main political opposition in the late 1920s, and sent Don Sturzo into exile. (Bob Santamaria's early thinking was heavily influenced by the Don Sturzo model.) The Catholic Church signed a Concordat with Mussolini in 1929, and kept seeking a *modus vivendi* with his regime so it could continue to operate both in Italy and world-wide. But continuing attacks on the church lessened its regard for the regime.

In reviewing a book favourably describing Mussolini as an arresting, dynamic, imperious 'Napoleon turned pugilist' figure,

The Advocate's literary editor Patrick O'Leary was dubious, asking in *The Advocate*, 27 September, 1923: 'Will similar forces to those that made him unmake this brilliant and gasconading figure?...The posturing suggests a want of balance and [of] a real constructive sense of statesmanship'. In reviewing Don Sturzo's book *Italy and Fascism* O'Leary wrote that 'Fascism is not the entirely admirable political system its apologists represent it to be.' (*The Advocate*, 3 November 1927) O'Leary very early on saw through dictators like Mussolini, at a time when some Catholic writers, and *The Advocate*, were sympathetic to them. Arthur Calwell wrote, in a letter to *The Advocate* (4 March, 1926), that 'Mussolini is not a patriot, merely a parricide'. He then documented the many attacks Mussolini had made on the Catholic Church. To the *Advocate* article's argument that Mussolini had pacified Italy, Calwell replied: 'Mussolini has certainly "pacified" Italy with the cudgel and the bayonet, and by the suppression of the freedom of election, of Parliamentary discussion, of the press and of association.' *The Advocate* editorially replied conceding many of Calwell's points, but maintained that Italy's post-war progress had been due to him. It described Calwell's letter as 'somewhat heated'. It may have been, but more to the point it was true.

The Conservative 1920s

In contrast to events in Europe, the decade of the 1920s in Australia was quiet, stable and non-radical; society was catching its breath again after the First World War. Protestants had lost more than Catholics in the financial crash of the 1890s, and as fervent supporters of the war they were more prone to war weariness after it. This double deficit meant that, in comparison, the rising Catholic middle and professional classes of the eastern suburbs gained confidence between the wars. Contrary to the belief that Catholics acted tribally, information provided in Janet McCalman's *Journeyings* reveals that middle class Catholics mixed outside their own group more than those from other faiths. One aim of ordinary Australians was to be respectable, which meant adhering to mainstream values. Conservative governments ruled in the Federal and Victorian Parliaments. Traditionalists like

12 St Patrick's Day procession through Melbourne streets in 1925. (MDHC)

Robert Menzies and Richard Casey, who saw themselves as in tune with the mood of the time, were emerging in Victoria, while Labor figures like Scullin and Brennan had to wait in the wings. For these reasons Catholics were not publicly noticeable in this period. They were still looked down on in some quarters as shirkers when the Empire was in mortal danger during the war. Kathleen Fitzpatrick's *Solid Bluestone Foundation* reveals a predictable split on these matters in her mixed-marriage Buxton family. When Kathleen's parents met socially at a Catholic church and decided to marry, 'from

Grandpa's [Buxton] point of view the whole affair reeked of Popery from the first and also practically of treason, because [my] father was as keen on Gladstone and Home Rule for Ireland as Grandpa was on Disraeli and the Empire.'[10]

Catholics felt they had to go quiet, or at least quieter; the earlier Irish nationalist rhetoric was less heard. To differentiate themselves in Australia Catholics had to revert to a *Bulletin*-type 'Australia First' nationalism, which Mannix and Scullin publicly adopted. In 1925 the widely read James Scullin gave talks promoting Australian literature. But there is a gap in the social record in this period. George Johnston, Hal Porter and Graham McInnes produced magnificently detailed reminiscences of growing up in the suburbs of Melbourne, but they were from Protestant Empire loyalist families. No account of equivalent depth of lower middle class Catholic families between the wars seems to exist. Kathleen Fitzpatrick's history of the extended Buxton clan, *Solid Bluestone Foundations*, is an exemplary study, but an account of an untypical wealthy, mixed-marriage family.

The literary void was partly filled for Victorian Catholics by the bush ballad collection *Around the Boree Log* of the Riverina priest Fr Patrick Hartigan writing as 'John O'Brien'. These popular poems sentimentalized fading bush ways, just as the songs Melbourne Catholics sang romanticized fading Irish ways: The Rose of Tralee, Danny Boy, Molly Malone, The Mountains of Mourne, Galway Bay, When Irish Eyes Are Smiling, and the drawing room ballads of Thomas Moore. At this period the worldview lovingly created in Mary Grant Bruce's *Billabong* series – comfortable, middle class, insular, Anglo-Australian – came to hold sway, even among Catholics. Marion Miller Knowles wrote ten novels and ten volumes of poetry. Her first two books of fiction, *Barbara Halliday* and *Shamrock and Wattle Bloom,* focussing on the large Irish Catholic mining community of her childhood at Wood's Point, are her best. In poetry she vigorously eulogized our First World War involvement. Like Knowles, Patrick O'Leary was so consumed by the constant demands of journalism that he did not live to record his life's

---

[10] Kathleen Fitzpatrick, *Solid Bluestone Foundations*, p. 56.

variegated experiences. Neither Scullin nor Frank Brennan wrote memoirs; Ned Hogan's are narrowly political.

The 1920s were a period of reasonable expansion for the archdiocese, especially in school enrolments. Primary school pupils still totalled six times more than secondary ones. The number of brothers and priests in religious orders doubled. Churches were added in a ring of developing suburbs at Frankston, Elwood, Balaclava, Armadale, Murrumbeena, Ringwood and Kensington.

	1920	1930
Parishes	81	101
Diocesan priests	151	154
Religious priests	45	94
Brothers	82	158
Nuns	1030	1275
Primary schools	125	143
Secondary schools	37	41
Secondary school pupils	5058	6491
Primary School pupils	30,204	37,650
Total pupils	35,438	44,480

The Rise of the Catholics

The 1920s witnessed the increasing prominence of Catholics in the Victorian Labor branch (but not in government). The fact they were now referred to as 'the Catholics' revealed how much they had previously been on the outer in a party dominated by evangelicals, secularists, ideological radicals and State Aid opponents. Paul Strangio comments:

> Ambitious, young Catholic males were storming its [the ALP's] ramparts by the 1920s ... It included three of the ablest Catholics who made their way through the party in the interwar era – Calwell, WP (Bill) Barry and HM (Bert) Cremean...This influx occurred with a climate in which the religious prejudices and political realignments of the Great War had transformed one-time stereotypes into unshakeable and self-perpetuating axioms: Catholics voted and joined

the ALP whereas non-Catholics were for the non-Labor parties…[Catholics] came from neighbourhoods where the clustering of working class Catholics and Labor's entrenched political ascendancy not only made for fused religious and political identities, but created opportunities for the politically ambitious, conventionally beginning at the level of the local ALP or trade union branch. [11]

Addressing a CYMS gathering in October 1924 Mannnix developed one of his familiar themes: 'They [young Catholics] should not be narrow minded or parochial, but should have a wide outlook, and in social, political and patriotic work they should take their part.' This would make them not only good sons and good Catholics, but also good citizens. Mannix, himself a product of the Christian Brothers in Ireland, consciously encouraged a network of Brother's products in Labor ranks. He reprimanded Jesuit schools for not producing a similar cohort in public life.

One big factor in the rise of the Catholics was the kudos they had gained for their successful effort, led by Mannix, in stopping Hughes on conscription and driving him out of the party. Previously the Catholics has been seen in party's eyes as conservative (as they still were on many social issues), but they had now established their radical credentials and become, as in the United States, a powerful, even dominant force in Tammany Hall style local politics. The state ALP needed a new group to make itself electable. It's remarkable that all the electorally successful Victorian Labor Leaders in the first half of the twentieth century (Prendergast, Hogan, Scullin, Curtin and John Cain senior) were of Irish background, all originally Catholic, and all originally not from Melbourne, but from the goldfields region of western Victoria. [12] Melbourne itself produced no noticeable Labor leader. Its most promising product, John Curtin, originally from Creswick, had become a secular radical in the Victorian Socialist

---

[11] Paul Strangio, *Neither Power Nor Glory*, p. 154.

[12] George Michael Prendergast's Irish parents' Christian names Luke and Mary suggest a Catholic background – 98% of Irish Prendergasts were Catholic. However his State School education in Australia, and his marriage in an Anglican church suggest he was not raised as a Catholic. Though formally called George in the press, among friends he was known as 'Mick'.

Party and then moved to Perth in 1917 to recover from personal problems and from the Melbourne maelstrom.

The country stronghold of Irish Catholicism was the Ballarat region. The Eureka rebels led by Peter Lalor had a strong Irish Catholic element. The Eureka rebellion was retrospectively hallowed as the birthplace of organized working class solidarity in Australia. As gold mining declined, the surrounding districts of Bungaree (potatoes) and Ballan, Wallace and Gordon (small farms) became Irish Catholic enclaves. In Melbourne large, well organized Irish Catholic networks existed in inner suburbs like North Melbourne, Richmond, South Melbourne and Collingwood, whose legendary football club had a strong Catholic flavour, sponsored as it was by John Wren. Jock McHale, a product of CBC Parade and a champion footballer in his own right, coached the club for a record thirty-eight years to eight premierships, including four consecutive ones in 1927-30. Jack and Frank Galbally played football for Collingwood, and so became acquainted with Wren; in addition Jack knew Wren's son at Newman College.

Victorian Politics

In the 1920s Victorian politics witnessed a triangular contest between three groups: the Labor, Country and Conservative parties (the latter variously known at the Nationalist, the UAP and the Liberals). As it was rare for any party to get an absolute majority of seats, government was marked by a changing constellation of unsatisfactory coalitions, whereby the largest party had to rule with a coalition partner it had little in common with except a shared dislike of the third party. As the two non-Labor parties were conservative, the Labor Party, even though it sometimes obtained the highest vote, rarely ruled in the 1920s, and then only as a minority government. Moreover, electorates in Victoria were weighted to rural constituencies, and Labor could hope to win country seats mainly in the old goldfields constituencies around Ballarat and Bendigo. As a result aspiring Victorian Catholic politicians, who naturally aligned themselves with Labor, had slim pickings for much of the 1920s. Even getting pre-selection in the ALP was difficult; in the mid 1920s Calwell tried for the state seat of

Fitzroy, but was defeated by the left winger Maurice Blackburn. The situation was not quite as dismal for Catholics in federal politics. Hughes formed the National Party and ruled as Prime Minister until 1923, when Stanley Melbourne Bruce took over until he lost government in October 1929 over a rash attempt to dismantle the arbitration system.

In 1924 a minority State Labor government under George Prendergast briefly came to power. Born in 1854 to an Irish family on the western goldfields at Stawell, the Ballarat journalist Prendergast was seventy when he became Premier in 1924, having spent four decades in trade union and party politics, including involvement with the Eight Hours Committee, the Celtic Club and the United Irish League. Future Labor Premiers Ned Hogan and John Cain senior were ministers in this government. But the ideologically pure Labor party machine argued against Anzac Day celebrations and against 'militarism' which spooked the two other parties, and the Prendergast ministry fell after only four months. The Country Party under John Allan, a farmer from Kyabram, then formed a coalition government for two and a half years until 1927.

In 1927 Labor under Edmund 'Ned' Hogan, born in 1883, came to power backed by Albert Dunstan's breakaway County Party grouping. A sportsman with a genial but strong personality and 6 foot 4 inches (194 cm) tall, he came from the Ballan Irish Catholics east of Ballarat. Like his Ballarat counterpart Scullin, he had read widely and studied social problems. After a stint in Kalgoorlie where he learnt public speaking and political organization as a union official, he returned in 1912 and was elected member for Warrenheip in 1913, a seat he held for thirty years, as well as farming at Ballan. With other Catholics he had climbed the ranks of the ALP in the 1920s: Victorian ALP president in 1922, minister in the Prendergast government of 1924, Parliamentary party leader in 1926 and Premier next year. Hogan was said by some to be a Wren man. After a short McPherson government interlude for a year in 1929, Hogan again became Premier, this time for a two and half year term.

From the mid 1920s the Australian economy began to deteriorate; as a result the Premier Ned Hogan believed that unemployment

13 At a garden party at St Mary's Hall in 1928: from left Lady Morrell,
Archbishop Mannix, the Lord Mayor Sir Stephen Morrell, the Premier E.J.
Hogan, the Apostolic Delegate Archbishop Cattaneo, Fr Jeremiah Murphy SJ,
and Melbourne University Chancellor Sir John MacFarland. (MDHC)

was the biggest problem facing the nation. T.M. Burke and Frank
Maher, a recent graduate, argued for an insurance scheme for
the unemployed. Burke, of the Develop Australia League, was
with Scullin and Hogan the leading Victorian Catholic thinker on
economic matters. He argued, as did Scullin, that Australia needed an
'Australia First' program, with manufacturing industries encouraged
and given tariff protection. Tom Brennan, brother of Frank and an
aspiring conservative politician, spoke against this protectionist,
go-it-alone policy, advocating two-way trade between nations.
Tom Brennan pointed out that the great fear that ending protection
between the states at Federation would cause economic disaster had
not eventuated. *The Advocate* editorially took the line that tariff
protection hadn't worked, and in addition it disliked industrialization
which it saw as a blight; it believed we needed agricultural pursuits
and a rural way of life as our base, a position later institutionalized
as the National Catholic Rural Movement.

On the Depression and its causes Mannix did not display his customary analytic confidence, as he lacked economic knowledge. He followed Burke's protectionist 'Australian first' line. But he did make one telling point. We had spent too much on the First World War, being propelled into spending 'to the last shilling' by British imperial advocates in order to prop up war-time Britain. We were now in debt because of this. Yet it was those same advocates of profligate war-time spending, Mannix pointed out, who were first to insist we should pay back English bond holders. Mannix advocated moderate policies like lower wages and lower interest rates; all owners and workers should cooperate and both should sacrifice something. He opposed radical solutions like overthrowing capitalism.

Brennan and Scullin

The two most prominent Victorian Labor figures were Frank Brennan (b. 1873) and James Scullin (b. 1876) – their careers seemed to run in tandem. They had moved to Melbourne from the goldfields areas of Bendigo and Ballarat respectively, and were well known in both Catholic and Labor organizations at the same time, which sometimes caused conflicts of interest. Though they disagreed with Mannix on how to achieve State Aid, both had been strong Mannix supporters on the Easter rebellion and conscription. Their personalities differed: Brennan was dapper, flamboyant and popular, excelling at speech-making and in running organizations, whereas Scullin was quieter, more studious, a great reader with a range of interests (such as economics and literature) beyond the political. Both were products of the CYMS.

Frank Brennan came from an extraordinarily talented family which amounted to a clan. One brother Tom was an *Advocate* editor who supported conscription and became a long-time conservative member of the Federal Parliament. Three other brothers distinguished themselves as journalists and lawyers, and their sister Anna was one of the first women to graduate in law, becoming a leading figure in Catholic women's affairs. After graduating in law in 1901, Frank specialized in union and conciliation matters, by 1907 he was president of the CYMS and a member of the ALP, for which he gained the Federal seat of Batman in 1911. Two years later he married (with Mannix, who rarely officiated at weddings, as celebrant,) Sheila O'Donnell, daughter of Dr Nicholas O'Donnell, Australia's foremost Irish scholar and activist. At this stage people would have expected a more successful political future for him than for Scullin.

Scullin had a slower start to his career, remaining in the country longer. He inherited an Irish love of learning, developing his interests and public speaking abilities through the local Ballarat CYMS branch. Like Hogan and Prendergast he worked at manual jobs in his youth. While running a grocery shop in Ballarat he joined the Political Labor Council and then became an organizer for the Australian Workers Union in western Victoria. He won the Federal set of Corangamite in 1910, impressing people with his knowledge, but lost it in 1913. After this defeat he became, like Prendergast, a Ballarat journalist, editing a Labor daily newspaper the *Ballarat Echo* for the local miners' union, taking a radical line, opposing conscription and supporting the Irish cause. He also joined a Catholic Study Club which explored the insights of *Rerum Novarum* and other tracts on Catholic economic and social principles. He became Victorian ALP president in 1918-9, and on the death of the Labor leader Frank Tudor succeeded to the Federal set of Yarra in 1922, moving to live in Melbourne. Scullin was a decent modest man, abstemious, with few interests outside politics and reading. He specialized in taxation issues, federal state relations and the general economic outlook. By 1927 with the economy showing worrying signs he was, though in caucus for only five years, elected Federal Deputy Leader, replacing the Victorian Frank Anstey, a radical socialist whose policies Catholics disliked. In 1928 Scullin, because of his economic knowledge, became federal Labor leader, leapfrogging over Frank Brennan who had been in caucus for seventeen years.

Arthur Calwell

The group of Melbourne Catholic politicians born around the turn of the century and based around Arthur Calwell, Pat Kennelly,

Frank McManus and the Cremeans came a generation after Brennan and Scullin. Between the wars they first rose to prominence as party officials; their move into parliament came relatively late in their careers. Born in West Melbourne in 1896 to a father of Ulster Protestant descent and an Irish Catholic mother, Calwell soon experienced the first of the many setbacks and tragedies which dogged his long career. At six he almost died from diphtheria, an ailment which left him with a distinctive throaty voice. His mother died in 1910 when he was sixteen. He was educated at St Joseph's CBC, North Melbourne, and was to become the most prominent of an influential cohort of politicians educated at that college. He joined the Victorian public service in 1913 and stayed in it until 1940, though this was not his original intention. When in 1915 at the age of nineteen he became secretary of the Melbourne branch of the ALP, he never imagined he would have to wait a quarter of a century for a parliamentary seat. In 1921 he married Margaret Murphy, but she died a short time later, another great personal tragedy. Between the wars he held many important party positions, including membership of the State and Federal central executives, and Victorian party president.

Calwell's party career ran in parallel to an equally influential career in the public service, being secretary and president of the Victorian and national public service associations respectively. In 1932 he married the Irishwomen Elizabeth ('Bessie') Marren, who as 'Cecilia' edited the women's pages of *The Tribune* newspaper. They were part of a small group who in the wake of de Valera's 1932 election victory formed the Victorian Irish Association, and published its journal *The Irish Review* from 1933 to 1953. Calwell studied Gaelic and spoke it on public platforms. The Irish connection was a life-long interest, a third pursuit to go with his extensive ALP and public service commitments. He later became a stalwart of the League for an Undivided Ireland. He was close to Dr Mannix whom he admired almost inordinately.

His flourishing career in the Labor Party led him to expect in the 1920s that he would soon inherit the Federal seat of Melbourne, held by Dr William Maloney since 1904. Dr Maloney had an intriguing background, being the illegitimate son of the wealthy squatter William 'Big' Clarke of Rupertswood, and a Catholic lady Jane Maloney. Maloney had first sat in the Victorian parliament in 1889, so by the mid 1920s his career in two parliaments had already stretched for 35 years. Maloney was moreover a political light-weight who wasn't cabinet material. But Maloney hung on to his seat forever, never resigning until he died in 1940 aged 86, after fifty years in two parliaments. Calwell admired Maloney, and didn't try to ease him out. The two decade wait stalled Calwell's political career, frustrating his ambitions, another great setback. How Calwell was viewed by Melbourne Catholics at the time is conveyed in the following passage from *The Advocate*, 4 April, 1929:

> Mr Arthur A. Calwell, who has just been appointed vice-president of the Victorian Labour party, has had much experience as a debater in the ranks of the C.Y.M.S and the A.N.A. There are few better platform speakers in the Labour Party in Victoria today than Mr Calwell, whose flair for politics and economics, of which he is a keen student, is almost certain to secure for him a seat sooner or later in one of the legislative halls...During the two conscription campaigns Mr. Calwell was a tower of strength to the anti-militarist cause, and his support of the movement for Irish liberty has never wavered. A Big Australian, who will in wider spheres serve his country with brilliance and devotion if given the opportunity, is Arthur Calwell.

He wasn't given the opportunity for another decade.

Kennelly gained a Victorian seat only in 1938. Like Calwell, Frank McManus made his way up the ranks of the Victorian Labor organization between the wars without gaining parliamentary pre-selection. McManus's career was described in *The Advocate*, 29 October, 1931:

> Mr F.P. McManus, well known in the CYMS, of which he has been a prominent and distinguished member for some years, added to his laurels by winning the champion debate competition at South-street, Ballarat. Mr McManus, who is a school teacher, is one of the best informed of the younger

Catholic laymen. His addresses have a depth and substance which are not always to be found in the deliverance of even champion debaters. He is a thinker as well as a speaker.

Medicine & Law

St Vincent's Hospital was founded in Victoria Parade on the edge of the CBD in 1893 by Sydney based Sisters of Charity. The enterprise expanded by taking over adjoining houses, and in 1905 a new purpose built, three-storey hospital was erected. The hospital's founding spirit was Sister Mary Berchmans Daly, who came to Melbourne in 1889 and remained Mother Rectress until 1920. She was an outstanding administrator, having great charm and enthusiasm. She brought land on an adjacent block to found Mount St Evin's Private Hospital (now St Vincent's Private) in 1914, and also began the Catholic Ladies College nearby. A few years after her death in 1925 an extension was added to the hospital, with a clinical school headed by Dr Murray Morton for teaching medical students. This building included a better casualty ward, a new block for X-ray and pathology units, and less crowded facilities generally. An additional 150 beds were provided on the site of the old Cyclorama building. The hospital, whose activities were increasingly subject to government and university approval, was not an exclusively Catholic domain: half of the outpatients were not Catholics, most but not all the doctors were. Paying for the new buildings caused a financial crisis for the hospital in the late 1920s. The hospital's new advisory committee had been kept in the dark, nor were the medical staff consulted.

The outstanding medical figure in the hospital's early days was Sir Hugh Devine, who was born near Werribee in 1878 and educated at St Patrick's Ballarat. After completing a brilliant medical degree in 1906, he was briefly at St Vincent's until he undertook postgraduate studies in surgery in Austria, England and the US, returning in 1913 to a long career at the hospital, at which he was at various stages dean of the clinical school and senior honorary surgeon. His dexterous operating skills were of world standard. When in 1924 he visited the renowned William Mayo at the Mayo Clinic, other US surgeons came to witness his operating techniques. He was foremost among those specialists who established St Vincent's reputation. Devine, a general and gastro-intestinal surgeon, wrote medical text books and devised surgical instruments. He was the inaugural President of the Royal Australasian College of Surgeons (RACS), being instrumental in the College acquiring its distinctive triangular block on Spring St. Knighted in 1939, Devine had a genial personality and generously guided the emerging specialists at the hospital, and at the University's Medical School. He was a keen sportsman, keeping himself alert and fit. His son, John, also a surgeon and author of the book *The Rats of Tobruk*, died in mid-career in 1955. Sir Hugh's wife Mary died a year later, to his great anguish. Sir Hugh died in 1959; a Chair of Surgery was named in his honour.

An older specialist on the St Vincent's honorary staff, the eye surgeon Dr Leo Kenny, was with Devine a founder of the RACS, and its first secretary and treasurer. Dr Kenny, a cousin of Archbishop Carr, had arrived in Melbourne in 1870 as a boy. He had an extraordinarily long career in important positions in medical

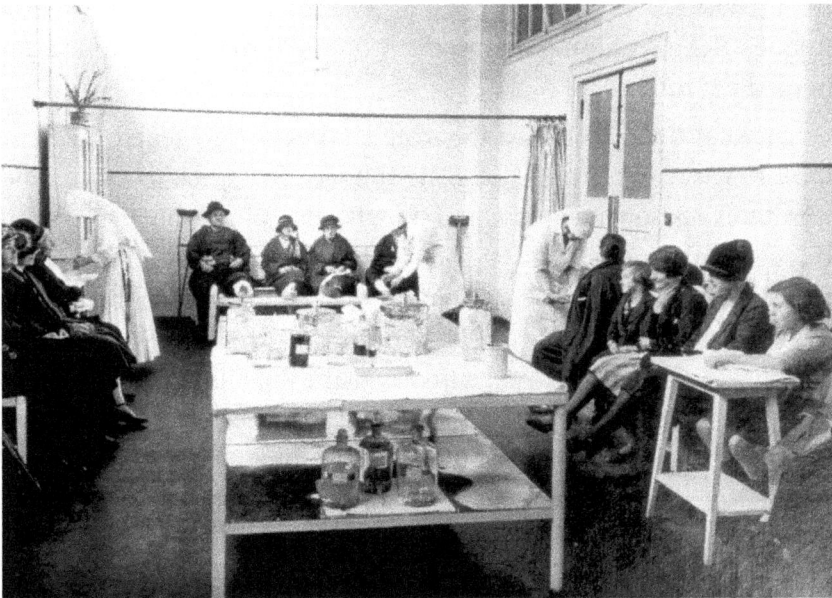

14 The dressing room for women patients at St Vincent's Hospital
in the 1920s. (St Vincent's)

and Catholic organizations, being as various stages President of the Victorian Branch of the British Medical Association, and active in the founding of the Cathedral Club, the ACF, Newman College and St Mary's Hall. For these activities Dr Kenny received three papal awards.

A family with an equally long history of activity at the hospital were three generations of the Brenan family. Alderman and Mrs Brenan, leaders of the Druids' Medical Benefit Society, were crucial in the establishment of St Vincent's; the Druid and Brenan Halls at the hospital commemorate them. Their son Dr Andrew Brenan was appointed to the hospital staff in 1913 on the out-patients staff as a clinical pathologist. A key presence around the hospital and an influential member of its advisory committee, his long career meant he acted as a source of advice for younger staff. Other prominent members of the St Vincent's staff between the wars included George Syme surgeon, Kevin O'Day and Edward Ryan, both eye specialists, Leo Doyle (whose surgical skill equalled Devine's), John Clareborough dental surgeon, Raymond Hennessy dermatologist, and John O'Sullivan radiologist. Dr John Eccles, a resident at St Vincent's in 1925, was awarded a Rhodes Scholarship and subsequently had a distinguished career in medical research.

Dr John Catarinich was the state's Director of Mental Hygiene from 1937 to 1951. Born in 1882 he attended St Patrick's College and was an exceptional sportsman, a bowls champion who also played league football and district cricket. He joined the Mental Health Department in 1907. Dr Catarinich spoke regularly in public forums before and after the Second World War on social issues, including marriage guidance, sex education and mental illness. He lectured to students at Corpus Christi seminary for many years. He had seven children, including Maurice a priest, Frank a doctor, and Joan a sculptress. Another daughter, Thea, married Dr Donald Rush in 1948; the Rush family had extensive medical and legal connections. Dr John Catarinich died in 1974 at the age of ninety-two. Dr John Garvan Hurley, a Collins St surgeon, held a number of government positions, including State Medical Officer during the 1930s.

Sir John Madden, Irish Catholic by background and establishment figure by disposition, had been Chief Justice of Victoria from 1893. The most eminent Catholic jurist of the early 20th century was Sir Leo Cussen. His father Maurice Cussen from Kerry had migrated to Sydney in 1841 and moved to a business in Portland. Born in 1859 Leo went to Hamilton College and then graduated in civil engineering in 1879. He was a good sportsman who enjoyed surveying trips in the countryside, but returned to university to complete degrees in arts and law, after which he studied for the bar under Madden. Cussen was sought after as a barrister for, among his many attributes, his great grasp of legal principles. His engineering skills helped in local government cases. He was a popular advocate whose legal knowledge became legendary; it was said that if a barrister 'had a difficult case and did not consult Cussen he was guilty of negligence'. Cussen never took silk. His appointment and performance as a Supreme Court judge from 1906 onwards increased his reputation. He was twice acting Chief Justice in the absence of Sir William Irvine.

While on the bench he embarked, largely in his spare time, on his life's work, first the immense task of consolidating the Victorian statutes, which appeared in five volumes in 1915. He then combed through thousands of English and Australian Acts dating back many centuries to assess which were applicable to Victoria, a task completed by 1929. He was knighted in 1922 at which *The Advocate* (5 January 1922) commented: 'It was commonly thought on the death of Sir John Madden that Sir Leo Cussen would have been appointed Chief Justice of Victoria...but ability does not always count in high appointments, particularly where the political pull is concerned'. (*The Advocate* had a habit of claiming sectarian slights against Catholic leaders whether they occurred or not, like J.J. Liston missing out on being elected Melbourne's Lord Mayor. The nadir of this habit was reached in an article on the French military leader Marshal Foch which had the mind-boggling headline: 'Anti-Clericalism May Have Caused Allies' Defeat' in the First World War. The claim was that Foch's early Jesuit education was held against him in his later military career.) Sir Leo Cussen died in 1939 at the age of seventy four while still a sitting judge. Dr Mannix presided at his funeral at St Patrick's, a public event after which there was a large procession. Sir Robert Menzies believed Cussen was 'one of the great judges of the English-speaking world' and Sir Owen Dixon that he should have been appointed Chief Justice of Victoria or Australia. He had been on many public bodies, including the National Gallery, Public Library and Museum, and was President of the Melbourne Cricket Club. The six sons and one daughter of Leo and Johanna Cussen produced a number of legal and medical practitioners. In 1964 the new Monash University established a Sir Leo Cussen chair of law, and in 1972 the Institute for Continuing Legal Education was named after him.

In 1931 Sir Frank Gavan Duffy was appointed Chief Justice of the High Court of Australia at the same time as Cussen was appointed acting Chief Justice of Victoria. Born in Dublin in 1852, Gavan Duffy was a son of Sir Charles Gavan Duffy, Young Ireland rebel and Premier of Victoria in 1871. Frank came to Australia as a young boy when his father emigrated here in 1855; after early schooling in Melbourne he completed his education at the Jesuit Stonyhurst College in Lancashire. Returning to Melbourne he graduated MA and LL.B, and by 1900 he was a KC and a leader of the bar. He was appointed to the High Court in 1913, knighted two years later, and appointed Chief Justice of Australia in 1931. Apparently in this case his early Jesuit education did not impede his rise to the top. Remarkably his brother George Gavan Duffy, a signatory of the Treaty of 1921, was appointed President of the High Court of Ireland, a position equivalent to his brother's. The Gavan Duffy family continued to be prominent in law and politics in Australia; one member published an account of the split in 2002.

In the year Sir Leo Cussen died, 1939, Norman O'Bryan, his successor as Melbourne's leading Catholic legal light, was appointed as a judge of the Supreme Court. Born in 1894 at South Melbourne, O'Bryan was educated at St Patrick's College and CBC Parade, and had, like Cussen, a stellar career from an early age at school and university. He graduated in 1915 with first class honours and the

Supreme Court Prize. After a spell as an officer in the First World War, he spent a year at the English bar, then returned to read with Cussen in 1920. In 1921 he had married Elsa Duncan who died six years later. A year later he married her sister Violet; both wives converted to Catholicism. O'Bryan became a successful barrister, methodical in preparation and forceful in court; he also lectured in law at the University of Melbourne, and became a member of the Bar Council. He was a sound 'common law' judge, who gave clear and fair explanations, often used in appeal cases during the later years of his long stint on the court (1939-1966). Tall and distinguished in appearance, he was popular among his peers.

Sir Eugene Gorman QC, known to his friends as Pat Gorman, another well-known Melbourne barrister before and after the Second World War, was a contemporary of Sir Norman O'Bryan. He was admitted to the bar in 1914, and like O'Bryan served in the First World War, during which he was awarded the Military Cross for bravery. In 1926 an articled clerk John Barry, later a judge, began to read for the Bar under Gorman. Barry noted in his diary at the time:

> Gorman is only a young man – an R.C. and a very decent little chap with it all. We gave him quite a lot of work so I am fairly well in with him. Gorman did the article clerks course in Bendigo and started in here after he returned from the war. He was Captain E. Gorman, there, and collected a French bride. His old man is fairly well sugared I believe.[13]

In the Second World War Gorman held the rank of Brigadier as Chief Inspector of Army Administration, and was active in the RSL and Legacy. He was a leader of the Victorian bar in common law, but he developed a number of other careers as well. He was vice-president of the Council for Civil Liberties, a body founded by the historian Brian Fitzpatrick, to whom Kathleen Fitzpatrick neé Pitt had been briefly and unhappily married. Gorman was Victorian consul for Greece, and had interests in racing, primary industry and business. Generous and charitable by nature, he was knighted in 1966. The first Red Mass for Catholic legal figures was held at St

---

[13] Mark Finnane, *JV Barry: A Life*, p. 43.

Patrick's Cathedral in 1938. The League of St Thomas More was set up for Catholic professional men such as lawyers. The Jesuits ran the Professional Men's Sodality, founded in 1872, which met at St Patrick's College; Dr Leo Kenny had been its Prefect (President) in the past.

4

THE EARLY 1930S:
THE CAMPION SOCIETY

The Scullin and Hogan Governments – Reactions to the Depression
– New Thinkers – The Campions – Dictators – Mannix As Aristocrat
– The 1934 Eucharistic Congress

The Scullin and Hogan Governments

The Federal Scullin and Victorian Hogan Labor governments both came to power after long periods of conservative rule, and unluckily, as economic conditions deteriorated on the eve of the great depression. As a result they had parallel trajectories and fates. The Scullin government was elected in October 1929 with a sweeping majority. In his cabinet seven out of thirteen ministers were Catholics, including Joseph Lyons, who often stopped over in Melbourne on trips between Tasmania and Canberra, and the Treasurer Ted Theodore from Queensland, both former state Premiers. *The Advocate* went overboard in praise of Scullin; Mannix was more restrained, perhaps sensing how daunting the problems thrown up by the depression would be.

Ned Hogan was elected Premier of Victoria two months after Scullin in December 1929, but only as a minority government with Country Party support. The two Labor governments were left to pay back debts run up by their conservative predecessors (the opposite of the situation in our era). Both leaders and their ministries were conversant with internal economic matters such as taxation, and federal-state and employer-employee relations, but not with global problems like national debt, repayments to overseas bondholders, and new solutions which economists like Keynes and Schumpeter were advocating. Theodore tried to implement a mild stimulus program, but the Commonwealth Bank, the Senate and overseas interests stymied this. The Scullin and Hogan governments were defeated by a

15 James Scullin centre, with Frank Brennan in white shoes, among Federal
Labor politicians in Canberra in the later 1920s. (NLA - pic-an 2367513)

similar combination of factors. They were forced by their weakened
position to support the orthodox, belt-tightening economics of the
Premiers' Plan and Sir Otto Niemeyer, who represented British
financial interests. This path included deflationary measures such
as reducing wages, interest rates and borrowing, paying off debts,
and hoping that austerity was the road to recovery. These policies
were naturally not acceptable to the Labor movement, which
wanted to stimulate the economy through a program of immediate
employment. World economic factors, out of Australia's control,
were the determinant. Federal Caucus split in early 1931, with
Lyons joining the conservatives to form a United Australia Party
government, which governed for the rest of the 1930s.

Hogan agreed to the traditional economics of the Premiers' Plan.
Criticized by Trades Hall and the State Executive of his own party,
his government, assailed from both sides, gradually lost confidence
and was crushed in the election of April 1932. It was replaced by
Sir Stanley Argyle's conservative UAP government, of which Robert
Menzies was an influential member. The personal health of both
Scullin and Hogan was undermined by the irreconcilable demands
made on them. In office for a total of almost four years in his two terms,
Hogan had led the first substantial Victorian ALP government, but fell

out with Trades Hall over policy issues. After his electoral defeat he was expelled from the party. He thereafter joined the Country Party, becoming a minister in some subsequent Dunstan governments. The ALP was in power federally for only three of the twenty-two years between the wars, and for only four years in Victorian politics, seven years in a total of forty-four, an extremely disappointing effort. Hogan remained interested in politics, in the 1950s writing frequent letters-to-the-editor, and publishing pamphlets against Communism and in favour of State Aid. He wrote a short memoir, and a book *What's Wrong with Australia*? (1953). He died in 1964 aged 81.

In 1934 four Tobin brothers of North Melbourne moved into the funeral direction business, as they were laying out their deceased fellow Catholics who could not afford burial expenses. The firm eventually opened offices in Kensington, Essendon and Mentone as well, all areas with high Catholic numbers. Michael Mulqueen of Bendigo became principal of a Bendigo undertakers company after marrying into the family of its owners. In 1939 he moved the Mulqueen funeral business to Brunswick. For the funerals of buildings Melbourne had the firm of Whelan the Wrecker. Three Whelan brothers took over the family firm on the death in 1939 of their father, James Whelan, who had founded the business in the 1890s. The firm's income came from preserving and reselling items like doors and window frames as well as from demolishing structures. Both the Tobin and Whelan firms expanded after the Second World War.

Reactions to the Depression

The inability of governments to solve the problems thrown up by the Great Depression provoked thinkers into developing new solutions to endemic unemployment, poverty and social disruption. This involved them in reassessing how Western societies functioned. Catholic thinkers had usually been absent from the public conversation on these matters, as they had only reluctantly accepted liberalism, modernism and the separation of church and state, and generally abhorred the ideas of Marx, Freud and Darwin. They had become quiescent, having given up hope that a Catholic view of the world could again prevail. But the depression resurrected their interest. Their great chance lay in the papal encyclicals *Rerum Novarum* (1891) and *Quadragesimo Anno* (1931) which argued for a system based on devolution of power, and worker-employer co-operation rather than antagonism. Such attitudes had been current in Catholic circles since the mid 19th century, but with limited effect.

The depression would have been expected to produce gloom, but paradoxically it inaugurated a new burst of optimism. Thinkers of the right and left thought in terms of wide ranging historical vistas, of large forces rising and declining. They felt a sense of hope that the depression had dynamited the old structures, clearing the way for a fresh start. The left rejoiced that capitalism had been destroyed, the right that 19th century liberalism had been swept away. A new world could now be built from scratch. What a time it was to be alive; a phoenix might arise out of the depression ashes if fresh ideas were implemented.

Where to look for this vision? Italy had had Don Sturzo and the PPI, and its early experiment in Catholic social action, but they had been knocked out by Mussolini. Similarly in Germany a Catholic Centre party had arisen out of the innovative social thinking of Ludwig Windhorst and Bishop von Ketteler of Mainz in the later nineteenth century, but Hitler swept away all parties except his own. (The PPI and the German Centre Party emerged from the ruins of the Second World War as the ruling Italian and German Christian Democratic parties.) In the 1930s living Catholic ideas thus had to come from English and French sources. These originated from the Belloc, Chesterton and Christopher Dawson grouping in England, and in France and Belgium from the JOCist movement (*Jeunesse Ouvrière Chrêtienne*), which we know as the Young Christian Workers, led by Canon (later Cardinal) Joseph Cardijn. Both movements envisaged lay renewal from below.

The JOCists formed active groups called cells, often in industrial areas, and were more radically anti-capitalist in their social thinking than equivalent groups in Anglo-Saxon counties, as France was in a parlous condition. It was the West European country worst hit by the fighting in the First World War, which physically devastated its landscape and people. In addition, in the century after the French Revolution the Catholic Church had lost the allegiance of the large French industrial working class (a development which, as Santamaria was to point out, had not occurred in Australia). In England, Catholic ideas had been on the outer, until they made a comeback led by converts such as Cardinal Newman, Monsignor Knox and G.K. Chesterton. Belloc's French ancestry and fondness for traditional French ways meant the English group idealized a pre-Reformation pan-European unity, a wider perspective than the usual insular English one. Francophone Catholicism, in the shape of original thinkers like Leon Bloy, Charles Peguy, Jacques Maritain and Paul Claudel, led the world in Catholic thought.

Mannix spoke repeatedly against the rise of Communist ideas engendered by the depression, the first indication of a stance that was to become more central to his thoughts in the 1940s. As early as June 1933 he warned an Old Paradians' Communion breakfast:

> They had been told on reliable authority that the menace of revolution and Communism existed in Australia. They [Paradians] could be relied upon to throw their weight and influence against anything that menaced religion and the ultimate good of Australia. He would appeal to the Paradians to exercise their individual and collective influence in factories and political and economic circles in opposing [Communist activities].

This exhortation is important in revealing Mannix was aware of the danger of Communism in Australia before most observers, and was from this juncture exhorting young Catholics to take Movement-like concerted industrial and political action. He had devised this strategy before Catholic Action was formally on the scene, and was therefore not merely a Santamaria puppet in this matter, as some later alleged.

New Thinkers

At this juncture three important Catholic thinkers in Australia, Dr Justin Simonds (NSW), Paul McGuire (SA) and Denys Jackson (Vic), all independently came across these new European ideas and were enthused by them. By a fortuitous set of circumstances – Denys Jackson's move to Melbourne in 1928, Dr Simonds' appointment to Melbourne in 1942, and Paul McGuire's close connection with Bob Santamaria – the Melbourne Archdiocese became the focal point of these ideas, and later the focal point of disputes about them.

Justin Simonds was born in 1890 and ordained in 1912. During Cardinal Moran's funeral in 1911, Simonds, participating as an acolyte, accidently slipped into the open grave. As he was hauled out the Master of Ceremonies admonished him, saying: 'That grave's only for the Cardinal!' This turned out to be not just a warning but a prophecy. Simonds became Professor of Sacred Scripture at Springwood Seminary and Dean of Manly Seminary in Sydney in 1921. From 1928 to 1930 he studied at Louvain Catholic University in Belgium, gaining a doctorate on the Church fathers. While there he became an enthusiast for the JOCist movement, of which Louvain was a stronghold, interests he furthered while Rector at Springwood on his return. By the time he was appointed Archbishop of Hobart in 1937, he was considered Australia's leading clerical expert on Catholic Action matters. At his inauguration Simonds showed he was ahead of the pack in seeing the totalitarian ideologies of Fascism and Communism not as left and right opposites but as similar, in that both divinized the state as all powerful.

In the early 1930s Paul McGuire was developing Catholic Action groups in Adelaide. Born in 1903 and a product of CBC Wakefield Street, he had four brothers who were killed in the First World War, which understandably affected him deeply. A star at Adelaide University in drama and as a debater in the 1920s, he became a journalist writing for the Sydney *Bulletin* and the Adelaide Catholic paper *The Southern Cross*. In 1927 he married Frances Cheadle who converted; they formed an intellectual partnership. McGuire was influenced by both the English and French models of Catholic Action. The McGuires went to live in London in 1928, where he survived on his journalism and turning out detective novels, at the same time helping with Frank Sheed's Catholic Evidence Guild. McGuire took up the Chesterbelloc model of promoting the glories of traditionalist Catholicism. In Belgium he met Canon Cardijn, founder of the

JOCists, and was similarly impressed. Back in Adelaide in 1932 the McGuires founded the Catholic Guild for Social Studies, the first Catholic Action program in Australia, with groups in parishes, workplaces and schools on the French/Belgian model. JOCists believed members had to study a social problem before acting on it. In 1938 McGuire helped Santamaria set up the official Catholic Action organization. Santamaria adapted McGuire's title, as the Movement's first name was the Catholic Social Studies Movement.

Denys Jackson, born in 1899 in Liverpool to a High Anglican family, had joined the Catholic Church during the First World War. He completed an honours degree at Liverpool University in medieval history, and became a teaching colleague of a fellow convert, Monsignor Ronald Knox, and an exponent of the English Catholic revival. He emigrated to Victoria as a high school teacher in 1926. His appointment to the staff of *The Advocate* in 1934 and to *The Tribune* a year later began a controversial writing and speaking career of enormous output, in which he argued the traditionalist Catholic case over the next four decades in many forums. He had prodigious learning, and a rapid journalistic facility which enabled him to assess current affairs in the light of his historical worldview. In all these attributes he reminded many of his hero G.K. Chesterton, whose shambling gait and endearing eccentricities he came to share in later life. Jackson was a regular visitor to Raheen over the decades.

Jackson followed the English Chesterton-Belloc social thinking at the time, which was conservative, anti-industrial and backward looking, in contrast to the more progressive and urban French views. These English Catholics wanted to retain a capitalist framework as they abhorred its alternatives – socialism, anarchism and Communism – but they wished to modify capitalist behaviour. They didn't feel at home with the tenor of modern life, objecting to increased economic centralization, to industrial ventures and urban conglomerations flourishing at the expense of craft industries and country living, and to the state accumulating control over all areas of life. One part of their solution was admiration for medieval times. They hankered after a more perfect world before the Industrial Revolution, the Enlightenment and the Reformation, where church

and monarch ruled in harmony under God's auspices. It was a world
of inspiring Gothic cathedrals, monasteries as key economic units,
new Catholic orders with specific reform missions, and an absence
of heresy and doubt. Rural life should be the norm, with minimal
division of labour. The high point of European history from this
point of view was the naval battle of Lepanto in 1571, when further
Muslim encroachment in south-east Europe was curtailed, and their
basic text was James Walsh's *The Thirteenth Greatest of Centuries*.

On one reading this was the last gasp of the old Catholic hope
that one day we might again live in a totally Christianized society.
But the Chesterbellocians knew, though they never quite admitted it,
medieval ways were never going to be replicated in the contemporary
world – it remained as a vision. So they developed an economic
blueprint, a modified version of their medieval ideals, which they
thought, if implemented, would go some way to soften rampant
capitalism and restore a sane balance. The plan was a mixture of
ideas labelled 'distributism', 'subsidiarity', 'guild socialism' and
'corporatism', seen as compatible with each other. Distributists
believed that agriculture, not industry, and private property should
be the basis of an economy, that wealth should be not concentrated
as at present but distributed (by worker co-ownership of business in
co-operatives, for example), which would protect capitalism from its
tendency to exploit and monopolize. Private savings would create
independent citizens owning their own homes or small farms. The
notion of subsidiarity, or devolution, that all functions should occur
at the lowest possible local level (for example, decentralisation),
was promoted by the Catholic Church (which just happened to itself
be a highly centralized and top-down organization). Guild socialism
advocated an alliance of producers and consumers: 'The workers,
organized into occupational unions or guilds, should control the work
of production; the consumers, represented by the state, should own
the means of production.' Each guild or union would have pride in
its own craftsmanship. In a corporatist society each economic sector
would form itself into a corporation of owners and workers who
would come to agreements with each other, and these self-regulating
corporations would in turn negotiate with the government. Mussolini

had gone further and formed a corporate state, a hierarchical system where corporations reported to him, thus bypassing parliamentary government. *Quadragesimo Anno* had argued for such occupation-based groups, but the Vatican thought Italian Fascism had gone too far in this direction, stifling private initiative, exalting the state, and favouring the Fascist Party. Dr T.J. Kiernan, later the first Irish Ambassador to Australia, argued a pro-encyclical and anti-Mussolini case in *The Advocate* of 25 May, 1933.[14]

The variety of Catholic Action views, encompassing those from radical to conservative, were in some cases at odds with each other. Australian Catholic thinkers tended to cherry-pick ideas from the offerings available according to their individual tastes. Bob Santamaria for example combined medievalist and distributist views in forming the National Catholic Rural Movement in 1940, but more JOCist-type entrist strategies for the Movement. These disparate ideas were mingled together as they were being developed in the 1930s, and it was only later in the 1950s that the incompatibility of some of them became apparent under the pressure of events.

The Campions

In the early 1930s a group of Melbourne Catholic university students and recent law/arts graduates, clustered around Newman College and the Newman Society, worried about these questions, and were enthused by the solutions proposed by Catholic social teachings. Gerard Heffey, Murray McInerney, Frank Maher, Ray Triado and John Merlo were among the most prominent at the beginning. They began an informal group to understand contemporary society, and to see its problems in the light of European and church history. They knew Catholics had meekly accepted modern secular ways as par for the course in contemporary life, even though they felt uncomfortable with them. The group decided not to accept defeat as in the past. Perhaps the Christian message could once again permeate society as it had in patristic, medieval and counter-reformation times. Perhaps they could set off a spark, fired by enthusiasm for a radical renewal.

---

[14] For the history of these ideas see Colin Jory, *The Campion Society*, 1986, and Race Matthews, *Of Labour and Liberty*, 2017.

16 Denys Jackson spoke regularly on the 'Catholic Hour' as well as being a prolific columnist. (MHDC)

Denys Jackson first became prominent in 1931 at a meeting of the group which was soon to formalize itself as the ground-breaking Campion Society. Judge Murray McInerney remembered:

> Jackson sparked [the meeting] into life with fireworks about Latin culture and the neo-scholasticism of Maritain – a display which dazzled and delighted the younger men, who in the words of Gerard Heffey 'started to read, to come under the spell of Belloc and Dawson. The glorious and tumultuous past of the Church unravelled before us. We infected one another with enthusiasm, became filled with scorn of a decadent paganism'. (*The Advocate*, 13 November, 1986)

Jackson wrote an influential article 'Reflections on Christianity in the New Age' (*The Advocate,* 10 August, 1933) which crystalized the mood of the times as a 'sense of the instability of the institutions on which our civilization is founded…Western culture already stands on the defensive, in fear of a coming siege.' Europe had been created by the church after the fall of the Roman Empire, he reminded his readers, when it tamed the prevailing pagan barbarian rulers; a similarly dire situation prevailed today. The spiritual bond which holds Europe together goes beyond nationalism, which seeks to usurp the role of God: 'Catholics must regain control of the world of thought'.

As an English Catholic of Anglican background Jackson was important in offering a different perspective to the prevailing Irish Catholic monopoly in the archdiocese. In his 'swan song' piece in 1980 he remembered:

> In the Australia we saw, Catholics of Irish stock had played a worthy part...but they lived in a spiritual ghetto, cut off from their fellow Christians of the British Reformed Churches, and recent memories of conflicts in the old land [Ireland] embittered the separation. [Catholics had to] form a united front against secular atheistic humanism.

Ireland at the time, engrossed in its own independence struggle, was not producing any new insights into social problems in the way Catholic thinkers in England and France were. The new group decided not to name themselves after an Irish saint. They considered the English martyr St Thomas More, but were worried he might be confused with the Irish balladist of the same name. So they chose the name 'Campion' after the English Jesuit thinker and martyr, who had displayed bravery in dark times. This was a watershed moment in the history of the Australian Catholic thought. Previously Melbourne had been an independent Irish fiefdom. Now the archdiocese was to move to an assertive, internationalist, public policy orientation, while Sydney continued to defer to the strain of Irish Jansenist piety which marked Archbishop Kelly's personality.

The Campion Society, which began in May 1931, formed study groups based on the history of the church, its recent loss of influence, and on contemporary social thought, including *Quadragesimo Anno*. Following Denys Jackson, they absorbed the writings of the English Catholic revival. Continental thinking, especially French, was another influence, including the JOCist notion of permeating one's milieu with Catholic ideals. Fr Hackett SJ, with his inspiring personality and store of publications at the Catholic Central Library, encouraged them, and soon became their chaplain. New members who became prominent as the Society expanded included William Knowles (son of Marion Miller Knowles), Val Adami, Kevin Kelly, Frank Misel, Bob Santamaria, Arthur Adams, Keith Mitchell, and Frank Murphy. Wider contacts were made with aspiring priests at the Werribee seminary, with Newman College and the Newman Society, and with the CYMS (Michael Chamberlin was its president at the time), thus joining two different strata (professional and lower middle class) of Melbourne Catholics together. Members' views began to be heard on the 'Catholic Hour' and at university debates. The Campions did not have a formulated plan of action based on cells, like the JOCist groups in France. Nonetheless they decided not be defensive, but to be assertive and outgoing in facing the public in open forums. In all this they resembled other ideological ginger groups of the left and right at the time, active partisans embroiled in the current ferment of ideas. Looking back they thought the Campion experience the great time of their lives.

The purpose of the Campions' study and participation in public forums was, in Frank Maher's words, as a 'training school for the leaders of Catholic thought and action throughout Victoria', a program which came to fruition in the setting up of Catholic Action in 1938. Apart from Paul McGuire's South Australian organization, there was no equivalent group in other states. In December 1934 Mannix established an Episcopal Sub-Committee 'for the purpose of evolving practical plans for Catholic Action'. In the same year he approved the Campions as a Catholic society. They were continuing the Melbourne tradition of lay initiative.

In 1932 two further bodies designed to spread Catholic ideas were launched. The Catholic Evidence Guild in Australia had been founded by Frank Sheed in 1925 in Sydney to promote Catholic apologetic views in contentious public forums, like the Sydney Domain and later Melbourne's Yarra bank. Kevin Kelly and Brian Harkin established a Melbourne branch of the Guild in 1932. Strong supporters included Frank Murphy and Fr James Murtagh, both soon to become *Advocate* journalists, and Fr Bernard Stewart, son of the *Austral Light* writer and convert Ronald Stewart, and later Bishop of Sandhurst. The Campions avoided the exclusively apologetics approach of the Catholic Evidence Guild. Sheed had moved to London and married Maisie Ward, who descended from a High Anglican family of converts prominent in the Oxford Revival Movement. The Sheeds founded the influential English Catholic publishing house Sheed & Ward, crucial in promoting the ideas of the current Catholic revival.

In the same year the long running radio program the 'Catholic Hour' began on 3AW, initiated by Fr Hackett and Dr Matthew Beovich, diocesan inspector of schools, and later Archbishop of Adelaide. It was broadcast on Sunday evenings, with a mixture of music, recordings of the Mass and talks on current affairs and religious topics. A section of the program, 'Question Box', where listeners' queries were answered, was initially conducted by Fr Jeremiah Murphy SJ of Newman College. Fr Henry Johnston SJ and Denys Jackson were regular contributors over the decades. Dr Percy Jones remembered:

> Joe Lyons organized some of the priests to persuade the Archbishop to take a weekly hour on one of the stations. He wanted us to have 3AW. 3AW derives from Allans, the music people, the *Age* and J.C. Williamsons... The Catholic Church was to have an hour of broadcasting every Sunday night for a nominal fee.[15]

Jones was made musical director of the program in 1940.

Dictators

Just as the Campions were grappling with depression-induced social problems, they were assailed by a new threat, the rise of Europe's dictators. Lenin and Mussolini had come to power in the meltdown caused by world war one, and Hitler in the implosion caused by the depression. These were a new type of dictator, addicted to deploying world historical panoramas to justify their aim of total control. The Catholic reaction was often to excuse those on the ideological right, and condemn those on the left, as the church saw itself as an integral

---

[15] Donald Cave, *Percy Jones*, p. 32.

part of the conservative European order. This bias led it on many occasions to misread the situation. We can now see that the totalitarian ideologies of Communism and Fascism had a lot in common with each other. The crucial struggle was not between left and right, but between monsters of all stripes who suppressed liberties and on the other hand free democracies, as a few commentators like George Orwell understood at the time.

One standard Catholic reaction was to judge each new regime primarily on its attitude to religion, and on the extent it would allow the Catholic Church and its congregations freedom to practice. This instinct for self-preservation was an understandable, if dangerously limited, approach. Religious people condemned these new regimes primarily as atheistic. But most political philosophies since the Enlightenment had been non-religious, and sometimes anti-religious. The new totalitarian regimes were objectionable not primarily because they attacked God, but because they attacked men. One had to judge these dictators on what they actually did, not on their professed aims, which were usually a double-think camouflage for their real intentions. In looking at reactions to these events at the time, we, having the benefit of hindsight, should be wary of rushing to judgement, as many commentators understandably got these unprecedented events wrong.

In the early 1930s Melbourne Catholic attitudes were still overall in favour of Mussolini. Fascism, it was argued, was healthy because it got rid of decadent liberalism: there was 'much to be said for the government of a dictator' because Mussolini got things done. Mussolini and the Pope were alike as both were 'live wires' and the 'strong men' of Italy. A Concordat signed between the Vatican and the regime would, Dr Beovich hoped, curb Mussolini's attempt to dragoon religion into becoming a state enterprise. It didn't. (*The Advocate*, 7 January and 10 November 1932)

Catholics were much less sympathetic to Hitler, and overall unfavourable. He had restored order, reduced unemployment, and purged the Communists. An *Advocate* editorial sympathetic to Hitler as a victim of the Versailles reparations (21 September 1933) was embarrassingly supported in a letter from a group of 'Hitler

Sympathisers in Melbourne'. But as *The Advocate* also reported, German Catholic clerics were warning against Nazism's egoism and self-deification. Nazism wanted a purely 'German Church' based on Nordic not Christian values, its nationalism was fanatical not unifying, it was excessively harsh on the Jews, and it was overall a menace to Europe. The Catholic Church signed a Concordat with the regime in 1933 in which it agreed to tolerate the Nazi program in exchange for freedom to practice the faith, a bad bargain. Mannix wrote to the head of Melbourne Jewish community as early as 1932 expressing sympathy for their plight under Hitler. It was disappointing therefore that *The Advocate* ran a piece on 31 January 1935 ridiculously claiming that a Judeo-Masonic nexus had caused the Catholic monarchs of Austria and Spain to be driven from their thrones, had divided Ireland and solidified a Prussian hegemony in Germany. The Campions, though enthused in a general way by Denys Jackson, had a better record than him or *The Advocate* on these matters; they didn't as a rule fall for the new ideologies.

In 1934 Denys Jackson was given a position on *The Advocate* staff and rapidly took over from the far-sighted Patrick O'Leary the role of chief opinion former, writing so many prominent editorials and articles that he was acting as de facto editor. Jackson was a fluent and stimulating commentator, who thought on a world scale. In that regard he greatly enhanced the paper. It was his opinions that were the problem. As a monarchist Jackson opposed democracy and so agreed with Hitler's demolition of it. Tough measures were need in a crisis, he argued, a corporate state had been established in Germany, and Western propaganda against Hitler was untrue. On the other hand Jackson worried that Hitler was anti-religious and that a new barbarism would descend on Germany in the future. In a review of a book on Bolshevism by Waldemar Gurian, Patrick O'Leary understood that Communism's outrages were not arbitrary and accidental, but derived from its theory. Jackson's qualified excuses for Nazism revealed he did not appreciate this point. He introduced a new uncomfortable appeasement tone into *The Advocate*, he wrote too sympathetically on Germany and Italy to the exclusion of other issues, and he let his own strong personal views become editorial policy, to such an extent that the paper's managing editor Fr Moynihan terminated his position on the paper in early 1935. As Jackson had left his teaching profession he now had no employment, so Mannix arranged to have him appointed editor of the other Catholic paper, *The Tribune,* but he continued to publish extensively in *The Advocate.* In all these matters we must remember that the totalitarian regimes did not display themselves in their full horror till the second half of the 1930s.

Mannix as Aristocrat

Between the wars Mannix dominated the Australian Catholic Church; he had no coadjutor and no rivals. Sydney's Archbishop Kelly was old and ailing, and never had a wide-ranging grasp of things. As the connection with Ireland lessened, Mannix imperceptibly acted more as the remote aristocrat and less as the tribal chieftain. The roles of tribal chieftain and aristocrat are different: the first relies on closeness to the populace and the second relies on distance from it, but both can be deployed in the one personality. As happened with the careers of de Gaulle and de Valera as well as Mannix, a successful counter-governmental strategy can become the transition mechanism from tribal leader to ruler. Mannix gradually withdrew part of himself, though not his voice and influence, from the public domain and rendered himself untouchable, and perhaps unknowable. He was self-contained – his sources of inner strength seemed not to derive primarily from human contact. Cocooned in cold austere Raheen, he continued the monastic regimen of his Maynooth days. By giving priests and laity permission to do their own thing, he was the superintendent but not the engine room of the great energies of his domain. Melbourne produced its own momentum. Asa Briggs pointed out in his book *Victorian Cities* that in 1834 no European foot had stepped on its soil, yet such was its extraordinary rise that fifty years later Melbourne was one of the great metropolises of the British Empire.

In Australia Mannix was technically an aristocrat, a Prince Bishop in the European mould with his own coat of arms. But even before he became a prelate he was known at the Maynooth seminary as the

'Roman emperor'; like de Gaulle he was a natural born aristocrat. A Maynooth student, G. Brendáin, wrote of Mannix in *Austral Light*, September, 1912, that he had 'a temperamental reserve often taken for coldness, in the imperial manner which impressed but awed, and suggested hauteur, in the manifest dignity of his personality'. Mannix had a patrician demeanour before his elevation to the rank; his consecration as an archbishop therefore confirmed him as an aristocrat as much as it made him one. The Prime Ministers Bruce and Menzies were the only Australian politicians of the time who had, like Mannix, a naturally patrician superiority. All had a certain aura and distance around them. One couldn't saunter up unannounced to Mannix or to Menzies, as one could to, say, Bob Hawke, as both Mannix and Menzies were wholly outside the beer-drinking, back-slapping egalitarianism of demotic Australia.

17 Archbishop Mannix's favourite photograph of himself, in walking rig on his way to the cathedral. (MDHC)

Mannix gradually affected the theatrical style of a European grandee – the regal bearing, silken top hat adding to his considerable height, black cape and silver cane, doling out trinkets to the plebs on his strolls through Collingwood. His favourite photograph of himself shows him in this rig. He even allowed a Melbourne physician who had treated him to advertise his medical services 'by appointment to Archbishop Mannix', in the style of services by appointment to the Governor or Buckingham Palace. He did not drive but was chauffeured to his many speaking engagements. Mannix did not socialize, he did not go to dinner parties, he did not frequent vice-regal functions as Archbishop Carr had done. He told Calwell he would never mix socially with the British-Australian ascendency while Ireland remained partitioned. As time was not healing that wound, Mannix was 'nursing his wrath to keep it warm'. As a consequence Raheen with its prominent red tower became a sort of counter to the official Government House with its white one. At Raheen Mannix had no court, no lesser nobles, no clerical retainers or flunkeys. We are accustomed to think traditional power hierarchies took the form of a pyramid. But Mannix's had a flattened structure; below him there was a gap, and then all, with the exception of his Vicar General, were equal. He allowed no successor, no rivals, no powerful barons to develop, as Carr had with Fr Patrick Phelan who climbed the pyramid successively as Dean, Vicar General, Monsignor and eventually Bishop. Mannix allowed his coadjutor, Archbishop Simonds, forced on him by Rome in 1942, minimal say. Menzies ran his cabinet and Bob Santamaria ran the National Civic Council the same way. A flattened ruling structure, rule by separation rather than closeness, is necessarily neither good nor bad, it's just the way a commanding personality usually runs things, keeping himself above the fray.

Mannix's distance from events allowed him to adopt the role of wry social satirist. Here he is having a sly shot at the wowser atmosphere of Melbourne, especially Sabbatarianism:

> As everybody is aware, Sunday in Melbourne is a day of gloom. It is because the vast majority of the people remain in bed. Speaking generally, the only people who get up on Sunday morning to go to church are Catholics. A stranger passing through Melbourne on a Sunday morning and seeing numbers of people hurrying in the various streets could come to only one conclusion – that there was a Catholic church around the corner. (*The Advocate*, 15 September 1932)

The unstated rebuke here is that non-Catholics aren't as religiously observant. Mannix became a master of the humorous putdown, the deadpan comment with a sting in the tail. He once said in the presence of his closest friend Fr Hackett: 'I always knew the doctrine of the Trinity was a great mystery, but I never realized how mysterious it was until I heard Fr Hackett giving a sermon on it'. Mannix is always one jump ahead of us. Normally we think at some stage we understand what makes a person tick, but it's best to admit we are still learning about him. We never quite have him taped. The prison chaplain Fr John Brosnan said that Mannix was so remarkable that when in his presence he couldn't take his eyes off him, and the number of books and articles on Mannix shows that even in death this still obtains.

The 1930s was a time when many of the people who had come out from Ireland in the previous century were passing away. The peak of Irish migration to Australia was the 1860s to the 1880s. Very few (such as J.J. Liston, Dr Kenny and Fr J.J. Malone) were left, and very few were now coming out. When William McMahon, a founder of the Australian Catholic Federation and *The Tribune* newspaper, died in 1933, Dr Mannix spoke at his funeral of Melbourne Catholics as 'a body such as I had never yet come into contact with in any other country I have visited – men not merely willing to give money, but ready to give their services day and night in the cause of the Church.' The rise of the Campion Society, encouraged by Mannix, was one sign that this Melbourne tradition was still flourishing. He gave them the nod, then took a step back and let them proceed on their own. Mannix's name was often mentioned in Ireland during the election campaign that led to de Valera's ascendency as leader of Ireland in 1932. Mannix announced he was pleased that Ireland was at last free after the traumas of the previous decade. Patrick O'Leary and Arthur Calwell were the principal speakers at a large meeting to celebrate de Valera's victory, organized by the Irish Association of Australia and held at St Patrick's Hall in March 1932.

The 1934 Eucharistic Congress

Catholics loved public celebrations. 1925 had been a Holy Year based in Rome, Chicago had staged a massive international Catholic congress in 1926, and in 1928 Sydney held a Eucharistic Congress, all of which Mannix and other bishops attended. The European habit of public religious processions, such as those on the feast of Corpus Christi, when the Host or a statue is reverently carried through the streets, had been continued in the New World. The Salesians held an annual Eucharistic pageant at their Sunbury mansion Rupertswood, at which the participants dressed up in white and paraded around the grounds on floats decorated with banners and ribbons. Schools staged elaborate tableaus at annual speech nights, and parishes conducted May and Spring Queen competitions. In later years public Catholic festivals included the 'Credo', a dramatized play performed at the MCG in 1939, the centenary celebrations of Catholicism in Victoria, and Fr Peyton's Family Crusade extravaganzas at the MCG in the 1950s.

1934 was the centenary of Victoria's European founding, and as its contribution to the State celebrations the Catholic Archdiocese decided to hold a large Eucharistic congress in December. In Anglo-Saxon societies, triumphalist religious displays were distasteful to the more austere Reformed Churches which abhorred colourful vestments, ciboria, decorated canopies, images of the Virgin and other 'graven images'. The annual St Patrick's Day procession caused annoyance on these grounds. Such displays of religious pageantry were too 'in your face' for the Anglican Archbishop Frederick Head, who was moved to write to Mannix in November 1934 asking him not to process the Host through Melbourne streets as planned at the Eucharistic Congress, as this would offend 'many of your fellow Christians'. Mannix replied that such processions were commonly approved around the world, and Head should instead devote his energies to persuading his fellow Christians that the proceedings were in order. Mannix added that he proposed to publish their exchange of letters. Alarmed at this, Head then arranged for a joint letter on the matter from the heads of the Anglican, Methodist and Presbyterian churches be published, stating that the normal tolerance of religion did not apply in this case, and that the procession 'will stir historical memories of the most painful kind', a remark Mannix described as 'deplorable'. The state Attorney General, Robert Menzies, approved the procession.

The public face of the congress, attended by 37 bishops, was a number of massive gatherings and demonstrations. The first was the welcome to the Papal Legate, the Irish Primate Cardinal MacRory, who was driven through crowded streets lined with cheering members of various Catholic organizations. Men's and women's outdoor Masses

18 The Papal Legate to the Congress, Cardinal MacRory, takes precedence; in the back row second left is Dr Leo Kenny attired as a papal knight, and second from the right is Fr Jeremiah Murphy, SJ. (MDHC)

each attracted crowds of 150,000. The Congress climaxed with a Eucharistic procession, and Benediction celebrated from Mount St Evin's Private Hospital balcony in front of a congregation estimated at half a million people. The remainder of the congress was taken up with a series of lectures and ancillary events, including civic receptions. The theme of the proceedings was 'Catholic Action', though of the many lectures at the main sessions only two, given by bishops, were on the topic, and neither understood the problems in their contemporary form, as the Campions did. Kevin Kelly and Paul McGuire spoke more knowledgeably on Catholic Action at a Newman Society gathering during the congress. The congress proceedings seemed an old fashioned, backward look, hardly related to a time when the dictators were ravaging civilization, including religion, in Europe.

The priest later most strongly identified with Melbourne Catholic festivities, Fr Percy Jones, was studying in Rome at this stage. He had secured outstanding results in his final year school exams at the age of fifteen in 1929, with honours in his humanities and music subjects, and with an Exhibition and a University free place. *The Advocate* and *The Tribune* produced identically worded accounts of his success: 'His excellent work in music earned for him the approbation and flattering comment of the examiners who awarded him the coveted University exhibition. Percy, though an artist of the keyboard, shows a well-balanced range of subjects, in his scholastic programme and in the sports arena.' (*The Advocate*, 13 March, 1930) The stilted extravagant prose style suggests this encomium was penned by his father. As the young Percy now wished to become a priest his father went straight to the top by taking him to see Mannix, who envisaged Percy eventually being in charge of music for the Archdiocese, which came to pass. So instead of entering the Werribee seminary Mannix sent him straight off to Propaganda College, Rome, to study for his ordination and then complete a Doctorate on Sacred Music. In Italy Jones studied the church's musical tradition from Gregorian chant onwards, and in particular absorbed the Benedictine approach of integrating music and liturgy. In 1933 his younger brother Basil Jones, then eighteen, was awarded the Victorian violin grand championship; like his brother he would go on to a distinguished musical career.

Bernard Heinze, a Catholic from a family of German origin, a former pupil of St Patrick's College Ballarat, and a generation older than Jones, was already making a success of a musical career. He had studied in London and Italy, and served in the First World War. Between the wars he assumed three important musical posts. In 1926 at the age of only 32 he was appointed Ormond Professor of Music at the University of Melbourne. In 1933 he became chief conductor of the Melbourne Symphony Orchestra, holding both positions until the 1950s. He was also director-general of music at the ABC, speaking on radio 3LO-3AR and helping to form state symphony orchestras. In these posts he did much to bring classical music to a larger audience in Australia. He worked closely with Fr Percy Jones on the latter's return. In 1932 Heinze married Valerie Hennessy, daughter of Sir David Hennessy, a prominent businessman and former Catholic Lord Mayor of Melbourne. Heinze was himself knighted in 1949.

5

THE LATE 1930s:
CATHOLIC ACTION

Mussolini – The Spanish Civil War – The Catholic Worker *– Catholic Action – The Prehistory of the Movement – Personalities – Charities and Churches*

Mussolini

From the mid 1930s to the mid 1940s, international affairs dominated many people's thoughts. Things got much worse in Europe. The dictators now acted much more blatantly, persecuting innocent citizens, including their own, on a large scale. Stalin began a massive concentration camp empire. Hitler did the same in his sphere, while expanding to invade neighbouring countries. Mussolini went on imperialistic adventures in Libya and Abyssinia, while the Japanese invaded Manchuria and central China with great ferocity, and then moved down on south-east Asia. Such expansionist outrages led to another world war, and six years of desperate struggle to defeat the aggressors militarily. These unexpected developments took precedence over all others, even in geographically isolated Australia, where our troops had to prepare to fight the Germans in Europe and then the Japanese on our own doorstep.

The Advocate continued to give Mussolini favourable coverage, as in an article headed: "Mussolini is Always Right!' Italy's Confidence in its Duce'. This praise continued in more muted form when he embarked on imperial expansion. Italy had established a small colony in Abyssinia in the late 19th century. Mussolini used the excuse of local attacks on this colony to launch a takeover of the county, his real motive being personal and national glory. The League of Nations dithered and did not stop him. An *Advocate* editorial of 11 July 1935 did not support his move, was neutral on the issue of colonialism, but, disagreeing with Britain's strong stance against

Italy, believed the matter was not worth fighting over. The well-known Catholic author J.B. Morton ('the Beachcomber'), supported Mussolini's anti-democracy attitude in an article reproduced in *The Advocate* of 1 April 1937.

Denys Jackson justified the takeover of Abyssinia in *The Advocate,* and later when he became editor of *The Tribune*; he continued to write his *Advocate* column under the pen name 'Sulla'. Sulla was a Roman dictator who appealed over the head of the ruling elite directly to the masses. As a monarchist Jackson believed that a strong man, like Mussolini, could arbitrate among the squabbling factions below him. On 17 October 1935, an *Advocate* editorial argued against British objections to the Abyssinian adventure. In the same issue Jackson strongly supported the Italian move:

> Abyssinia would inevitably, sooner or later, be subjected to "development" by European peoples, and experience showed that if exploitation were to take place, it was best that it should be accompanied by definite responsibilities for orderly administration. Italy had the best right to undertake this task, for which she was well fitted; and in achieving her own aims she would also give security and peace to Abyssinia herself.

Jackson does not come out of this well. Neither did the high profile Sydney Catholic surgeon Dr Herbert 'Paddy' Moran, famous as the rugby union footballer who had captained the first Wallaby team to England. Moran went to Italy at this stage, met Mussolini a number of times, published a book *Letters from Rome*, and worked as freelance doctor in Abyssinia in 1936.

When Japan invaded Manchuria, Jackson used similar arguments to his Abyssinian ones: though we may deplore Japan's brutal actions, pressure from the West has helped the militarist faction in Japan get the upper hand. As a monarchist Jackson wrote a column praising the character of the Emperor Hirohito of Japan after his country had invaded its neighbour. An *Advocate* editorial of January 7, 1937, accused those who said Hitler might invade Czechoslovakia of scaremongering. Jackson kept directing his animus against the West for being non-conciliatory, instead of against the aggressors

Germany, Italy and Japan; by this means he indirectly provided excuses for their actions. His dislike of liberal democracy meant he was fishing in dangerous waters. Overall *Advocate* editorials and Mannix were more sensible.

The Spanish Civil War

In 1937 Pope Pius XI issued an encyclical, *Divini Redemptoris*, condemning Communism. Most Melbourne Catholics supported the Franco side during the Spanish Civil War because the Republicans sacked church properties and persecuted clerics, and because Catholics believed the Republican government was a prelude to a Soviet-supporting Communist regime in Spain. In addition the Popular Front government of Leon Blum in adjacent France was seen as potentially falling prey to Communism. For Catholics Spain was a rerun of the Mexican tragedy. *The Advocate* featured a headline on 29 October, 1936: 'Last Crusade Holy War for Catholic Spain. Enemy Worse Than The Saracen.' Long memories of medieval crusades, Muslim Spain and the Ottoman threat to Europe were surfacing here.

The gulf in Spain between Catholic traditionalists and anti-clerical socialists had been getting steadily wider, as both sides took turns at unsuccessfully governing a deeply divided society. When in mid 1936 General Francisco Franco launched a military coup against the Republican government, the country was plunged into an extremely bitter civil war of a complex kind. The staunchly Catholic and traditionalist Basques found themselves, for example, on the Republican side, and the Stalinist Communists purged their socialist allies in Catalonia. The Spanish Catholic Church supported Franco's Nationalist objectives. European ideologues of the left and right saw Spain as a testing ground for their own worldviews, imposing on the country their own templates which often did not take account of Spanish conditions. The Spanish conflict caused a divide in the Australian Labor movement, with the unions pro-Republican and the Catholics pro-Franco.

Melbourne Catholics were active at the University of Melbourne, where opinion ran overall in favour of the Republican forces in

19 Paul McGuire, an early exponent of Catholic Action, and later Australian Ambassador to Italy (MDHC).

Spain. Matters came to a head during a dramatic debate on the war in Spain on 22 March 1937, which attracted widespread attention and came to be regarded as symptomatic of the era. Kevin Kelly, Stan Ingwersen and Bob Santamaria, all prominent Campions, supported the Franco side, while Nettie Palmer, Jack Legge and Dr Gerard O'Day, an ex-Catholic, the latter two Communists, supported the Republican side. Nettie Palmer's husband Vance was a friend of Patrick O'Leary, who had invited him to write *The Advocate's* foreign affairs column in the 1920s. Now his wife Nettie announced there were no anti-Catholic atrocities in Spain, which *The Advocate* rightly found baffling.

The Catholics, comprising about two-thirds of the large audience, were well organized at the debate. The Catholic team, experienced debaters, presented their case coherently, whereas the opposing team's approach was more scattergun, with O'Dea making the tactical mistake of belittling the Catholic Church. At the end of a highly charged meeting the organized Catholic side won the vote, at which they shouted out in unison 'Long Live Christ the King', a triumphalist slogan defiantly repeated on Santamaria's funeral booklet six decades later. Militant organized Catholicism had announced itself on the public stage. Similar debates were held in Geelong and Ballarat, and in Adelaide organized by Paul McGuire.

In this period of great disturbance which challenged accepted verities, wild swings in belief were common. Gerard O'Day was a former Catholic turned Communist, and a bitter opponent of the Catholic Church. Since Newman's time a number of prominent people, mainly High Anglicans, including G.K. Chesterton, Monsignor Ronald Knox, Arnold Lunn, Douglas Hyde and

Evelyn Waugh in England, and Denys Jackson now in Australia, had converted to Catholicism, becoming staunch defenders of the church's beliefs. Catholics trumpeted these defections as the wave of the future. But were they? On the other hand people raised as Catholics like John Curtin, Gerald O'Day, the judge John Barry and the foreign affairs commentator Dr Peter Russo were leaving the church as they became more radical in their thinking, just as some Sinn Feiners had in Ireland. Those who had relinquished Catholicism ranged on a spectrum from those who remained generally religious to those who became agnostics or atheists. Some embraced secular 'religions' like socialism and Communism which held out the promise of the Kingdom of Heaven on earth. Later Communist union leaders like O'Shea, Malone, Healy and Gallagher had surnames betraying their Irish Catholic origins. Another example was Muriel Heagney, of Irish Catholic upbringing and part of Richmond ALP branch, who spent the interwar years in radical union activities and became sympathetic to Soviet Communism. This small breakaway group was an early crack in the hitherto impregnable fortress of Australian Catholicism, foreshadowing a wider relinquishing of allegiance, for different reasons, from the 1970s onwards.

Denys Jackson, a supporter of appeasement, provided excuses for Hitler all the way to the Munich pact, blaming Austrians, Jews, Czechs and other victims of Hitler for not being accommodating enough. In late 1938 he was arguing that Munich meant war was not likely. In late 1942 at the darkest stage of the war, he was still more sympathetic to Petain and Vichy France than to de Gaulle and the Free French forces. Overall Jackson took the line that Fascism was the lesser of two evils compared with Communism, a view common on the right at the time. Patrick O'Leary had much clearer insights during this bewildering period, seeing the calamity in both the Nazi and Communist approaches, but as he was only the literary editor on *The Advocate*, he had less influence on current affairs commentary than Jackson. The young Fr John Kelly, who like O'Leary read and thought a lot, noted perceptively in his diary in March 1939: 'Nazi-ism seems only one degree removed from Communism'. By 1944 (*The Advocate*, 24 May 1944) Jackson had realized that totalitarianism (which included both Fascism and Communism) was the enemy, but a bit late, as the die had been cast. In his final appearance in old age on the 'Catholic Hour' in May 1980, Jackson admitted he had got things wrong in the 1930s:

> I erred in failing to realize the basically anti-Christian features in Italian Fascism, and in imagining the Church could deal with Hitler, and Europe could live with him. My strong sense of the world-ranging menace of Communism, to which so many liberal thinkers, and even Christians, seemed blind, helped to obscure for me the imminent threat of the Axis Powers. (*The Advocate*, 29 May, 1980)

The *Catholic Worker*

When in 1935 the Campions had the idea of a new journal, Bob Santamaria, a young and junior figure, took it on, his first venture in a unique political career which was to stretch over six decades. Santamaria, from Brunswick and educated at CBC North Melbourne, had competed a brilliant degree in Law/Arts. First published in February 1936, the title of the paper echoed Dorothy Day's US *Catholic Worker*. Following Papal encyclicals, it focused on bettering the conditions of the employed and unemployed, and provided a forum for the worries of workers and unions. The young Santamaria now met Mannix, half a century (two generations) older than him, for the first time, a momentous conjunction, as Mannix later said Santamaria was the most intelligent person he had ever met, and Santamaria said he revered Mannix more than his own father. It was the beginning of a close association which lasted until Mannix's death almost three decades later.

The *Catholic Worker* defended the Catholic Church, following the church's line of opposing both inequitable capitalism and strike-prone Communism as the 'illegitimate offspring of the same diseased materialism'. Santamaria wrote most of the early copy for the *Catholic Worker* himself, and because the paper had passion and informed insights, it was an extraordinary success, selling 27,000 copies an issue six months after it began. But in October 1937 some Campions, led by Kevin Kelly, reacted to this success by taking the sole editorship off Santamaria, reducing him to one of an editorial collective, a curious move given the paper's outstanding debut. Santamaria then gradually severed connection with the paper. As the parties did not differ over issues, this seems most likely a personality clash, arising out of envy of Santamaria's success, and difficulties in coping with his superior energies. The *Catholic Worker* then became the mouthpiece of the Campions and their successors, the progressive Catholics, and the leading organ of Catholic anti-Santamaria sentiment, a campaign which Kelly and some of his colleagues kept up for decades.

This pattern of events was repeated when the Campions suggested to the hierarchy in 1937 the formation of a large-scale Catholic Action organization which everyone, including the leading Campions, expected they would lead. The youthful Santamaria was surprisingly made deputy, and by 1946 he was head of Catholic Action, as well as running the industrial Movement, the Rural Movement and publishing his own paper, which still exists, whereas the Campions, except for Frank Maher, had no official positions. Santamaria had blindsided them. The weakness of the Campions was that they had no action program, as their aim was confined to lifting awareness through study and debates with others. Santamaria produced the *Catholic Worker* for them, their most successful operation. With no organizational role left the Campion Society dwindled, not the first time in history a group spawned an offspring which consumed its begetter. Santamaria's colleagues found him, as others found him later, uncoalitionable, uncontrollable and unbeatable; it was the latter which rankled most. Santamaria's opponents always gave, in retrospect, political objections to what he did, but their complaints were as much personal as political, and initially over the *Catholic Worker*, not over the Movement. The ALP had a political split in 1954-5, but the internal *Catholic Worker* stand-off was the genesis of a split among Melbourne Catholics before the political one.

Catholic Action

Under the pressure of the world-wide depression the insights of *Quadragesimo Anno* were condensed by the Pope in 1934 into a new round of Catholic Action, an attempt to change a whole society by the organized action of Catholics in the social and public spheres. The Pope described Catholic Action as 'in its very nature, above and outside all political parties, being directed not to achieve or protect the particular interests of special groups'. He added that 'that does not prevent individual Catholics taking part in organizations of a political character'. A year later the Pope tried to make this distinction clearer by saying Catholics should engage in 'non party politics which has in view the *polis*, the advancement of the common good.' (*The Advocate*, 19 April 1934 and 2 May 1935) Difficulty in understanding and then following this rather fuzzy distinction was to cause much of the fallout over the Movement at the time of the split and after. 'Catholic Action' was a phrase that, uniquely in Australia, was to become a headline and household word here because of this.

The Campions put out an ACTS pamphlet *Prelude to Catholic Action* in 1936. Kelly and McInerney wrote to *The Advocate* in mid 1937 calling for an official Catholic Action organization to be set up. A Campion memorandum of late 1937 was sent to Mannix to this end. It had two aims, first to generally energize Catholics for concerted public action, and second to draw attention to 'a crisis among the working classes, fraught with danger to Catholics', by which was meant Communist union gains. When the Catholic Action organization was set up in early 1938 in Melbourne by the Catholic bishops, its employees Maher and Santamaria worked under the supervision of Archbishop Simonds, appointed Episcopal delegate in charge of Catholic Action, who was at the time more knowledgeable on these matters than Maher or the 23-year-old Santamaria. Maher became in effect the Catholic Action house manager, Santamaria its political activist out and about. Paul McGuire was called in by Santamaria to tour the eastern states in 1938 to help set up the new organization. McGuire then went on a USA lecture tour in 1939 speaking on the 'Catholic Revolution'. In the same year he co-authored a book *Restoring All Things – a Guide to Catholic Action*.

The Catholic Action secretariat was set up as a national body, but the Sydney archdiocese decided to go its own way rather than be run from Melbourne, an early hint of differences. Catholic Action was based on the belief that every vocation had attributes specific to it, and so had to develop along its own lines. Groups were therefore organized by workplace and occupation rather than by parish. Cells of each specialized movement met regularly with a specific agenda. Officials from headquarters and local leaders (sometimes called 'militants') attempted to expand the cell system. The early period was devoted to setting up specific movements, the principal ones being the Young Catholic Students (YCS), the Young Christian Workers (YCW), the National Catholic Girls' Movement (NCGM), and the National Catholic Rural Movement (NCRM). It was intended that each of these bodies be on a national scale, but they were strongest in Melbourne and the eastern states. Older Catholic bodies, like the Legion of Mary and The Grail, both based on personal piety, for years strenuously resisted being taken under the Catholic Action umbrella.

Catholic Action developed a comprehensive socio-economic analysis of the needs of Australian society. Economic problems which interested Catholic Action officials included inflation, the living wage, and work conditions. Catholic Action encouraged worker participation in management, industrial councils, the breaking up of business monopolies, and the redistribution of wealth. Ownership was to be restored to workers and smaller farmers, with emphasis on a just living wage and on co-operatives. Catholic Action opposed women moving into the war-time workforce, supported women as mothers in the home, and reinforced traditional moral views on the importance of the family, and the dangers of sex and contraception. In foreign affairs Catholic Action opposed the White Australia policy, and supported anti-colonial and anti-Communist movements in Asian countries. Though membership of the various movements of Catholic Action was confined to Catholics, attempts were made to collaborate on these goals with other denominations.

One example of a new body was the National Catholic Rural Movement (NCRM) set up by Santamaria in 1940. It was based on the ideal of a pre-Reformation, pre-industrial, craft-based Christendom current at the time. Such a style of life would preserve, it was hoped, religious belief, which declined in the cities, as the European experience had shown. Santamaria wrote *The Earth Our Mother* (1945) and Denys Jackson wrote an ACTS pamphlet *Australian Dream* in this vein. Ray Triado at Whitlands and Fr John Heffey (brother of the Campion Gerard Heffey) at Gladysdale formed small Catholic farming communities in the Victorian countryside along these lines. The San Isidore settlement near Wagga and the Maryknoll settlement of Fr Pooley near Pakenham were more structured examples. Santamaria never distinguished between Catholic Action organizations and the Industrial Movement, so the NCRM carried out Movement functions in the regions. One of the principal advisors to the NCRM, as well as the National Farmers Federation, was James Tehan, from a family clan with large holdings in central Victoria. Tehan had been a friend of Frank Maher at Newman College in the 1920s. His daughter-in-law Marie Tehan was a Kennett government minister, and his grandson Dan Tehan became a minister in the Federal Liberal Turnbull government in 2016. The extended Catholic Gorman family similarly held properties in central Victoria as well as in the Riverina.

The Prehistory of the Movement

The later 1930s presaged disasters to come: Hitler had taken over Austria and Czechoslovakia and was now moving on Poland. A new large scale war looked imminent. Remembering the carnage of 1914-1918, world leaders, including the newly anointed Pope Pius XII, called for peace. Responding to the Pope's call Santamaria, acting through the Catholic Action organization, formed a Central Catholic Peace Commission with Dr Leo Kenny as chairman. It organized an enormous peace rally which 60,000 people attended at the Exhibition Buildings on Sunday 28 May, 1939. This function was the second public appearance of Bob Santamaria; on the platform with him were Dr Mannix, Robert Menzies, Prime Minister at the time, and Albert Dunstan, Premier of Victoria. Santamaria, the first speaker, argued that in the critical European situation at the time all parties should disarm and go once again to the conference table to avert a world catastrophe. A motion moved by Santamaria and Denys Jackson asking Menzies to convey these sentiments to world leaders was supported by Bert Cremean, Deputy Leader of State Labor Party, and others. The last speaker was Mannix who declared *inter alia*: 'I am still a democrat, even though, in these days, democracy is with many people at a discount and in disfavour'. The motion for peace was passed and a telegram sent to the Pope. The Nazi-Soviet pact a few months later in August shattered these hopes. Hitler and Stalin were not interested in peace, only a breathing space as they prepared to invade Poland and divide it up. By unilaterally offering to disarm and calling for peace the Western allies were making peace less likely. In later decades Santamaria regretted the position he took at this time. During the Vietnam War he argued that simply calling for peace objectively helped an aggressor, in this case the North Vietnamese Communist regime, just as those who had naively called for peace in 1939 had helped Hitler. Civilian populations needed freedom in order to have peace.

The controversial Industrial Movement, an unofficial political operation organized by Bob Santamaria, deputy head of CA, to defeat Communist takeovers of key unions and of the ALP, was set up at the time. It was, confusingly, run from the Catholic Action office though its status as a CA body was unclear. Santamaria called it the 'Movement' because he believed in dynamic bodies which lived dangerously in always questing after new goals; if they ceased to initiate and rested on their laurels, they would die. When did the Movement begin? Santamaria claimed that he began it in August 1941, but that was actually the time he put it on an organized basis. The Movement had a prehistory. By 1937 awareness of how Communists had penetrated the Republican government in Spain led to worries that a similar white-anting of the ALP and the unions was already occurring in Australia. A correspondent wrote to *The Advocate* on 12 August 1937:

> If Catholic unionists and Catholic Laborites and other anti-Communist unionists and Laborites were to attend the meetings of their organizations and take an interest, intelligent and instructed, in them, the Communist leaven in the all too stolid as well as solid mass of Laborites would quickly prove inoperative.

This is exactly the *modus operandi* of the future Movement. At the same time the Campion Society memorandum requesting the bishops to start up a Catholic Action organization had as one of its two aims action against Communists in the unions. It warned that trade unions were 'steadily coming under the control of the Communists'. The new CA body should aim at 'preventing a Communist or pagan capture of unionism in Australia'. It would do this by watching Communist activities and reporting on them. This reveals a Movement-type anti-Communist body was officially proposed from the very start by the Campions.

A further Campion memorandum defining this anti-Communist activity stated that unionists should be educated in Catholic social ideas: 'Out of these trained workers will soon arise groups in individual unions...The [Catholic Action] Bureau cannot do more than train militants; it must scrupulously avoid politics and can only indirectly direct group tactics.' This, the distinction announced by the Pope, was taken up by Archbishop Simonds. In the month Catholic Action was being founded, January 1938, Simonds went into print in *The Advocate*, stating that one of its aims as 'beneficent social action...outside and above political parties'. Insisting on this distinction, on which the Movement venture later foundered, was one of the highlights of Simonds' career. Next month, February 1938, at the time he was appointed deputy head of the newly formed CA secretariat, Santamaria offered in *The Advocate* his unique definition of Catholic Action as 'the new-found determination of Australian Catholic unionists to fight the Communist aggression against the industrial movement'. No secrecy here! This reveals Santamaria had the idea of the Movement in the forefront of his mind at least from early 1938.

Individual efforts by Catholics to oppose Communism in the unions were in existence from 1938. At this stage Calwell was one of the first to organize groups to combat the pro-Communist left, not only in unions, as is well known, but in the ALP itself, as he and others were having their own political pre-selections and careers threatened by far left entrism. So Calwell was at this stage an initiator and supporter of Movement strategies. At the suggestion of Calwell, Frank Keating organized in the Boilermakers Union against the Communists at the Newport railway workshops; Keating later claimed to have founded the Movement. Santamaria was in contact with Bert Cremean, Deputy Leader of the Victorian Labor Party, on these matters. Cremean and Calwell's involvement meant the Victorian Labor Party was in the know from the beginning. In the next few years similar groups were begun in industrial areas like Newcastle and Broken Hill, and by Fr Paddy Ryan in Sydney. The Nazi-Soviet pact of August 1939 added a new dimension to the Movement's operations. When the Second World War broke out some months later, Communists around the world were supporting their ally Hitler against the Western allies. Communists in Australia were not only trying to take over unions for their own ends, they were now also sabotaging our war effort against Germany. Early Movement activity therefore involved national security as well as internal union politics. The existence of the Movement had not been disclosed. Nonetheless the left wing Labor Federal MP Maurice Blackburn wrote in the Melbourne *Argus* on 30 September 1941:

> I am told that a body known as 'Catholic Action' has nothing to do with politics. But the same name is used by Catholics as well as non-Catholics to describe that energy, organized or not, which unremittingly but unsuccessfully attempts to influence the votes of Catholics in Labor organisations.

Blackburn's letter makes it clear that Movement activities had been going on for some time before 1941, that they were directed from the CA office, and that this was known to its targets.

In 1941 there had been a slip up. In a speech reported in *The Advocate,* 1 May 1941, Denys Jackson referred to 'the Catholic Rural Movement, which has made useful contact with other Christian bodies for joint action in maintaining Christian social principles and applying them to public life'. In the next issue of *The Advocate* it was announced that Jackson 'has since learnt that no connection exists between these two movements'. It seems that Jackson, who was close to Santamaria, had inadvertently let the cat out of the bag by linking the Rural Movement with Santamaria's industrial Movement's activities. We now know that the NCRM did in fact act as the Movement's arm in non-metropolitan areas.

Personalities

On returning to Melbourne in 1939 after being ordained and studying music in Italy, Percy Jones was appointed Diocesan Director of Music and Director of the St Patrick's Cathedral choir, appointments he held for the next quarter of a century. He appreciated having had a much wider exposure to life-changing experiences during his seminary years than those provided at Werribee; it made him more free-wheeling in style than most other Melbourne priests. In his Melbourne appointments Jones worked on improvements in liturgical music, as a result of which he produced in 1942 a melody and accompaniment edition of the *Australian Hymnal,* which included motets, and Latin, Marian and vernacular hymns. In the 1940s he organized an annual Diocesan Plainsong Festival with choirs from Catholic schools taking part. He was in charge of the musical recordings played on the 'Catholic Hour' from 1940; he believed more religious music should be played on ABC radio. In the 1940s he also became a pioneer collector of Australian folk songs, including 'Click Go The Shears' and 'The Springtime It Brings on the Shearing', publishing a collection with the American folk singer Burl Ives. On the other hand he made a surprising attack on jazz and blues music, saying these appealed to low emotions and should be regulated.

Jones' manifold activities meant he became a familiar figure in circles wider than the Catholic Church. He remained close to Mannix for the rest of his life. Like Mannix Jones praised the energy of the Melbourne church: 'When I came back, and this is what impressed me, was the immense vitality of the lay church in Melbourne. It seemed to just blossom everywhere...The number of organizations which existed, many of which I became involved in myself, is amazing'. Jones listed as examples the Legion of Mary, the Campion Society, Catholic Action and the Therry Society, and concluded: 'Extraordinary people came to be associated with these movements, marvellous thinkers who gave a maturity to the Church.'[16] In 1950 Jones was appointed Vice Director of the Conservatorium of Music at the University of Melbourne under the Ormond Professor of

[16] Donald Cave, *Percy Jones,* p. 27.

20 The US folk singer Burl Ives and Rev. Dr Percy Jones, who collaborated
on a collection of Australian folksongs, pictured in 1952. (MDHC)

Music Sir Bernard Heinze. His brother Basil Jones became Director
of the equivalent institution in Brisbane.

Dr Matthew Beovich, born in 1896, was appointed Archbishop of
Adelaide in December 1939. He had been educated at the influential
CBC North Melbourne stable, studied for the priesthood in Rome
at Propaganda College where he was ordained in 1922, and was
awarded doctorates in Divinity and Philosophy. From 1923 he was
stationed in the Melbourne Catholic Education Office, becoming
Director of Catholic Education from 1933 until his Adelaide posting.
He had a special interest in migrants because of his Croatian heritage.

George Duke Walton, playwright and theatre director, was the most important person in Melbourne Catholic theatrical circles in the 1930s. Born in 1906 and also educated at CBC North Melbourne, he was an architect by profession and by temperament a deeply religious, even mystical, person partial to Marian devotion. Captivated by St Thomas More he wrote a play on him 'But New Beginning' staged in Melbourne by the St Aloysius Players in 1935. In 1937 Walton founded the Therry Society for drama and liturgy which was of interest to Catholics. The Paraclete Arts Group was begun in 1941 to promote Catholic interest in literature, music and culture generally. In 1936 Walton was the producer of the Belgian religious pageant 'Credo' to an audience of 30,000 in an Auckland stadium as part of the New Zealand centenary celebrations. The drama is based on forces aligned against Christianity in the modern world. He restaged the pageant, designing his own sets, at the Melbourne Cricket Ground in 1939 in front of 70,000 people. Dr Percy Jones had worked closely with the dramatist George Walton, whom he admired because Walton 'did a superb job in introducing young Catholics to the role of Catholic culture', but Jones thought Walton too 'absorbed in the spiritual-liturgical aspects of drama' at the expense of theatrical impact.[17] In 1944 Walton moved to Adelaide to help run Catholic Action there, as he saw his theatre work as an artistic expression of Catholic Action. Later Walton went to live at Fatima with his wife, formerly Molly Minogue, where they helped at the Carmelite Fathers' hostel. He died there in 1961.

The Advocate moved into new offices in a'Beckett Street in 1937. Fr James Murtagh was appointed assistant editor in 1936, and Frank Murphy joined the staff in the next year; they became life-long friends. Miss Caroline Goulding was in charge of the paper's social columns; her sister Jean was secretary to the editor. Caroline wrote a page on wide ranging topics each issue under the name 'Catherine Kaye'. She took a trip to Europe in 1935 and sent back articles on her experiences, especially those in central Europe. Marion Miler Knowles had retired from *The Advocate* in the late 1920s after a

---

[17] Donald Cave, op. cit., p. 29.

21 The staff of *The Advocate* and other Catholic organizations in their new building, 1937. Front row from left: Fr J. Murtagh, Fr F. Moynihan, Archbishop Mannix, Mons. J. Lonergan, Fr J. Hannan and a staff member. (MDHC)

long career on the paper. A testimonial fund was set up to act as her superannuation. Her *Selected Poems*, a volume organized by Lily Adams, mother of the Campion Arthur Adams, and comprising two hundred poems over 330 pages, part of her enormous output, was published in 1935.

Charities and Churches

Until the 1920s St Vincent's had been Melbourne's only large Catholic hospital. It underwent a series of extensions on its block in the early 1930s, and added the new St Brendan's Ward in 1937; a new casualty ward, planned for the early 1940s, was held up by the war. But because of space constraints it had to expand beyond its original site. Across the road from the main hospital a three-storey building called Somerset House near the fire station, which had operated as a private hospital, was purchased and converted into St Vincent's Maternity Hospital in 1937. Nearby in Grey Street, East Melbourne, the Mercy Private Hospital was built and opened in 1934 by the Sisters of Mercy with intermediate, private and maternity wards.

A program of building further hospitals was undertaken in the interwar years as the suburbs extended in a ring around the city. In 1921 the Sisters of Mercy bought a Federation mansion in Coonil Crescent, Malvern, from Frederick Hagelthorn, a prominent Catholic and a former Victorian Minister of Agriculture and Public Works. The building was converted into St Benedict's Hospital, and included an operating theatre. In 1947 the hospital was taken over by the Missionary Sisters of the Sacred Heart, usually known as the Cabrini Sisters after their founder Sister Frances Xavier Cabrini, who had been canonized the year before. This venture was arranged by the chaplain to the Italian community Fr Modotti. The existing hospital was expanded into the new Cabrini Hospital which was erected on the site in 1957. To cater for the northern suburbs the Missionary Sisters opened the five-storey Sacred Heart Hospital at Moreland, with surgical, medical and maternity wards, in 1939. Caritas Christi Hospice, for the dying rather than the chronically incurable, was opened in 1939 in Studley Park Road next to Raheen. In the same year the Blue Sisters founded a hospital in South Melbourne. A branch of the Guild of St Luke for doctors was formed in Melbourne in February 1935, with the veteran Dr Leo Kenny as Master. The surgeon Dr Herbert 'Paddy' Moran from Sydney came down to help before going off to Italy and Abyssinia.

The Catholic Church in the Melbourne archdiocese was so large and active it had at this stage about 80 organizations under its umbrella, forty of which had the word 'Catholic' in their title. Among these were many charitable organizations such as hospitals, orphanages, hospices, foundling homes and so on. The Grey Sisters had a Mothercraft Home at Canterbury and opened a Rest Home at Croydon in 1940. Near the fire station among the many other Catholic institutions were the Convent at Abbottsford, the Little Sisters of the Poor at Northcote, the Morning Star Boys' Home at Mornington, the Sisters of Nazareth at Camberwell, St Anthony's Home for boys at Kew, St Joseph's Homes at Canterbury and Broadmeadows, and the Salesian agricultural college at Rupertswood. In 1943 Marillac House in Brighton was established by the Daughters of Charity for mentally impaired children, there was a home for the deaf at Portsea, and for the blind at 'Villa Maria' in Prahran.

In the 1930s new needs were arising. Within Australia the unemployed, dropouts from society, the poor and in general depression victims had to be cared for. The government undertook a slum clearance program. In addition the increasingly disturbed state of Europe and elsewhere meant an increase in victims of war, of racial and religious persecution, and of social dislocation. New welfare services specifically designed for immigrants, refugees and displaced people were needed in response to the world crisis. Two Perth nurses, Norma Parker and Constance Moffit, involved in social work in their home state and trained overseas, came to Melbourne in the early 1930s. Parker approached her uncle, Joseph Westhoven, chairman of St Vincent's Hospital, and was employed to set up an Almoner's Department, to co-ordinate palliative welfare work with medical services. Parker and Moffit also utilized the Catholic Women's Social Guild (CWSG) to organize female welfare workers to cope with increasing social problems and family disruption. They improved professional expertise and, with the backing of Mons. Lonergan and the Campion Arthur Adams, co-ordinated the many Catholic welfare services, which had up till this time acted on an individual basis. On their recommendation Mannix approved the setting up of a Catholic Social Service Bureau in 1935.

A branch of the St Joan's Alliance for Catholic lay women active in social and political activity was founded in Melbourne in 1936. Its members were mainly single educated working women, like those in the CWSG, but it was not an official Catholic body, which gave it more latitude to promote ideas such as women's right to work and equal pay. The Alliance's mission fitted in well with the lay apostolate ethos of Catholic Action then being promoted by the church. Its first President was Enid Lyons, the Prime Minister's wife, and influential members included Anna Brennan, Julia Flynn, the social worker Teresa Wardell and Dr Inez Parer. The Grail, a religious community of lay women originating in Holland, ran courses of lectures and summer schools, and staged large religious pageants as forms of communal worship. Members wore a uniform and a badge but no veil. A Grail nucleus was established in Melbourne in 1939 and moved into a large Queen Anne style Tudor mansion 'Tay Creggan' in Hawthorn in 1940.

In the late 1930s Mannix spoke strongly in favour of Jews and refugees, and welcomed Australian government moves to help them. In September 1939 on the outbreak of war he founded the Catholic Welfare Organization (CWO), with Dr Leo Kenny as chairman, to provide services to the community during the war, particularly for those in the armed forces, and to co-ordinate the activities of the archdiocese's other charitable institutions. A Catholic War Veterans Association had been formed in 1936; its members met together in remembrance at Mass, and it naturally expanded its activities as war approached. The Catholic Migrants Committee assisted refugees coming from racial and political conflicts in Europe, helping minimize their difficulties of adjustment as they settled here.

Various Catholic friendly societies united to form the Catholic Friendly Societies of Victoria and the Catholic National Insurance Association, necessary under Commonwealth legislation. The Legion of Mary, founded in Dublin, had formed its first Melbourne branch in 1933; it aimed to sanctify its members and to help others through charitable works. The Legion, which opened its Regina Coeli Hostel for destitute women in North Melbourne, was organized on a parish basis to assist local clergy, and worked with other bodies like the St Vincent de Paul Society. The Holy Name Society was similarly organized on parish lines and, though it also had a spiritual mission, its main task became to provide a voluntary labour force at the call of the parish priest. The Legion of Mary and the Holy Name Society both markedly increased their numbers in the inter-war and post-war years.

The Archdiocese was still growing, but its rate of expansion was slowing down in the 1930s due to the depression and its after-effects, and to a lack of immigrants.

	1930	1940
Parishes	101	105
Diocesan priests	154	181
Religious priests	94	187
Brothers	158	181
Nuns	1275	1594
Primary schools	143	160
Secondary schools	41	41
Primary School pupils	37,650	33,865
Secondary school pupils	6,491	7,295
Total pupils	44,480	41,850

The Werribee seminary was now graduating local priests for ordination. New orders of priests arriving in Melbourne doubled their numbers which now equalled those of diocesan clergy. Primary school numbers dropped probably due to students leaving school early to seek work in the depression; in addition some families were too poor to support their children at a Catholic school.

In the 19th century stone and wood were the materials used for church construction. In the first half of the twentieth century, brick was commonly utilized, but the form of churches, both inside and outside, changed little. The basic shape was a rectangular box, with high walls, a regularly sloped roof of tiles or iron, and length emphasized rather than width. The altar was often enclosed in a small extension which also contained the sacristy. At the street end was a vestibule with steps leading off each side, or in larger churches directly from a large main door. Stained glass windows and sometimes a spire or tower above the altar end emphasized the vertical, transcendental aspirations of the faithful. The suburban church was the centrepiece of a group of buildings, with the parish primary school, presbytery and hall usually on the same block. Some affluent suburbs, such as Kew, could afford a large red-brick Eastern-style basilica, with a cruciform floor ground plan and a copper dome. St Dominic's in East Camberwell was a prominent bluestone Gothic structure. Many churches incorporated Byzantine, Romanesque,

Gothic, Baroque or Spanish Mission forms, or some mixture of these elements. These styles, known collectively as 'Medieval Revival', were transported to Australia, where they existed in forms modified from their European originals. Thomas Payne's Newman chapel and William Wardell's ES&A bank on the Collins-Queen Sts. corner employ Gothic revival elements in a less comprehensive way than Wardell's St Patrick Cathedral.

22 The pre-Vatican interior of St Mary's West Melbourne: the marble altar is rendered remote by the long nave, and by the intervening altar rails. The church's stained glass windows and soaring ceiling in French Gothic style are harmonized with its Italian-influenced granite pillars, intricate fittings and tinted walls. (MDHC)

Inside the church was often filled with a melange of devotional objects in the style Robin Boyd characterized as 'featurism', a welter of add-ons which threatened to overwhelm, or at least disguise, the basically plain design. The altar, remote from the congregation, was attached to the back wall, with the sanctuary cut off from the rest of the church by altar rails as a sacred space for the celebrant and his male attendants only. The altar was elaborately decorated in order for it to become the focal point of the interior; all visual

perspectives led to it. Richness of colour and decoration were pre-
eminent, with the sanctuary often generously decked out in marble.
A golden tabernacle, monstrance, silver chalices, sanctuary lamps,
and lectern, some of these objects embedded with precious stones,
were relics of the sumptuous decoration of a more aristocratic age.
As the decades passed pastel shades of interior décor replaced
earlier darker, sombre ones. The rest of the church was filled with
statues, stations of the cross, confessional boxes, an elevated pulpit,
baptismal font, paintings of holy figures, candle racks, bronze
plaques commemorating deceased parishioners, and other objects of
devotion. Some churches had side altars devoted to Our Lady, St.
Joseph or the church's titular saint, and even an 'altar of repose'.
Architecture, piety and liturgy were intertwined.

THE WAR YEARS

6

THE EARLY 1940S:
THE MOVEMENT

The War Years – The Movement – Mannix as Strategist – The Apostolic Delegate Panico – Simonds and Calwell – Three Central Europeans – War's End

The War Years

1941-2 was the low point for the allies in the Second World War. In June 1941 Hitler broke the recent Nazi-Soviet pact and invaded Russia; Soviet Russia was now no longer an enemy combatant, but part of the Allied coalition. Pearl Harbour was bombed in December 1941 and Singapore fell in February in 1942. These were the darkest days on both fronts, with grave repercussions for Australia which now had its sovereignty threatened. We had been slow to realize the danger posed by Japan. As Defence headquarters were in Melbourne Mannix remained Catholic Chaplain General. His deputy, Fr Tim McCarthy, was sent to the Middle East as Senior Chaplain AIF Overseas; Fr John Pierce was RAAF chaplain in London. Twelve military chaplains were initially appointed to the armed services, with their numbers increasing rapidly. The Catholic Welfare Organization provided amenities for soldiers at the Melbourne Showgrounds, Mt Martha and Seymour. Dr John Clareborough, a dental surgeon, was, like the barrister Eugene Gorman, promoted to brigadier, and commanded a number of brigades during the war.

The Menzies administration was replaced by the Curtin one in August 1941, the first federal Labor government since Scullin's defeat a decade earlier. Moreover there had not been a Victorian Labor administration since Ned Hogan's defeat in April 1932. Curtin, an anti-conscriptionist during the First World War, had been briefly gaoled in 1917. Now as Prime Minister he was a mainstream Laborite and Australian nationalist. During the period of the Nazi-

Soviet pact in 1939-41 the Communists and their left-wing allies, supporting Hitler as well as Stalin, had been hindering our war effort, especially at ports, where union members damaged equipment and delayed it being sent to our soldiers abroad. These acts of sabotage have been documented in Hal Colebatch's book *Australia's Secret War*. It was during this phase that Santamaria and others began to oppose Communist infiltration in the Labor movement.

In the months before the forming of the official Movement in August 1941, articles began appearing in *The Advocate* complaining of obstruction by Communists. A clear hint of Movement-like counter action is evident in an *Advocate* editorial of 9 May, 1940:

> Communists are being dismissed from munitions works; power is sought by the A.W.U. to enable unions to expel Communists; the Victorian Labor Party is investigating, through a special committee, Communist infiltration into Labor Party branches; efforts are being made to eradicate Communist influence in the militia; and the Federal Attorney General (W.M. Hughes) is expected to press for action against Communists.

The last sentence refers to Hughes' use of intelligence funds to support anti-Communist activities. An editorial on 14 November 1940, reported an announcement that the 'Commonwealth Investigation Branch is perfecting new plans to stamp it [the Communist Party] out of existence'. The editorial of 9 May 1940 also warned against 'the menace of the white-anting tactics which have been assiduously carried on in almost every department of the community – economic, social and political.' *The Advocate* of 13 February, 1941, ran an article headed: 'How Communists Carry on Underground. Red Column's Silent Sabotage'. The article was based on a Communist leaflet trying to foment class antagonism and civil strife at the most desperate stage of the war. *The Advocate* commented: 'The Labour movement in Australia is likely to suffer harm by allowing Communists to take a hand in its affairs'. On 24 July 1941, the paper reported the Minister for the Army, Mr Percy Spender, warning that Communists were 'working incessantly to bring about eventual overthrow of constitutional government' by organizing strikes, disaffection and industrial unrest. These reports together suggest some government-backed activity was afoot to end the apathy about Communist tactics. On the other hand Catholic spokesmen at the time dismissed Communist Party claims that Catholic Action was opposing it in the unions.

The Movement

World war two revived and changed Mannix. Australia was itself facing a crisis with the nation in danger, just as Ireland had been in the 1910s. And in Bob Santamaria he found a kindred soul, a fellow Cincinnatus who believed he had been *called* to save the nation from its mortal peril. Santamaria now became a surrogate for Mannix's new ambitions, as de Valera had once been. After decades when he had never taken Australian affairs close to his heart, they now took priority over Irish ones for the remaining decades of his life. The Movement was founded with Mannix's support in August 1941, a crucial date, the period of maximum peril for the Allies, the month Curtin took over from Menzies as PM. Like Mannix, Menzies had blown his chance to go down in history as the saviour of his nation. For both no amount of subsequent accolades could make up for missing out at a crucial moment in their nations' history.

The Movement was formed in the context of an external security crisis as well as the internal one: the Japanese southward thrust and the Communist-inspired union subversion of our war effort. Australian Communists were more respectable, since the Soviet Union was now our ally against Germany. But in alliance with other radical unionists Australian Communists continued their disruption, as they hoped increasing wartime chaos could provide a revolutionary opportunity. They had a controlling interest in maritime, transport, ironworkers and coal mining unions, all essential industries, which made their campaign of disruption especially damaging. The Federal government had naturally been alarmed by Communist activity.

This was shown in the same crucial month of August 1941 when documents revealed that funds from the Commonwealth Investigation Service (CIS), the body which was the forerunner of ASIO, had been supplied to Catholic Action and the Coal Miners

Federation in their fight against Communist influence in the unions. Billy Hughes, Attorney-General in the outgoing Menzies government, was in charge of the CIS funds. But when it became a public issue Hughes, the new Prime Minister Curtin, and Mannix all denied any religious organization had received any secret funds. But the embryonic Movement was not a religious organization at this stage, and *The Advocate* had already reported that both Mr Hughes and the Commonwealth Investigation Service were actively moving against the Communists. Documents in the National Archives, and David Horner's history of ASIO, *The Spy Catchers*, both reveal that during in the 1940s the Movement and the intelligence service worked in such close co-operation that each had an official stationed in the other's offices. Clearly the intelligence services needed Santamaria's unrivalled knowledge of Communist union inroads to combat the problem.

The man who had set up the government's secret intelligence unit in 1917 was Billy Hughes, when it was employed to harass people like John Curtin and Mannix's supporters. These three combatants from the First World War now found their roles radically rearranged in the second. The man in charge of the secret fund in 1941 was none other than its founder, Billy Hughes. Was Mannix, the leading opponent of people being press-ganged into the army by Billy Hughes in 1917, now taking the king's shilling from Hughes? As we are here dealing with three secretive organizations (the Communists, the Movement and the intelligence service), it is hard to determine what exactly was going on, but, given Communist union disruption of the war effort, one would have expected that Australia's intelligence organs would have been supporting opposition to Communist activities. We have here an apparent contrast between the early and later Mannix. In 1921 Mannix was backing a revolutionary group, Sinn Fein, trying to overthrow a government in Ireland; in 1941, only 20 years later, he was opposing a revolutionary group, the Communists, who were trying to undermine our government. Because both were well versed in counter-governmental strategies themselves, Mannix and Santamaria were among those people in Australia who best understood Communist standover methods, ballot rigging and other takeover tactics.

Santamaria had a two stage strategy. He remained head of Catholic Action, as his principal aim was to Christianize Australian society. But before this could be fully accomplished, he believed the Communist threat had to be eliminated, hence the Movement. Santamaria decided to form the Movement on an organized basis, with Archbishop Mannix's blessing and financial support, in the crucial month of August 1941, perhaps because he thought he could work more closely with the incoming federal Labor government, which better understood labour problems and which his supporters were already co-operating with. Santamaria named his co-founder of the Movement as Bert Cremean, deputy leader of the State Labor Party, an indication it was formed with the active support of the Victorian ALP. An influential official of this branch was the former Communist and now active anti-Communist Dinny Lovegrove.

The Movement has been thought of as an operation to cleanse the union movement of pro-Communist infiltration, but this is only half the story. It was also from the start an operation to cleanse the ALP as well. In his memoir Frank McManus reveals an organized left-Communist alliance almost succeeded in capturing the Victorian Labor Party in 1940, which scared Cremean, Kennelly and Lovegrove in to forming an 'ad hoc' group to secure help (from Vic Stout of the Trades Hall among others) to protect the party in the future. As part of this effort Cremean went to see Mannix, who referred him on to Santamaria. In this version it was the party not the unions, which was in danger of takeover.[18] Calwell and Cremean were part of this operation from the start to protect their ALP branch, and their own careers. A May 1940 *Advocate* editorial (already quoted) revealed that 'the Victorian Labor Party is investigating, through a special committee, Communist infiltration into Labor Party branches'.

Evidence backing this aspect of the Movement's founding also comes from the files of *The Advocate* at the time. On 23 August 1941, the month the Movement was founded, the Central Executive of the State Labor Party was reported to have banned its members joining Soviet front organizations, and Bert Cremean is reported condemning Communist subversion. In an editorial on

---

[18] Frank McManus, *The Tumult and the Shouting*, pp. 21-4.

11 September *The Advocate* warned: 'The Labor Party should not allow traitors to be nourished in its bosom. Prompt and decisive action now is needed'. *The Advocate* was alert to the fact that this was happening. Vic Stout, secretary of the Melbourne Trades Hall Council (THC), asked Santamaria and Bert Cremean to help him oppose Communists who were taking over unions and threatening to control the THC. Mannix gave support to the embryonic Movement, but its existence was deemed by the hierarchy, by the Labor party and by Movement members to be kept secret. To disguise its existence it was colloquially known among its members as 'the show'.

Santamaria's account is that he called a meeting to form the Movement with Bert Cremean, Stan Keon, Frank McManus, and Frank Hannan on his 26th birthday, 14 August 1941. The young Stan Keon, an important CYMS official, was brought into the Catholic Action/Movement fold at an early stage. Paul McGuire, a geo-political strategist and member of Naval Intelligence, helped. The existence of the Movement was hidden under the cover of Santamaria's Catholic Action activities. In 1942 Fr Paddy Ryan, a noted anti-Communist activist, was appointed Director of Lay Apostolate activities in the Sydney Archdiocese, and came under the supervision of its Catholic Social Science Bureau. Ryan's network became part of the approved Movement in September, 1945.

Freedom newspaper, later called *News Weekly*, began in 1943 as the mouthpiece of the organization, sometimes known at that time as the Freedom Movement. Movement members had to pledge themselves to obedience, secrecy and discipline, something required only of organizations with a special military or sacred mission. Santamaria's novel strategy was to base his Movement on a ready-made network, the Australia-wide Catholic parish system. Each parish had its own organizations, like the Holy Name Society, from which ready-made leaders and organizational expertise could be recruited. The list of parishioners could be used to summon those who belonged to a particular union. Parish members would be notified of relevant upcoming union meetings by Movement officials, who could arrange transport for them. Holy Name members were told not to wear the distinctive lapel badge of their sodality to union meetings, which would identify them as Catholic activists.

Communist influence in the union movement grew during the war years, reaching its height at the 1945 ACTU conference, where its supporters could virtually command a majority of the votes. On 13 May 1943, *The Advocate* announced: 'Catholics were the spearhead of the opposition [to Communism]. We should throw our weight behind our organization', a pretty clear indication to those who knew what was happening. In 1944 a Victorian Labor member John Mullens named Communists and their supporters in the Victorian parliament, and Cremean stated that Communism aimed to destroy bourgeois society and parliamentary democracy. Santamaria, Mullens, McManus and Cremean all called for action against the Communist danger in *The Tribune*.

Mannix as Strategist

What role did Mannix play in the formation of the Movement besides approving and funding it from 1941? In 1912-14 Mannix had been behind the founding of the Catholic pressure group, the Australian Catholic Federation (ACF). The ALP rebuffed the ACF, forbidding ALP members to be part of it. The ACF retaliated by creating a new body, the Catholic Workers Association, consisting of Catholics who were members of unions and the ALP (the same membership as the later Movement), to infiltrate the ALP to get their agendas approved. The same procedure of forming two bodies was replicated in 1941, when Catholic Action spawned the Movement which likewise tried to exert a strong influence on the Victorian ALP branch. As Mannix was a key figure behind the earlier manoeuvres, had an astute political intelligence and was, as we have seen, early in the 1930s alert to Communist manipulations, he may have had a more direct role in the formation of the Movement than has been previously realized.

Early on Mannix had a reputation as a firebrand extremist, but between the wars he, like Curtin, gradually emerged as a moderate, rejecting hot-headed proposals and taking care not to endorse current fads. During the Second World War Mannix said hate should not be the dominant emotion energizing Australians against the Germans and Japanese; we are all guilty in some ways in this war. He maintained a dignified detachment in the face of the inflamed propaganda of all sides common in times of crisis. It was not a war to defend Christianity, Mannix insisted; Russia was fighting to defend Russia, not democracy. He opposed both the White Australia policy and the use of atomic weapons.

The Apostolic Delegate Panico

The Apostolic Delegate in Australia from 1935 to 1948, Archbishop Giovanni Panico, played a role in Mannix's life analogous to that of Lloyd George in 1920, quarantining him and stripping him of supporters. Panico's job as a diplomat was to conduct relations with the Australian government on behalf of the Holy See, not to run the Australian church. But as the man on the ground he had other roles, for example, in making recommendations on key hierarchy appointments in Australia. Panico had twelve years in Australia, an unusually long term. He was energetic and relatively young, and took it upon himself to reorganize the Australian church and so become its de facto leader, a role which no previous Papal Nuncio had attempted. To implement his plan he needed to lessen the pre-eminence of the Mannix-led Irish clergy in the Australian Catholic church.[19]

In 1920 the Vatican under Pope Benedict XV had decreed that native clergy were to be preferred in all countries, explaining that 'the Church knows the value of a common fatherland, tongue and temperament between the missionary and those whom he wishes to bring into the fold'. The church had active missionary programs as it moved into Africa and Asia; there was, for instance, a big Irish mission in China. A Melbourne priest, Fr Romuald Hayes, had after ordination joined this mission as a member of the Columban Missionary Society; in 1932 he was appointed Bishop of Rockhampton, an early Australian born bishop. In Melbourne the Association for the Propagation of the Faith was active: the

---

[19] In her biography of Mannix Brenda Niall devotes two chapters 'The Vatican Chess Game' and 'The Cardinal's Red Hat' to Panico's extensive manoeuvres.

Missionaries of the Sacred Heart were in Papua, the Marists in Fiji, the Pallottines in the Kimberley. Monsignor James Hannan, from Melbourne but based in Sydney, was in charge of Australian missionary activity.

A white European priest going out to Africa or Asia was culturally remote from his new parishioners, but the gap between Irish Catholic clergy and their predominantly Irish Catholic flock in Australia was minimal. Australia had its first Australian-born bishop as early as 1897; by the time Panico was on the scene there had been six, so the problem hardly existed here. But the Pope's ruling in favour of local clergy gave Panico his opening. Acting under Vatican instructions Panico could diminish the dominant influence of Irish-born bishops, particularly Mannix, and appoint his own, less experienced, local choices in their place. Panico appointed Simonds to Hobart to be the first Australian-born archbishop in 1937. Some younger Australian priests, especially in Sydney, did resent the rigidity of Irish bishops and parish priests here. In addition the Vatican did not look favourably on Irish-born clergy involved in politics.

One of Panico's basic strategies was to isolate Mannix by removing his deputies, on whom as an old man he depended to administer his archdiocese. Monsignor John Lonergan had held many important posts, and as such was Mannix's deputy in the absence of a coadjutor bishop. In 1938 Mannix's reliance on the efficient Lonergan was terminated when Lonergan was appointed Bishop of Port Augusta. The next most important clerics in Melbourne were Dr Patrick Lyons and Dr Matthew Beovich, both of whom were soon promoted to bishoprics out of Victoria. Mannix now had to fill the deputy's job once again, and was running out of talent. So Fr Arthur Fox, not trained overseas nor even a home-grown thinker, was appointed to the major posts, consolidating in one deputy the enormous task of day-to-day management of an expanding see.

The other side of the coin was Sydney. A Sydney priest, Dr Thomas Gilroy, had been appointed Bishop of Port Augusta in 1934 only eleven years after his ordination. Meanwhile Panico manoeuvred the Sydney coadjutor, the Irish Archbishop Michael Sheehan, out of his post, and appointed Gilroy as Coadjutor Archbishop. Gilroy

23 The imperturbable Archbishop Kelly of Sydney, second from left,
separates two protagonists, Archbishop Panico on the right and Archbishop
Mannix, left, at a conference in the later 1930s. (MDHC)

succeeded Kelly on the latter's death in 1940. The overall effect of
Panico's moves was to reduce Mannix's and Melbourne's leadership
of the Australian church, and so in comparison to increase the
importance of Sydney.

Another Vatican/Panico coup was still to come. Simonds was
Hobart's reigning archbishop with full faculties. In the depths of
the war in 1942 Panico summoned him from Hobart to Sydney, to
tell him he was to be appointed Mannix's coadjutor in Melbourne.

Mannix was not to be informed, as he had a right to be. Simonds, a ruling archbishop, was thus demoted to be an assistant in another archdiocese, an unusual appointment and an attempt to corral Mannix, unsuccessful and disastrous as it turned out. Another reason for Simonds' transfer to Melbourne might have been for Simonds, the Episcopal delegate for Catholic Action, to keep a close watch on the controversial Movement activities already going on in the Catholic Action office in Melbourne.

24 Archbishops Simonds and Mannix give nothing away in this formal pose in October 1942, just after Simonds' Melbourne appointment was announced. (MDHC)

Mannix was almost eighty by this stage, and the Vatican may have presumed the 'Angel of Death' might soon relieve it of this turbulent priest. But for the next twenty years God, and Mannix, had other ideas. When Simonds arrived in Melbourne in 1943, *The Advocate* article ended by saying that 'the burden of office, which he [Mannix] has borne for so long, will be lightened by one so eminently and manifestly suited to assist him'. It was not to be. Mannix gave Simonds an enormous reception at Cathedral Hall, as well as the cathedral-like St Mary's in West Melbourne, a priest as full-time secretary and a car, and then did not consult him on crucial issues nor give him administrative power over the next two decades. The move, which had the effect of ruining Simonds' career, was so crude and transparent that Mannix, a consummate tactician, had no trouble swatting it away. Nonetheless Mannix does not come out well of this sidelining of Simonds, even though the problem was not something of his or Simonds' making. Simonds had to put up with Fox, his inferior in rank and talent, running the archdiocese instead of him. The effect of these changes was not merely to replace Irish bishops and priests with local ones, but to replace independently minded bishops with dutiful Romanized ones. The Vatican revealed itself an exponent of the cultural imperialism it claimed to be dismantling. When Simonds met the powerful figure of Monsignor Montini (later Pope Paul VI) at the Vatican in 1946, he was surprised to hear of the high esteem Mannix was now held in Rome. The Panico-Mannix contretemps had been a cause for regret there, with Montini implying Mannix had been badly treated.

Simonds and Calwell

It would have been far wiser and simpler for Panico, instead of all this complex manoeuvring, to have made Simonds, the outstanding cleric from NSW in the 1930s, Archbishop of Sydney after Kelly. Sydney required a strong and imaginative leader after Kelly had run it down, and Simonds was far more qualified for this task, with his Louvain learning, social and theological ideas, and seminary and leadership experience, than Gilroy. Simonds was overqualified for both his Hobart and Melbourne posts, and consequently his talents were wasted. The messy situation created by Panico in Australia's two premier sees was an underlying factor contributing to Melbourne-Sydney tensions in events leading up to the split.

A few months after Simonds arrived as second in charge in Melbourne in 1943, Arthur Calwell was promoted to the Federal Cabinet. Both now began new and difficult careers which would run curiously in parallel until both ended in 1967. After showing great early talent, both suffered a succession of setbacks. Both were now based in the North Melbourne area, both their careers were stalled for two decades by the longevity of Dr Maloney and Dr Mannix respectively, both worked as deputies under leaders (Mannix and Evatt) to whom they were ideologically opposed, and as a result both became leaders of their organizations too late, with their talents and expectations eventually unfulfilled.

Calwell, having belatedly entered Federal parliament in 1940, was not, to his chagrin, included in Curtin's first ministry in 1941. Calwell became an irritant, making a number of attacks, on issues like overseas conscription, on the new Labor administration. Curtin, who had a war to fight, dubbed him 'the hero of a hundred sham fights'. In late 1942 the *Radio Times*, an ABC journal, gave a garbled account, most likely from left-wing sources, of recent infighting:

> Calwell and [Denys] Jackson saw an opportunity to use the conscription issue to gain a new control over the Labour party, and finally remove Communist and anti-Catholic influence...the politicians of the Church failed to rally behind Calwell, the political leader of the Catholic Action section of the Church, and so a heavy blow was dealt to the Church's campaign against Socialism...Calwell and Jackson choose the wrong issue, and the Communists registered their first big victory over Catholic Action inside the Labour movement.

This report was strenuously denied by Denys Jackson and *The Advocate,* which stated categorically: 'Catholic Action groups are not a politically active secular body of the Church...There is no Catholic Action inside the Labour movement', comments which were hardly true. But the incident did reveal the Communists and their allies were well aware that Catholic Action (aka the Movement) was organizing against them, and that at that stage Calwell was a key figure in that endeavour. In 1943 Calwell was made Minister for Information, and in this role he supplied Santamaria with scarce newsprint paper for *Freedom*, Santamaria's Movement journal, a sign that Calwell was on side with Santamaria and the Movement at this stage.

The ALP careers of Calwell's Catholic colleagues were developing during this period. In 1938 Pat Keneally had been elected to an upper house seat in the Victorian parliament; he also became assistant secretary of the Victorian party in 1940, beginning a long influential period of simultaneous positions in the parliamentary and administrative wings. Frank McManus joined the Movement at its inception in 1941 and worked for it in the early 1940s while retaining his strong ALP ties. He became vice president of the Victorian ALP in 1947, which revealed the Movement was at that stage not on the outer in ALP circles.

In 1946 Gilroy, with a short six-year term as leader and no discernible achievements, was appointed a cardinal, instead of Mannix, an incumbent for almost three decades and acknowledged as an inspiring figure. The prophecy uttered at Moran's funeral was being fulfilled; the Sydney Cardinal's role was not for Simonds. Calwell, devoted to Mannix and a senior government minister, caused a stir by saying Mannix should have received the honour. Mannix then proceeded to outline Gilroy's CV, a piquant example of damning with faint praise:

> God looked after him. He protected him on the shell-raked shores of Gallipoli. [Mannix knew that Gilroy had in fact been a radio operator on a ship offshore.] God guided him to Propaganda College, that nursing mother of many prelates. For years, the future Cardinal was buried in the silent catacombs of the [Apostolic] Delegation, and, no doubt, that too was providential. But God has His own way of working out His designs. If there was to be an Australian Cardinal, his selection was inevitable.

The inference here was that Gilroy devoted himself to understanding the inner workings of the church for his own preferment rather than undertaking pastoral duties. Mannix then compared Gilroy with Cardinal Newman:

The one [Newman] was all his life a student, the other
[Gilroy] has been a man of action which left little time for
academic leisure. The one was 80 years before the cloud
of suspicion and calumny was lifted and he was created a
Cardinal; the other has reached the same goal by pleasant
ways and easy stages.[20]

This is not just a comparison between Newman and Gilroy, it is
more importantly an identification of Mannix himself with Newman.
Eight-two years old when he came out with this putdown, Mannix
knew the 'cloud of suspicion and calumny' had not been lifted from
himself. In the political sphere he had been sidelined by his absence
from Ireland; in the religious sphere he was sidelined by the Vatican.
Mannix's experience with Panico reinforced his tendency to display
a humorous derision for centres of authority both ecclesiastical and
secular. He remained wistfully resigned to his dual banishment. The
Cardinal's hat he missed out on, but never sought, was collateral
damage for his activities in Ireland and Australia.

Three Central Europeans

Three European Catholics with unique talents and outstanding
in their fields of endeavour spent the decade of the 1940s in
Melbourne. In 1939 Professor Arthur Schüller, a world renowned
Austrian radiologist, arrived at St Vincent's Hospital to work in the
neurosurgery department. The connection which led him to Australia
may have been the radiologist Dr John O'Sullivan, who had studied
under him in Vienna. From Brno the capital of Moravia, where he
was born in 1874, Schüller had moved to Vienna and graduated at
Vienna University in medicine with the highest honours in 1899.
His greatest achievement was to be the first person to successfully
x-ray the brain, surrounded as it is by bone impermeable to x-rays.
As a result he became 'without any shadow of doubt the father of
neuroradiology', as his biographer wrote. He was awarded a Doctor
of Medicine degree under the auspices of Emperor Franz Joseph of
Austria, a distinction given by the Emperor only twice during his
69 year reign. Schüller was a tall, handsome man, with an imposing

---

[20] *The Real Archbishop Mannix From the Sources*, pp. 232-3.

presence. After the first world he was appointed chief neurologist at a Vienna hospital while continuing his medical research which resulted in many path-breaking publications. In addition he and his wife Margarete were accomplished violinists. By the 1930s he was 'famous everywhere in the medical world'.

25 The world renowned radiologist Prof. Arthur Schüller and his wife Margarete at home in the suburb of Heidelberg. (St Vincent's)

Schüller was too old to operate at St Vincent's, being sixty-five when he arrived, but for the next two decades his advice during operations and elsewhere was invaluable because of his vast knowledge. He died in 1957, but it was only half a century later that the full story of Schüller's life was revealed. He and his wife, neé Margarete Stiassni, were Czech Jews. They had converted to Catholicism, a prerequisite for those aspiring to high places in the Austro-Hungarian empire. When Hitler invaded Austria, Professor Schüller was able to leave, but his wife tried to escape east from Czechoslovakia with their two sons in front of Hitler's invading armies. She succeeded but the two boys were taken by the Nazis and murdered. Margarete was eventually able to escape via a tortuous route. Schüller could have obtained a position anywhere in the world, but chose Australia as the place furthest from Europe. It is not clear how much of this saga the St Vincent's medical staff knew at the time. Understandably the Schüllers found it difficult to settle here. Margarete worked humbly as a domestic help, perhaps to expiate her guilt at having surrendered their two sons, and he suffered depression in his last years.

Fr Ernest Worms was a German Pallottine priest on the Kimberley mission from the 1930s to the 1960s. While serving as a priest there, both as parish priest of Broome and working in the field, he devoted his time to studying the Aborigines, and became through his extensive writings a renowned anthropologist and scholar on Australian Aboriginal customs. In the middle of his Australian career, for the decade from 1939 to 1949, he was appointed rector of the Pallottine headquarters in Studley Park Rd, Kew, almost opposite Raheen. This break from active missionary work enabled him to consolidate his research interests. Ernest Worms was born in 1891 in Westphalia, Germany. He was severely wounded in the First World War, which interrupted his studies for the priesthood. After ordination in 1920 at the age of 29, he studied languages under the Berlin university scholar Dr Herman Nekes, a fellow Pallottine priest who became his mentor. Fr Worms was appointed to Broome and the Kimberley mission in 1930 under a fellow German, Bishop Otto Raible, head the Kimberley Vicariate. Worms' area of study ranged beyond the Kimberley into the northern half of Western Australia, including remote desert communities. His first interest was the structure of Aboriginal languages, which provided an entry point into their customs and rituals. Many of his early findings were published in German journals. Fr Nekes came to Broome in 1935 to help Worms with his language studies.

His second main field of interest was the more difficult one of religious beliefs. Worms was ahead of his times. He did not try to banish Aboriginal beliefs from his charges and impose Christianity on them *holus bolus*. Instead he saw both Aboriginal and Christian belief systems as variants of the basic structure of all religions, as understood from his anthropological studies. This was unusual at the time because many influential anthropologists, such as Sir James Frazer and Sir Baldwin Spenser, were secularists who dismissed religious beliefs as akin to magic and superstition. Worms was able to reconcile native and Christian religious behaviour rather than putting then at odds. The missionary must, he believed, move towards the spirit world of Aborigines to understand and be accepted by them; the missionary must have 'a fine feeling into their sensitive minds'. Patience and strength were needed. He demonstrated that the earliest tribes in Australia, such as the Victorian ones, had a notion of a supreme being, whereas the beliefs of later arrivals may have been contaminated by other religious systems. Worms was impressive personally, tall, thin, suntanned and fit, with a wide face, high cheek bones, flaxen hair and the reserved and serious demeanour of a dedicated scholar. His personality and reverence for the Aboriginal tribes were reminiscent of Patrick White's fictional German explorer Voss. After returning to the Kimberley at the end of the war for a decade, Fr Worms became Rector of the Pallottine House at Manly in Sydney. He died in St Vincent's Hospital, Sydney, in 1963 aged 72. His two major works, on Aboriginal languages and religion, were published in German, and translated for their English editions after his death.

The biggest Catholic group to migrate to Australia after the Irish were the Italians, some of whom had arrived during the gold-rush decades. They continued to come here in the interwar decades because of lack of opportunities in Italy. One of Santamaria's interests when Catholic Action began was to look after the needs of the community from which he derived. In 1938 the distinguished Jesuit priest Fr Ugo (Hugo) Modotti, a native of Venice, came to Melbourne at the invitation of Dr Mannix as chaplain to Italian communities in Australia, basing himself at the Richmond parish. Fr Modotti had studied at the Gregorian University in Rome before being posted as a missionary to India, where he completed his Jesuit training. For sixteen years he was, among other positions, attached to the long standing Syrian Catholic Church in south-west India. The main problems Italians faced in Australia were internment during the war, irregular church attendance, and difficulties of assimilating to the wider Anglo-Australian community. An administrative problem was whether Italian Catholics should form their own separate organizations, or mix in normal parish life, a forerunner of a dilemma which would resurface with the much larger immigration influx after the war. In 1941 a play written by Fr Modotti, 'St Agnes', a martyr in Roman times, was translated by Dr Stewart and performed in St Ignatius' Hall, Richmond. Mannix wrote to Prime Minister Curtin in September 1943 praising the work Modotti and Calwell were doing to alleviate Italian difficulties.

Fr Modotti's Australian mission was caught in the crossfire between Archbishops Mannix and Panico. The Italian Panico accused his fellow countryman Fr Modotti of being a fascist. However one of the first things Modotti had done in Australia was to forbid Italians wearing black shirts at religious functions. Modotti had in addition become friendly with Arthur Calwell, and when Calwell regretted that Mannix had not received the Red Hat, Modotti was accused, without evidence, of being behind the Calwell statement. After Modotti returned to Italy in 1946 to recruit more Italian priests for Australia, he was never allowed back here, presumably because of a Panico veto. Fr Modotti was instrumental in arranging for the Italian Cabrini Sisters to come to Melbourne.

The War's End

The fortunes of war changed for the better in 1943 in both the European and Pacific spheres. Stalingrad was a German disaster, Rommel and his Afrika Corps were driven back, and a second front was opened in France after D-Day. The Pacific campaign was now paramount for Australia. The Japanese downward thrust was reversed as they were pushed back over the Kokoda trail, while the naval battles of the Coral Sea and Midway were equally crucial. In 1942 the Deputy Chaplain General Fr Tim McCarthy was brought back from the Middle East, and the chaplaincy structure rearranged. Panico attempted to replace Mannix with Simonds as Chaplain General, but Mannix was able to retain the top post. Over 120 chaplaincy position were established with 50 in reserve, with many chaplains sent to New Guinea. During the duration of the war the CWO, with Mrs Mary Daly as President and Dr Stewart as director, helped with provisions not supplied by the military authorities: 230 Mass kits, almost two million altar breads, over 3500 bottles of altar wine, 1500 pieces of altar linen, 200 vestments, almost 50,000 rosary beads, over 100,000 prayer books, as well as stationery items and 100,000 Christmas cards for the troops to send to their families at home.

A photo of a Melbourne army chaplain, Fr Alo Morgan, offering Mass in the jungle for troops about to embark on a major assault on Japanese positions at Wewak, New Guinea, was featured in *The Advocate* on 23 May 1945. This photo became well known as it was prominently displayed at the Australian War Memorial in Canberra for many decades. Fr Morgan witnessed the formal surrender of the Japanese General Adachi at Wewak in September 1945, recording his reflections in a letter sent home to his family:

> As I watched him slowly walking up to surrender, my mind went back to the mud and rain and jungle tracks – the sprawling bodies of lads killed in battle – the hurried burials in temporary graves – the dying at the medical posts. May God have mercy on them. We owe so much to them. It was they who paid the price...Thanks be to God that it is all over. A hopeful sign of the future I read in the fact that peace came to the world on 15 August – Our Lady's Day. May she guide a wandering world in the days ahead.[21]

After the war the CWO concentrated its energies on sending

---

[21] Tom Johnstone, *The Cross of Anzac*, p. 226.

26 The army chaplain Fr Alo Morgan celebrates Mass in 1945 for troops
about to engage the Japanese near Wewak, New Guinea. (MDHC)

clothing to relieve shortages in Europe. In addition Mannix
inaugurated an appeal for money to restore churches damaged in the
British Isles. In August 1945 the CWO held a Victory Social at its
Elizabeth St Hut, at which the Federal Minister and local member
Arthur Calwell congratulated those present on their outstanding
war effort. The president of the CWO became Dame Mary Daly
in 1951 in recognition of her work for the organization. She had
been educated at Mary's Mount, Ballarat, and married Dr J.J. Daly,
a nephew of Mother Berchmans Daly, the founder of St Vincent's
Hospital. Mrs Daly had taken an active interest in the hospital before
the war. In August 1945 two Thanksgiving Masses, which attracted
huge crowds, were celebrated at St Patrick's Cathedral to mark the
end of the war. The sermons at these Masses were given by returning
chaplains. After the war three Melbourne priests became the senior
chaplains: Fr Kevin Ellis (Navy), Fr Alo Morgan (Army) and Fr
Ken Morrison (Air Force), all of whom happened to come from the
suburb of Essendon. Fr Morgan became Deputy Chaplain General
under Mannix in 1955, and later Bishop of the newly formed Military
Vicariate in 1969.

On one occasion some years after the defeat of Germany and Japan, Mannix had in his audience the retired German and Dutch Bishops Gsell and Vesters, who had laboured for decades on the mission fields of northern Australia and New Guinea before having to flee south from the Japanese downward thrust. Mannix began in good humour by saying we have here today two *foreign* bishops, at which the audience laughed. (These two bishops had been members of the Australian church for decades, Gsell for longer than Mannix, and of course Mannix was himself a foreign bishop). We all know, Mannix continued, that in the Dark Ages the Germanic tribes were converted to Christianity by Irish missionaries. Only for us Irish these two bishops here would still be benighted pagans; nonetheless we welcome them. Welcomed, but ever so gently put in their place. Mannix was here playing with themes close to his heart about the rise and fall of nations, which he could only hint at so as not to offend his guests. The Irish had once had a key role in civilizing Europe, but over time these roles had been reversed. The Irish had been subjugated for seven centuries, but the Germans, latecomers, had become a dominant power in the 19th and 20th centuries. So the Germans, now again at the bottom of the heap, could appreciate the suffering we Irish had been through for so long.

The Country Party led by Sir Albert Dunstan governed Victoria for the whole of the war, as did Labour federally, led by John Curtin, Frank Forde and Ben Chifley, all of Irish Catholic descent. Curtin, who had relinquished religion as part of becoming a radical socialist in his youth in Melbourne, resumed a general religious disposition, including belief in an afterlife, during the war as his health declined. He died in July 1945. Another death near the war's end was that of the famous photographer Damien Parer, a product of St Kevin's CBC, and official AIF photographer, well known for his remarkable photographs of the North African and New Guinea campaigns. He was killed in September 1944 on the Palau Island group when working for Paramount News during the island-hopping mopping-up campaign in the Pacific.

Two months before Parer's death Patrick O'Leary, book lover, autodidact and literary editor of *The Advocate,* died at the age of fifty-six. Just before his own death he had published an article on his sister's death, which amounted to his literary last will and testament. O'Leary had become a fixture over a quarter of a century at the paper, and in many ways determined its tone. He was one of those who gave it a national reputation among Catholic journals. O'Leary kept on his person envelopes containing scraps of information on his many interests, his own moveable filing system. He perused old copies of the paper dredging up stories of Melbourne's Catholic past. His immense output every week covered literature, politics, history and current affairs, with (like Mannix) a calm and accurate perspective on current fashions. His company as a raconteur had been much in demand, with his engaging personality and vast repertoire of literary and personal reminiscences. O'Leary had been urged by his friends to write down his memories, but the demands of his large weekly output meant he never had the time nor leisure to do so.

It took a number of staff to replace O'Leary. As he became ill Frank Murphy, interested primarily in music, theatre and literature, took over (under the pseudonym 'Gregory Parable') many of O'Leary's pages and added another on current radio programs. Fr James Murtagh, who had returned after completing a post-graduate degree in sociology in the US, wrote on wider social questions and reviewed books. Martin Haley from Brisbane took over O'Leary's role as literary critic, and Dinny Minogue kept the 'Memories and Musings' column on early Victorian Catholic history going. Later a group of O'Leary's friends, including Florence Hagelthorne, Nettie Palmer, J.K. Moir, Joseph O'Dwyer, and O'Leary's wife and two sons formed a P.I.O'L Memorial Committee, which organized a volume of his essays in his memory. From his vast output about fifty essays were selected and appeared as *Bards in Bondage,* edited by a fellow poet and raconteur Joseph O'Dwyer, and published by John Gartner's The Hawthorn Press in 1954. In 1945 Fr Francis Moynihan completed twenty years as the paper's managing editor. Fr Murtagh and Frank Murphy became the paper's workhorses in the post-war decades, when a new and daunting challenge emerged. Up to this stage *The Advocate* had a high reputation as a paper of record and commentary. It was now to be presented with a choice of loyalty to its journalistic traditions or to the church. Would it be able to maintain its reputation for information and frank commentary as events surrounding the secret Movement gathered pace, or would it sit on the biggest story of all?

THE POST WAR YEARS

7

THE LATE 1940S:
SECRET STRUGGLES

Immigration – The Official Movement – The Chifley and Cain Governments – Union Struggles and Strikes – Internal Disputes – Kew and North Melbourne – Catholics in Public Life – Centenary Celebrations – Publications

Immigration

Even though the demands of war had receded, in the five years after the war the Catholic Welfare Organization sent 50,000 knitted items and a thousand food parcels to a devastated Europe, and tons of food and clothing to the Pope's appeal. The archdiocese's primary welfare energies were now channelled into the new Catholic Migration Committee (CMC), formed by the Australian hierarchy to help migrants with their applications to settle here, and with their travel, arrival and adjustment problems. On a trip overseas Simonds arranged for an office to be set up in London for this purpose. Fr Con Reis was in charge of the CMC in Melbourne. Nazareth House in Camberwell provided accommodation for 150 young migrant women, and a similar YCW migrant hostel was set up for men. An Australia-wide Catholic Social Service Bureau was established to tackle welfare issues within Australia; Fr Eric Perkins headed its Melbourne Bureau. Governments were increasingly taking a role in welfare and health services. The Catholic Church, with its long history of service in these areas, increasingly worked in co-operation with government departments, but kept its own welfare organizations separate, as differences arose from time to time on moral and financial issues.

Mannix differed from Calwell on the White Australia policy, which Mannix opposed:

> It is unfortunate that by a crude insistence on the White Australia policy in its present form we have given them [Asians] cause for resentment...We should surely make plain to our coloured friends that there is no colour bar in Australia, and that, as children of the Father, we recognize our brotherhood with all men.

Mannix and Calwell differed in particular over the O'Keefe case. A woman from the Celebes in Indonesia, Mrs Jacob, had married an Australian, John O'Keefe. Her two youngest children were allowed to stay in Australia, but the other six children and Mrs Jacob were ordered to be deported by Calwell, who stated that he did not want a 'mongrel Australia'. Mannix appealed to Calwell to cancel the decision, which was causing adverse publicity for Australia in the Asian press. After the 1949 Federal election the incoming Liberal government allowed the O'Keefe family to stay.

In the depression years of the early 1930s both Mannix and Calwell had understandably opposed large scale immigration to Australia, as it would at that stage have taken jobs from Australian workers. The Japanese advance had exposed our unfilled spaces; population increase had become a security issue. By the early 1940s Melbourne Catholic leaders were lamenting that Australia's population was barely replenishing itself. Catholics blamed 'race suicide', a catch-all slogan which included birth control, abortion and low birth rates. Little did they realize they would soon have a population explosion they could barely cope with. From 1945 Australia's Immigration Minister was Arthur Calwell, identified with the policy of 'populate or perish'. He successfully oversaw Australia's large post-war program; in a rocky career this was his greatest achievement. Calwell's department had at first tried to find immigrants from the British Isles and Western Europe, but many of these had already been accepted by the United States and Canada. As a result Australia received, in addition to a group of Jewish Holocaust survivors, displaced people from east, south and south-east Europe, including the Baltic states, Poland, Ukraine, Italy, Malta, Austria and Croatia, all countries with large Catholic populations, though that was not the scheme's aim. As most of the millions of post-war

27 Arthur Calwell married Elizabeth Marren, social editor of *The Tribune*, in 1932; they jointly published *The Irish Review* in the 1930s and 1940s. (MDHC)

immigrants settled in Melbourne and Sydney, this meant a sizeable increase in the archdiocese's numbers into the 1950s and onwards, as many immigrant families had young children.

The Official Movement

In the first seven years of the Catholic Action secretariat, from 1938 to 1945, Maher and Santamaria successfully brought into existence the various organizations which comprised it. The positive aim of Catholic Action was to permeate institutions across society with Christian social principles. Running in parallel with this permanent aim was the preliminary task of eliminating far left threats to Australian society. As a result Santamaria put his main energies from the early 1940s into the anti-Communist Movement. The war had just ended, but the post-war world heralded new problems. By the end of the decade an estimated 50 million Catholics in Eastern Europe suffered under Communist rule. At Yalta, as Mannix pointed out, one tyranny replaced another. Exhausted Asian countries were now similarly exposed to Communism in the form of Mao's Red Army. Communist parties had very strong followings in France and in Italy, where the new Christian Democratic Party had struggled to win at the polls. In Australia the Communist Party, emboldened by Stalin's successes, and by its own strong position in key unions, was ready to test its strength. Archbishop Mannix made a number of speeches in 1947 warning of Communist activities: 'Communism is a real danger and what has happened in other places could happen here'.

It was in this atmosphere in 1945 the Australian Bishops formally approved the Movement, funded it, kept it secret and replaced Archbishop Simonds as the Catholic Action supervisor with Bishop O'Collins, all decisions with dire consequences in the future. In Melbourne Simonds had few important positions, one of which was Episcopal delegate for Catholic Action, for which he was well qualified; in May 1943, soon after his arrival in Melbourne he had addressed Catholic Action leaders on the 'Theology of Catholic Action'. He was presumably removed as Episcopal delegate because of his known anti-Movement views. Bishop O'Collins was inexperienced in Catholic Action affairs, too close to Santamaria, and located in Ballarat, which made close supervision difficult. All states backed the Movement and contributed financially, but Sydney ran its own show. Santamaria needed the church for its finances, for its Australia-wide framework of dioceses, parishes and religious orders, and for the Catholic Action secretariat with its resources, which he controlled. Santamaria's overall argument was: if we don't try to save the country from the Communist menace, who else will? And if we do try, where else can we get resources and nation-wide structural support except from the Catholic Church?

Santamaria always considered the Movement part of Catholic Action, but the bishops ruled otherwise, which indicated unease on their part. Santamaria was designated as merely the liaison officer between the bishops' committee and the Movement, an arrangement which did not reflect his real power. Fr Hackett, a Catholic Action chaplain, acted as a link between Santamaria and Dr Mannix. In retrospect these were contradictory and unsatisfactory arrangements. The official separation between CA and non-CA movements was in practice rendered meaningless, as Santamaria was head of the overall Catholic Action, the lay leader of the NCRM, a Catholic Action body, and simultaneously head of the non-CA Movement. Santamaria played down the separation, and operated as though the three organizations were combined. His dominant role and personality became an issue, since he insisted that all movements report regularly to him, have their decisions approved by Catholic Action, and that the bishops' decisions be relayed back through him. In a typical bureaucratic manoeuvre, he controlled the traffic both ways.

The Movement was a highly organized and efficient operation, stripped down and, unlike the Catholic Action office, not bureaucratic. It had national, State and regional councils which directed groups in districts, unions and factories. By the early 1950s, it claimed 6000 members in 350 districts, and 100 factory and union groups. Members had to devote themselves to it as the principal activity in their lives, akin to a religious vocation; total dedication, like Santamaria's own, was demanded. They had to sacrifice themselves, take a pledge, and obey orders from headquarters without demur. Santamaria was also busy after the war setting up a network of institutions as background structures to his main activities. Among them were the Institute of Christian Studies, later called the Institute of Social Order (ISO) at the Jesuit's Belloc House, Kew, which was a training institute for Movement recruits. *Twentieth Century*, a quarterly publication, and the Newman Institute for adult education, were other initiatives. The ALP formed Industrial Groups in 1946, which were from that time the actual vehicle which fought Communist control in the unions. The Movement provided much of the backbone of the Groups.

The Chifley and Cain Governments

The post-war period saw Labor in power both federally and in Victoria, providing opportunities for advancement long denied Victoria's Catholic politicians. Benedict Joseph Chifley from Bathurst, a NSW Catholic stronghold, became Prime Minister on Curtin's death in July 1945 during the last months of the war. John Cain senior became Premier of Victoria in November 1945, leading a Labor government which with the support of independents lasted for two years. Cain had belonged in the distant past, like John Curtin, to the radical secularist Victorian Socialist Party. Like both Curtin and the current Prime Minister Benedict Chifley, Cain had been brought up in an Australian Irish Catholic milieu, but Cain's case differed from the others, as during his long political career he disclosed neither his Irish nor his Catholic background.

His father was an Irishman, Patrick Cane, and his mother Julia Brennan. After the death of his father when he was eight, Cane lived with relatives near Bacchus Marsh. When he was thirteen he left to work on farms in the Goulburn Valley. He moved to Melbourne in 1907 at the age of 25, where he became reticent about his childhood and background, changing his surname to Cain, which masked his Irish Catholic origins, although as Robert Murray's *Australian Dictionary of Biography* entry on him puts it, his 'stocky, strong frame, 'map of Ireland' face, leathery voice and determinedly 'plain man' style all indicated his origins as the son of an Irish-Australian hill farmer'. Like Chifley he was a habitually seen with an old pipe

28 John Cain senior, Labor Premier of Victoria 1945-7 and 1952-5, with
Archbishop Mannix. (MDHC)

and grey hat. He had been a minister in the Hogan government. Cain
held the centre ground in his party, uneasily balancing the radical
forces on his left and the Movement/Groupers on his right. But his
government fell in 1947 when the conservative opposition moved
against him as a way of objecting to Labor's federal program of
nationalizing the banks. Thomas Holloway's UAP government was
kept in power by the Country Party until 1950.

Pat Kennelly was Minister for Electrical Undertakings and Public
Works in the Cain government, while being simultaneously federal
and state secretary of the ALP from 1947 onwards. He was successful
at raising funds, a strategic advisor to both Cain and Chifley, and
a masterly factional operator, whose standard retort to factional
competitors was: 'You might have the logic, brother, but I have
the numbers'. After being rolled by the Movement in his Victorian
seat in 1952, he was elected to the Federal Senate in 1953. Frank
McManus, vice president of the Victorian ALP in 1947, was at the
same time a key Movement operative involved with Santamaria's
new training organization, the Institute of Social Order. The young
firebrand Stan Keon was at first a Calwell protégé. Coming up
through the CYMS and the Victorian Public Service Association,

Keon won the Richmond seat in the Victorian house in 1945, after which he attacked John Wren fiercely. In 1949 with John Mullens and Bill Bourke he was one of a posse of outspoken anti-Communist Victorian Groupers elected to the Federal parliament.

Union Struggles and Strikes

From 1945 onwards hints of the Movement's existence and its activities in the unions were becoming common. In 1945 a fake ballot paper for a Clerks' Union election was printed in a left-wing leaflet claiming the Catholic Church instructed Catholics to vote for the candidates indicated. At a rally of youth organized by the YCW and NCGM in July 1945 the main speaker said: 'Today, the challenge of Communism is thrown out to Australian youth, and as Catholics we accept the challenge'. During this period *The Advocate* devoted, on a regular basis, a section of its editorial page to well-informed accounts of the latest Communist industrial tactics; the style indicates they were written by Santamaria or one of his close Movement operatives. One such *Advocate* editorial comment on 27 June 1945, ended: 'The rank and file of Australian workers… only realize danger when it is directly under their noses. The recent success of the Communists is, perhaps, the best thing that could have happened. It is bringing an awakening, and already there are signs of exciting days ahead'.

In these years the Communist Party published a number of claims of Catholics organizing against them in union elections, all of which were laughed off by the Catholic press. In a reply to a 1946 Communist publication *Catholic Action at Work*, an *Advocate* article answered that it was only to be expected that Catholics would oppose the Communist Party in unions, but they were not out to capture the trade union movement as a whole. In June 1946 the Communist Party of Australia (CPA) attacked Cardinal Gilroy for saying that within ten years Australian Catholic workers would rise up to crush Communism. Stan Keon launched a stinging attack on Communism as a fifth column in July 1947. In retaliation he was thoroughly denounced by the Communists, which revealed they recognized him as a key opponent; Keon was defended in this instance by the Victorian ALP. *The Advocate* of 9 September, 1948, quoted a CPA circular which referred explicitly to 'The Movement' which organized Catholics in the Clerks Union. At the Victorian Royal Commission into Communism in 1949, the Communist defector Cecil Sharpley praised the Industrial Groups but warned: 'I see a danger to the whole ALP Group movement, however, in the sectarian activities of a number of fanatics.' On 16 June 1949, an *Advocate* editorial disingenuously commented on his statement: 'This vague and cryptic sentence was the occasion of much discussion among Catholics readers.'

Post-war reconstruction in Australia was the beginning of a period of great prosperity for the rest of the century, but union disruption remained a roadblock. Far-left union white-anting had previously been a threat to our war effort and to our external security; it was now a threat to our internal recovery after the war. At the height of its power the CPA had around 20,000 members. With control of many unions in strategic and essential services like transport, shipping and coal mining, the Communist unions made one last great attempt for power in the late 1940s, by challenging the Federal Chiefly government with a series of massive co-ordinated strikes, which were eventually unsuccessful. This was the Movement's finest hour, as it was now not a lone force as in the past, but backed by the Industrial Groups. The ALP power brokers and moderate union leaders were on side, not just because they were patriotic Australians, but because their livelihoods, power and political careers in the Labor movement were threatened by Communist gains.

The Chifley government and Australian public opinion supported Grouper activity. The main union struggles were in NSW, on the coal fields of the Hunter Valley, and on the docks at Balmain in Sydney. The Movement was active in the Latrobe Valley power stations. The Movement-backed grouper Laurie Short was defeated in the ballot for national secretary of the Federated Ironworkers Association in 1949, but he appealed to the courts under new legislation on the grounds of ballot rigging; in 1951 the court declared him elected and exposed Communist vote manipulation for all to see. The Communists had overplayed their hand. This was the turning of the tide, one of the first big heavy industry unions to be returned to moderate hands.

Because of the later uproar over the split, crucial victories over extremist disruption in many unions were never properly acknowledged. Instead of the Groupers (a combination of Labor and Movement activists) being thanked for this, the term 'Grouper' itself soon became a derogatory epithet. There is, astoundingly, no book describing the successful, decade long struggle to defeat widespread far-left and Communist union domination, arguably the most important event in 20th century union history in Australia. After the split so many people were anxious to blame Santamaria that this success was conveniently ignored. Worse, because the Communist threat had been defeated, commentators began to argue there had never been a threat and that Santamaria had been exaggerating things for his own purposes. Santamaria was in a Catch-22 position, a victim of his own success. Fr Ted Stormon SJ made this point in 1953:

> These people [critics of Santamaria] are equivalently saying that Catholic Action, etc. are jeopardising democratic liberties in their fanatical pursuit of Communists, and then saying that, in any case, we don't have to worry much about Communists in Australia because the [Santamaria] people themselves and in particular the unions are cleaning them up.[22]

For these reasons Santamaria's greatest achievement has not been properly recognized. Breaking this disruption was an essential precondition of Australia's great prosperity in the post-war decades.

Internal Disputes

One argument against Movement tactics was that it imitated improper Communist tactics in unions, such as ballot-box rigging and manipulation of voting rolls. The Movement counter-argument was that Communist tactics meant the constitution of a union had been abrogated, so Rafferty's rules were OK until normality was restored, otherwise a union would remain in Communist hands forever. In a national emergency when you were flying by the seat

---

[22] B.A. Santamaria, *Your Most Obedient Servant*, p. 542.

of your pants, Santamaria argued, you didn't have time to have an academic discussion on the finer points of what Jacques Maritain and other political thinkers had written on the topic.

The Movement, a large operation involving thousands of people in different states, was, remarkably, kept secret from the general public for sixteen years, from 1938 to 1954. One accusation against Santamaria after the split was that the secret Movement was an underhand conspiracy of some kind, too illegitimate to see the light of day, with the added implication, given Santamaria's Sicilian provenance, that it was a Mafia-like operation, which made it doubly out of bounds in a decent Anglo-Saxon society. Santamaria himself came to realize, as the Movement became more successful, that secrecy was a poisoned chalice. Vincent Buckley, a Movement opponent, neatly expressed in a circular syllogism the hopelessly entangled position the church had got itself into: 'The Movement could not be mentioned/*Because it was not known to exist.* It could not to be criticised/*Because it was known to have the bishops' special favour.* It could not be actively opposed/*Because the bishops did not want it mentioned.*'

The Deputy Leader of the Opposition, Arthur Calwell, knew about it because he had been one of the first into the field. Everyone knew about it, said Mannix after the split, everyone, that is, except the public. Clyde Cameron recalled that when in 1951 he was the first to mention Santamaria at a Caucus meeting, Calwell warned him never to mention that name again. What Evatt belatedly 'exposed' in 1954 Blackburn had publicized in 1941, and the Communists had outed through various pamphlets on Catholic Action. After the split, many of Santamaria's Catholic opponents focussed on disagreeing with his tactics, never admitting their general support in the past. After all it was the Campions who first put the idea of the Movement to the bishops.

Santamaria tried to get other Catholic Action organizations to work towards the goals of the Movement, which itself was formally designated as not part of CA. The YCW, led by Fr Lombard, and the university Newman Society, led by Fr Golden, SJ, rebelled against the Catholic Action/Movement symbiosis. Groups such as the

YCW based their apostolate on the formula devised by the Belgian priest Monsignor Cardijn to change the 'milieu' in which Catholics operated. JOCist ideas were based on actions by individuals and small groups, which Santamaria argued were ineffective in complex modern societies, where large-scale organizations were the key. Santamaria took the idea of Catholic Action further, some said too far, by developing a kind of activity which he called 'the apostolate of institutions'. Institutions had to be permeated, not just the milieu. This difference in strategy meant Santamaria lost the support of the YCW and the Newman Society, the two bodies he most needed for recruits to the Movement.

Kew and North Melbourne

In the post war years the suburbs of North Melbourne and Kew, two contrasting centres of Catholic activity, took on added importance. North Melbourne, originally the working class hub of Melbourne's transport and livestock industries, expanded its role as the epicentre of Catholic political activity in the Labor movement. With the cathedral-like St Mary's towering over it, it had historically been the centre of Irish Catholic Melbourne. It had become a Christian Brothers fiefdom with the founding of St Joseph's CBC North Melbourne in 1903, a crucial node of influence, as the school drew pupils from the highly Catholic north-western and northern suburbs. In later life McManus fondly referred to North Melbourne as his 'native land'. CBC North was equally a breeding ground of clerical leaders, with four bishops (Lyons, Beovich, Stewart and Morgan) coming from that stable. At the school's 50th year celebrations in 1953 its students were praised for their 'virile, unapologetic and uncompromising faith' and for their leadership in the public service, municipal councils, parliaments and the professions.

Contrasting with North Melbourne was the upper class parish of Kew, and in particular the enclave of Studley Park. Barry Humphries was to dub the predominately Protestant eastern region of the city the 'dress circle' suburbs of Melbourne. A motorist driving up the Studley Park hill from the Collingwood flats had to run the gauntlet of a Catholic guard-of-honour of boom-time mansions, with Raheen

29 Archbishop Beovich, Bishop Lyons and Bishop Stewart, all CBC North Melbourne old boys, with the school's principal Br Crowle, left, in 1953. (MDHC)

on the left side, and Burke Hall, Campion Hall and the Pallottine Fathers headquarters on the right. Many Catholic orders were setting up their houses in Kew, including the Franciscan retreat house 'La Verna', the Jesuit 'Belloc House' and the Cluny Sisters all in Sackville St, a Redemptorist monastery nearby, the enclosed Carmelite Sisters in Studley Park, and the Sisters of St Joseph in Princes Street.

A small Catholic professional enclave was located in Studley Park. In her memoir *Life Studies* the biographer Brenda Niall, whose father Dr Frank Niall was a Collins St physician, describes growing up there in her opening chapter, 'On Kew Hill'. Nearby lived the eye specialist Dr Edward Ryan, the barrister-politician Jack Galbally, the businessmen John Wren, T.M. Burke and Michael Chamberlin, and the Cody and Parer families. Among Kew's non-Catholics were the Prime Minster after 1949, Robert Menzies, and the business magnate Sir Essington Lewis who both lived in Studley Park, and Billy Hughes, in his sixth decade in parliament, in Cotham Rd, Kew. Mannix told Calwell he was hurt that Menzies never visited him at Raheen, but his old foe Billy Hughes did. Santamaria dropped in regularly on his way home to North Balwyn. No other suburb in Australia housed such a collection of powerful public figures. Other affluent Catholics of the business and professional classes lived in the eastern suburbs stretching south from Kew, Deepdene and Balwyn to Camberwell and Malvern.

Catholics in Public Life

Mannix spoke regularly at Xavier College speech nights. In 1947 and again in 1950 he expressed disappointment that Old Xavierians did not have the prominence in public life he had hoped for. Xavier products ought to be the leaven of society, he believed, they needed to lead more and to assert themselves. But the difficulties forestalling Mannix's wish were well illustrated by the career of the Lord Mayor of Melbourne, the businessman Sir Francis Connelly. He had been educated at both CBC North Melbourne and Xavier, after which he joined the family grain stores business in Brunswick. Connelly travelled the world becoming an expert at the bulk handling of grain and wheat. In 1927 he had married Lurline Hennessy, a daughter of Sir David Hennessey, also a Brunswick businessman and a Catholic Lord Mayor of Melbourne during the First World War. Like his father-in-law, Connelly served a number of terms as Melbourne's Lord Mayor, in his case in the later 1940s. As his wife had died by this stage, he asked Sir Bernard Heinze's wife, the sister of his late wife, to accompany him as Lady Mayoress on formal occasions.

Connelly was one of those instrumental in initiating Melbourne's successful bid for the 1956 Olympic Games; for this and other accomplishments he was knighted in 1948. Though popular, influential and gregarious, he stood unsuccessfully three times for pre-selection on the conservative side. It was very hard for a Catholic, even one as accomplished as Connelly, to be selected for a winnable non-Labor seat. A rare exception was Tom Brennan, former *Advocate* editor, who had been a senator and minister in the Lyons government. In 1953 Robert Solly from St Patrick's College and the CYMS became Melbourne's third Catholic Lord Mayor. In 1956 George Hannan became a Liberal Party Senator. There may have been a few other prominent non-Labor Catholic politicians, but at any time they could be counted on the fingers of one hand.

Mannix spoke on a theme similar to his Xavier addresses when talking at Newman College in 1947. While acknowledging the College had produced successful doctors and lawyers, he went on to say: 'But where we have not succeeded is in getting representation on the staff of the University.' The difficulty, Mannix suggested, was that Catholic students who had carried off prizes in their courses did not have the financial resources to travel overseas to complete post-graduate courses. The remedy was a fund to achieve this. A scheme for Archbishop Mannix Scholarships was devised, for which donations were soon collected. The first three winners were John Mulvaney, who eventually became a leading archaeologist and a Professor at the Australian National University, and Max Charlesworth and Vincent Buckley, who both became academics at the University of Melbourne and were, ironically, critics of the Mannix-backed Movement.

It was also hard to advance within the Catholic Church in Melbourne, as Mannix did not believe in promoting accomplished priests, except the Vicar General, to the next rank of monsignor, nor in recommending papal awards for lay people. Fr James Hannan had slipped through the net, as he had been based in Sydney. He was a Melbourne priest well-known throughout Catholic Australia for his role in promoting the missions. Educated at Assumption College and Werribee, he gained doctorates at Propaganda College in Rome, where he was ordained in 1929. In charge of missions for the whole country, he successfully ran the Society for Propagation of the Faith, raising money for the Kimberley, Pacific islands and New Guinea missions. Fr Hannan was raised to the rank of domestic prelate, with the title of monsignor by the Apostolic Delegate in 1940; this entitled him to wear a purple stock and other regalia similar to that of a bishop. After the war Hannan appealed for Australian priests to become missionaries, and set an example by himself volunteering for the Solomons, then returned to serve as parish priest at South Yarra some years later.

Mannix preferred, as we have seen, to have all the main offices of the Archdiocese residing in one or two priests immediately below him. Few others were promoted. The Melbourne poet, Fr J.J. Malone, had written a well-received book of his travels through Asia called

The Purple East. Mannix was known to refer with derision to the Sydney archdiocese, which under Gilroy had two dozen monsignori, as 'the purple east'. The reason usually advanced for his aversion to appointing monsignors was that he did not wish to seek permission from Rome for their appointment. A more likely reason is he wanted no barons with independent fiefdoms and rivalries to flourish. On one occasion Mons. Hannan is said to have gunned his smart red sports car into the drive at Raheen and come to a screeching halt amid the smell of burning rubber and flying gravel. From the front porch Mannix quipped: 'If that's a domestic prelate, I wouldn't like to see a wild one.' That story has gone the rounds, but who knows if it actually happened. The point of the many Mannix anecdotes (now known as Mannicdotes) is not whether they are true or not, but the fact that they proliferated, thus adding to the mystique which surrounded him. Mannix didn't put himself out; he made you come to him, and when you did he said little – you had to do the talking. He was a master of the long pause and of silence. Not revealing himself of course added immeasurably to his mystique. How much Mannix consciously created an air of mystery around himself can never be known, but he was wily enough not to be entirely innocent in this regard.

Centenary Celebrations

The senior priest of the archdiocese, the poet and author Fr J.J. Malone, died in the centenary year of 1948. He hailed from Kildare which he often recalled in his poems. He had been one the few priests in Melbourne who had supported Mannix in taking the radical line of sympathizing with the Easter Rising in 1916. Malone had a distinguished literary career. His poems were collected as *Wild-Briar and Wattle Bloom,* indicating his dual allegiance to Ireland and Australia, and his essays were collected as *Talks About Poets and Poetry*. His detailed studies of the poets Henry Kendall and Adam Lindsay Gorton were early examples of Australian literary criticism. In his later years Fr Malone became a revered figure among Melbourne priests, some of whom knew his poems, especially the popular 'The day I rode to Gaffney's Creek, beside the Goulburn water'. Mannix delivered his panegyric.

30 The Children's Mass at the Exhibition Building during the 1948 centenary celebrations. (MDHC)

In 1948, the centenary of the Melbourne diocese established in 1847, and the installation of Goold in 1848, were celebrated. This included the by now customary round of High Masses, receptions, processions, concerts, talks and other large public events. Dr Percy Jones trained a choir of 200 singers, called the Catholic Philharmonic Society, to perform an Oratorio, 'The Franciscan Triptych', at a pageant on the final night of proceedings. Distinguished visitors to the celebrations included Mannix's old comrade, Eamon de Valera, now President of Ireland, Cardinal Spellman of New York, and the singer Fr Sydney MacEwan from Scotland. The US radio performer Mons. Fulton Sheen spoke on the dangers of Communism. There were exhibitions of religious art and illuminated manuscripts. A highlight of the celebrations was a morality pageant 'No Mean City', which re-enacted the early struggles of the Catholic Church and community in Victoria; Dr Percy Jones composed the incidental music. The play was staged at Caulfield Racecourse in front of a crowd of 100,000, with another 50,000 turned away. The centenary celebrations were conducted in an atmosphere of mild self-congratulation, indicating the church had made it at last, in contrast to the attitude of defiance Mannix had tapped into soon after his arrival in Australia. Publications associated with the centenary included Frank Murphy's biography of Mannix designed by the Hawthorn Press, an illustrated history of the diocese, and a special centenary number of *The Advocate*.

A well-known Melbourne Catholic, Mr John Hannan, was also celebrating his centenary in 1948. He had been baptized by Melbourne's first priest, Fr Geoghegan, and confirmed by its first bishop, Dr Goold. The Hannan family farm had been situated on the shores of the bay on land which became the army's Williamstown rifle range. Hannan remembered the time when a plough was first used at Parkville; few houses north of the Victoria Market existed at that stage. He and his wife, who died at 93 in 1943, had ten children. Two grandsons had become priests; one was Fr Kevin Hannan, indexer of *The Advocate*, who himself died at the age of 99.

The person with the most knowledge of the inner working of the archdiocese at the time of the centenary ceremonies was the cathedral sacristan Hubert Cooney, who held the post for 54 years. From a Fitzroy family, he was educated at St Patrick's East Melbourne, and had taken up the positions of librarian and sacristan at the age of 20 in 1894 under Archbishop Carr. He arranged the ceremonies for Mannix's arrival in 1913, and was present at Carr's death bed in 1917. He was sacristan when the cathedral was consecrated in 1897, and when the spires were completed in 1939. His extra duties included counting the cathedral collections, assisting with the accounts, and compiling the annual diocesan entry in the *Australasian Catholic Directory*. Cooney was renowned as a dignified master of ceremonies, always humble and obliging, with an enormous knowledge of liturgy and its rubrics. He was a scholar, knowledgeable in Latin, French, Italian and Spanish, who amassed an impressive collection of books which he bequeathed to Corpus Christi Werribee. Cooney went on pilgrimage to Rome in the Holy Year of 1950, and died in the following year, at the age of 76.

One outcome of de Valera's visit was the setting up in Melbourne, at his instigation, of a new pressure group on the Irish question 'The

League for an Undivided Ireland'. De Valera, with Mannix's support, had based his whole political career on abrogating the treaty with Britain in 1921, which had left the six county rump of Ulster in British hands. The partition of Ireland had been (and still is) a running sore. For de Valera, now President and aging, Ulster was his last piece of unfinished business. The League was an attempt to revitalize the issue here; Arthur Calwell became a strong supporter. The League tried to keep the Northern Ireland issue alive in Melbourne until the Derry riots of the late 1960s and Bloody Sunday in 1972 reignited the whole matter.

The Irish academic Dr Thomas Kiernan was appointed Irish Ambassador to Australia in 1946; earlier he had been a correspondent for *The Advocate*, recruited by its managing editor Fr Moynihan. Dr Kiernan's wife Delia Murphy was a noted singer of traditional Irish ballads, which she performed at a concert in the Melbourne Town Hall assisted by the ubiquitous Dr Percy Jones, and accompanied on the violin by his brother Basil Jones. Kiernan published his book *Irish Exiles in Australia* in 1954. The Kiernans' son Colm became an academic historian in Australia, writing studies on Calwell and Mannix, and on Irish-Australian relations.

The archdiocese continued its pattern of growth in parishes, and in those in the religious life.

	1940	1950
Parishes	105	121
Diocesan priests	181	239
Religious priests	187	230
Brothers	181	259
Nuns	1594	1730
Primary schools	160	163
Secondary schools	41	44
Primary School pupils	33,865	33,016
Secondary school pupils	7,295	13,082
Total Pupils	41,850	47,083

These figures reveal a levelling off of primary school students, probably a delayed result of depression and war, and a doubling in the number of secondary students, consistent with producing a professional middle class, but housed in about the same number of secondary schools, which suggests overcrowding.

Publications

Melbourne Catholics had an acute sense of the church's long history. They were taught to look back as a way of orienting themselves; the Latin tag *Laudator temporis acti* was often invoked. Each week *The Advocate* ran a column 'Memoirs and Musings', begun by Patrick O'Leary, recycling stories of the early church in Victoria from old *Advocate* files. Controversies on where the first Mass was held in Melbourne, and where the first priest Fr Geoghegan was buried, raged for months. The *Advocate* office was full of journalists who doubled as historians. One was Dinny Minogue, who wrote on the early church in Victoria. Another on the staff with historical interests was Fr James Murtagh, who in 1946 published a book *Australia: The Catholic Chapter*, an analysis of social trends in Australian history leading up to Catholic Action in the 1930s. His lifelong friend Frank Murphy continued as literary editor, writing a Mannix biography published in 1948, and a great number of articles, principally book reviews and theatre critiques, as he was a devotee of Gilbert and Sullivan. Murtagh and Murphy had parallel careers on *The Advocate* over the decades. Fr Murtagh was also researching a biography of Mannix but had not completed it by the time of his death in 1971. Fr Walter Ebsworth had published a history of the cathedral in 1939. His series on the early church in Victoria first appeared in *The Advocate* to celebrate the centenary of the Archdiocese in 1948. They were collected in book form and published in 1972 as *Pioneer Catholic Victoria*. Fr Ebsworth, the long term pastor of St Peter's Toorak, later incorporated Fr Murtagh's researches into his massive life of Mannix.

John Gartner, a traditionalist Catholic, founded the small Hawthorn Press with its distinctive colophon in the 1940s. An apprentice printer and linotype operator on *The Advocate*, he became interested in old printing fonts, typography, book design and fine paper, part of the revivalist movement begun in England by artists like William Morris. In reacting against modern cheap mass production, they favoured personally crafted objects which were works of art in their own right. The Catholic medieval revival of the 1930s was part of this movement; Dr Percy Jones's interest in Gregorian chant and older church liturgies had similar origins. Gartner, who was in touch with writers, artists and engravers, began producing limited, high quality editions on a small hand-fed press. Hawthorn Press books concentrated on literary works, such as the Patrick O'Leary memorial volume, but others, such as one of Santamaria's books, were also published. Another influenced by the revival of old ways was the Melbourne Catholic architect Thomas Payne, who, attracted to the clean lines of medieval Gothic, designed the chapel at Newman College. The exterior of his stone-clad chapel, though not its height, is in harmony with the unique Walter Burley Griffin style of the College. Payne's St Monica's Church in Moonee Ponds is a larger version of his Newman chapel. Payne had come to prominence when the foreman in charge of completing the spires on St Patrick's Cathedral died in 1939, and Payne was called on to complete the job. He has also designed St Paschal's College at Box Hill, St Teresa's Essendon, and the Carmelite monastery at Donvale.

In 1947 the long-term managing editor of *The Advocate*, Fr Francis Moynihan, died unexpectedly while on holiday in Kerry, his native county in Ireland. He had studied for the priesthood, like many Irish priests who came to Australia, at All Hallows seminary, and completed degrees in arts and education at the National University of Ireland. He was ordained in 1918 and came to Melbourne in the same year. As well as parish work (his final post was Clifton Hill), he edited the *Tribune* from 1924 for a year before he took up his *Advocate* position. He was also involved in the ACTS, the 'Catholic Hour' and Catholic Insurances. Fr Moynihan was a good administrator and organizer, but his greatest gift was to attract talent to the paper, both permanent staff, and local and overseas columnists. Fr Moynihan was quiet and unostentatious, his name was rarely mentioned in the paper, and his value became known to readers only on his death, when a four-page spread on him appeared in *The Advocate*.

The paper's founder Joseph Winter had created a remarkable institution, and between the wars Fr Moynihan and Patrick O'Leary had lifted it to a new level. Australian writers praised *The Advocate* as providing some of the best commentary on Australian literature. It was widely recognized that Moynihan's two decade's oversight were a golden age for the paper; its pages reflected the vibrancy of the Archdiocese itself. Both Moynihan and O'Leary died unexpectedly and young, O'Leary at 56 in 1944, and Moynihan at 53 three years later. Their deaths left a great hole to fill. Fr Denis Murphy, who replaced Moynihan as managing editor, had a similar career to him: Irish born, seminarian at All Hallows, a parish priest in Melbourne and involved with the 'Catholic Hour' and the ACTS.

8

THE EARLY 1950S: THE GREAT SPLIT

The Political Scene – The Population Explosion – Businessmen –
Thinkers and Writers – Power Without Glory *– The Alleged Takeover*
of the ALP – Preliminaries to the Split – The Great Split

The Political Scene

After the Second World War the importance of the European
sphere, traditionally our focus, diminished and we became more
oriented to Asian affairs. Scarcely had we seen off the Japanese
thrust south, than Communism began to make its appearance in
Asia. In 1948 Mao's Red Army took over in China, and precipitated
the Korean War. In Indo China after the French lost the battle of
Dien Bien Phu to Ho Chi Minh's forces, Vietnam was, like Korea,
divided into Communist and non-Communist states. It was in this
atmosphere of worry about worldwide Communist expansion that
much of Australian politics was conducted. Menzies unsuccessfully
attempted to ban the Australian Communist Party. Petrov's defection
in 1954 and his exposure of a Soviet spy ring heightened tensions.

Robert Menzies was returned to office as Prime Minister in 1949
on the back of opposition to bank nationalization, and the public's
weariness with strikes, even though it was the Chifley Labor
government which had put them down. Santamaria visited Harold
Holt, the new Minister for Labour, to ensure effective legislation
on free union ballots was implemented. Menzies, trying to put
together a new majority constituency, was aware of keeping union
and Communist activities in the public mind. One link man was
Richard Casey, Minister for External Affairs, who knew Santamaria
at this time. Another was Paul McGuire, appointed as an advisor
to Menzies, with an earlier career in Catholic Action and Naval
Intelligence. McGuire now tick-tacked with Santamaria, keeping the

169

government and the Movement informed of each other's activities. McGuire also worked closely with Dame Enid Lyons, promoted to cabinet to attract the women's and the Catholic vote. In 1953 McGuire was nominated as Australian Ambassador to Ireland, but was not accepted over a dispute about Ireland's status, so was made Ambassador to Italy and the Vatican instead.

With Chifley's death in 1951, Dr Evatt was elected leader of the Federal Labor Party, but his closeness to the left did not inspire confidence among Catholics. Calwell was elected deputy leader, but having the mercurial Evatt as leader proved another setback in his career. Calwell and Simonds were now both unhappy deputies in their organizations. By a terrible coincidence Calwell had lost his only son Arthur to leukaemia at the age of eleven in 1948, and Kennelly lost his son Neil aged 13 in a car accident in 1952, at the time the Movement rolled him in his state seat. These personal tragedies, coming in the midst of bruising internal political struggles, embittered both even more against Santamaria and the Movement.

The Population Explosion

The large post-war immigration came from many countries which were predominately Catholic. Many migrants settled in the poorer inner, western and northern suburbs, already Catholic strongholds. They felt at home in this milieu; having religion in common aided assimilation, sometimes through intermarriage. Catholic population figures began to soar. Firstly there was the original Catholic population which had been growing from a base of about 20% by high natural increase. Then there was the post-war baby boomer phenomenon. On top of these factors was the immigrant influx. The epicentre of this demographic change was the Federal electorate of Maribyrnong, centred on Essendon, whose Catholic population in the 1950s exceeded 40%, with some pockets reaching 45%, among the highest ever in Australia. St Aloysius' North Melbourne, St Columba's Essendon and Santa Maria Convent Northcote were girls' secondary colleges whose mission was to cater for the lower and middle classes in this region. For boys the area was the domain of the Christian Brothers, who had established CBC North Melbourne in 1904.

With foresight the Brothers had set up another school, St Bernard's CBC Moonee Ponds in 1940, just before this post-war population expansion. Soon after it opened St Bernard's couldn't cope. It had a small campus, with one tarmac school yard the size of about half a dozen tennis courts to cater for hundreds of pupils, and without room for expansion. There were no sports ovals, so the school had get permission for students to play in the adjacent Queens Park. Temporary wooden buildings became permanent, corridors were filled in to make new classrooms, classes of seventy in one room were common by the mid-1950s, and lay teachers had to be employed because brothers, unlike pupils, were in short supply. By the late 1950s the school, less than 20 years old, had grown to 600 students and was turning away 200 applicants a year. In the early 1960s the pressure of numbers forced it to open a new, more spacious campus further out at West Essendon on the fringe of the suburbs.[23]

In the fifties Catholic school enrolments doubled, with the result that the problems at St Bernard's were experienced everywhere, if not always in such extreme form. In 1955 a new Catholic primary school was begun at West Heidelberg. It enrolled 550 pupils in its first year; in the next year its numbers jumped to over 700. In some schools New Australian children outnumbered the rest. In the decade after the war 40 new parishes were formed in Melbourne. In the developing outer suburbs the parish school was often built first, with a couple of classrooms serving as a location for Sunday Mass until a church could be completed. The Catholic education system was bursting at the seams. A Schools Provident Fund was set up in 1956 to provide funds for schools to borrow. This emergency was one reason why governments finally brought in state aid for Catholic schools in the next decade. They had no option – it was as much necessity as generosity. At the instigation of Bishop Lyons of Sale, eight parishes in the Berwick-Pakenham-Koo Wee Rup area of west Gippsland were transferred into the Gippsland diocese in 1959, to ease the pressure of Melbourne's rapid post-war expansion, and to boost the Gippsland diocese's modest numbers.

---

[23] See Chapter 4 'Crisis of Accommodation' in Paul J. Rule, *To Learn And To Do: A History of St Bernard's College 1940-1980*, West Essendon, 1980.

31 School children form a living rosary at the Melbourne Cricket Ground in November 1951. (MDHC)

The Catholic profile at the time was high allegiance to the church and high church attendance on Sunday, in contrast to the Protestant churches with high allegiance but lower attendance. The Catholic Church therefore spent some of its energies consolidating a faith already strong. Following Bishop Fulton Sheen's visit in 1948, another world-travelling American Catholic preacher, Fr Patrick Peyton, came to Melbourne in 1951 and 1953 with his Rosary crusade and slogan 'The family that prays together stays together'. He filled the MCG in 1951 with a display of school children dressed in white forming a gigantic set of rosary beads. A morality play, *Chain of Light*, written by Ronald Conway, was staged before an audience of 80,000. In the same year the Pioneer Total Abstinence organization was introduced into the archdiocese. In contrast the Protestant churches invited the crusading US evangelist Billy Graham to jolt their less committed congregations into reviving their church-going through the shock therapy of an instantaneous 'decision for Christ'.

The other direction of Catholic energies was fulfilling its catholic (that is, universal) mission. As the church was in this era in expansion mode, special emphasis was put on conversion. In September 1952 a conference on this topic, sponsored by the Legion of Mary, was held at Sacre Coeur Convent; it agreed that the times provided opportunities for the instruction of non-Catholics. The archdiocese took pride in announcing ever increasing numbers: Catholics schools were growing at a faster rate than State ones, the world figure for Catholics was approaching half a billion. Organizations like the Catholic Evidence Guild and the Legion of Mary sought local converts, and the Society for the Propagation of the Faith supported missionary activity in Asia and the Pacific. Fr Phillip Crosbie of the Columban Fathers became a local hero on his return in 1953, after being imprisoned for three years under harsh conditions by the North Korean Communist regime.

In the past migrant groups, like the Lebanese and Italians, had brought their own chaplains with them, and worshipped as communities based on a particular ethnicity rather than on parishes. Post-war migrant groups did this in the early stages. Capuchins arrived in 1949, and by 1962 had built their church and shrine to St Anthony in Power St, Hawthorn, near the Yarra. The Scalabrinians took over the All Saints Church in Fitzroy in 1963. Both orders catered particularly for Italians. Dr Percy Jones, who spoke Italian after his time studying in Rome, was appointed parish priest at St George's Carlton, a post-war Italian stronghold. A migrant chaplain was subject to the bishop in the diocese in which he operated, but his role might diminish and even disappear as his flock assimilated; this had happened with the earlier Lebanese Maronite community.

As a general rule the archdiocese favoured the parish, a geographical unit, not the immigrant community, as the basis of diocesan organization. This helped assimilation, and in addition many Catholic social services were delivered via the parish. There were a few exceptions to this rule. Fr Ivan Prasko arrived as chaplain to the Ukrainian Uniate Church, a separate church in union with the Holy See. Fr Prasko was appointed its bishop in 1958, with his church in North Melbourne. (In later times a military vicariate for those in the armed services was set up in 1969, and an ordinariate for Anglican converts in 2012, as exceptional, non-geographical quasi-dioceses.) Another problem was that some immigrant groups, such as southern Europeans, had high allegiance but low attendance rates.

By the end of the 20th century Australian Catholics themselves had moved to this profile, so rescue of the faithful, not conversion, became the church's prime missionary activity.

Businessmen

Shortly after Collingwood won the VFL premiership in 1953 following a seventeen year drought, both its long-term patron John Wren and long-term coach Jock McHale died. Wren was described in an obituary in favourable terms: a great donor to charities, a man who lived frugally, and who supported Mannix in the tense years during the First World War. Another prominent Catholic businessman from the early years of the century, T.M. Burke, had died in 1949. Like Wren, Burke became a leading donor to Catholic charities. He promoted education, especially technical training, his name became almost a household word, his public reputation was much better than Wren's, and he was more closely aligned to the church. Burke was awarded a CMG in 1942, and was consul for Poland among his many positions. Both Wren and Burke had their funeral masses at St Patrick's Cathedral.

In a speech given in 1948 the businessmen Michael Chamberlin outlined his view of industrial relations from the point of view of employers. Business must take social concerns into account as well as profits in post-war reconstruction; sectional interests must be reconciled, not inflamed as the Communists aimed to do; a capital-labour bridge should be established. The 'higher unity' mentioned in Papal encyclicals was essential, as both sides had a duty 'to provide constantly for the common welfare and the needs of the community'. Michael Chamberlin was Manager of the National Trustees, Executors & Agency Co from 1933. He was chairman or director of bodies like City Mutual, T.M. Burke's companies and the Roman Catholic Trusts Corporation. He helped Catholic charities and other bodies, and was a member of the boards of St Vincent's Hospital, Newman College and later Mannix College at Monash University. He was close to Santamaria, being a key figure in his fund-raising operations.

Other Catholic businessmen at this stage with similar, if lesser,

profiles were Walter Broderick and Percy Page, both backers of
Santamaria. Wally Broderick owned a business in Fitzroy recycling
the leavings from the Richmond brewery to be sold as feed and
fertilizer. His horse, the filly Light Fingers, won the Melbourne
Cup in 1965, the first of trainer Bart Cummings' dozen Melbourne
Cups. In the mid 1950s Broderick arranged the purchase of a farm
near Yarra Glen for the Cistercian monastery at Tarrawarra. Wally
Broderick's grand-daughter Maree King married Bob Santamaria's
youngest son, Paul. Percy Page was in business as a printer, and in
sport a football administrator. He was secretary of the Richmond
Football Club from 1924 to 1931, after which he took Richmond's
coach 'Checker' Hughes to Melbourne FC when he moved to become
secretary there, inaugurating a golden age at that club when the two
were instrumental in winning three consecutive premierships in
1939-41. In 1931 Percy Page was co-designer of the McIntyre-Page
VFL finals system based on four teams. In the 1940s he was honorary
secretary of the St Vincent's Hospital public appeal for funds. His
firm printed one of Santamaria's early pamphlets. Sir Bernard
Callinan, from St Kevin's CBC, had gained an engineering degree
before joining the army. He became a war hero by leading Sparrow
Force, a small group of Australian commandos who operated as
guerrillas behind the lines in Japanese-occupied Timor, living off
the land while harassing the enemy. For this he was awarded the
DSO and Military Cross. In civilian life he held many positions,
on bodies such as the State Electricity Commission, Colonial Sugar
Refinery, the ABC and La Trobe University. He was President of
the MCC from 1980 to 1985. When Sir Michael Chamberlin died
in 1972 Callinan took over his role as fund-raiser for Santamaria's
National Civil Council.

Matt and Pat Cody continued the liquor and mining interests
inherited from their father, a Wren business partner. Pat Cody
featured prominently as a witness favourable to Wren in the libel
trial over Frank Hardy's novel *Power Without Glory*. Stan Keon
came from the Hogan liquor family; his Hogan mother had married
a Keon. Eldon Hogan, at this time secretary of both the Newman
Society and the Archbishop Mannix Scholarship fund, and well

known as a Xavier administrator and cadet supervisor, came from the same Hogan family as Keon.

Thinkers and Writers

Four of the five Irish Jesuits who had arrived in the early 1920s died in the years around 1950. Fr Albert Power, who had from the early 1920s been a dominant figure at the Werribee seminary as rector and theologian, died in 1948. Fr Eustace Boylan, schoolteacher, and long-time editor of the Jesuit devotional magazines *The Messenger* and *The Madonna*, passed away a year later. Fr Jeremiah Murphy had become a fixture as Rector of Newman College for almost three decades. He had guided generations of young Melbourne Catholics into the professions between the wars, adding a final layer to the Catholic educational structure set up by Goold, Carr and Mannix. He had a mild, pleasant personality, was influential on campus, and gave valued advice on many university committees. On his departure the Vice Chancellor, Sir George Paton, called him 'the University's senior statesman', the University conferred on him an honorary Doctor of Laws, and the government awarded him a CMG. He died in 1955 soon after leaving Newman College.

Fr William Hackett died in car accident in Kew in July 1954 a few months before the split; he was at the time chaplain to the Movement. An engaging and inspiring priest with a distinctive personality, Hackett had been instrumental in the Catholic intellectual revival of the 1930s. An Irish rebel and de Valera supporter he had been Mannix's closest companion, visiting him at Raheen regularly in the evenings to chat, and accompanying him on annual summer holidays at Portsea. Santamaria replaced Hackett as Mannix's confidant for the remaining decade of Mannix's life. The survivor of the five early Jesuits was the ubiquitous Fr Henry Johnston, who continued in his familiar role as public advocate for the faith for years to come.

Two famous economists lived in Australia in the 1950s. The prominent English Catholic economist and political broadcaster, Barbara Ward, married Commander Robert Jackson in England. They took up residence in Melbourne. Jackson, from Victoria, was a convert to Catholicism. A former deputy to the UN Secretary General Trygve Lie, he worked for the federal Ministry of National Development. The Jacksons moved to Pakistan in 1952 to advise the government there on developmental programs. They became close to Santamaria during their Melbourne sojourn, as did the renowned economist Colin Clark. Clark, another convert who had grown up in Queensland, became widely admired when in 1940 he published his *Conditions of Economic Growth*. Clark is credited with having devised the measurement of Gross Domestic Product (GDP), used for comparing the economies of different countries. Back in Queensland from the late 1930s he advised Santamaria on policies for the NCRM, though they differed on rural economics. After another spell in England in the fifties and sixties, he took up a position at Monash University in the 1970s.

In 1955 a large Catholic Life Exhibition was held in the Exhibition Buildings. A popular Catholic journalist at the time was E. W. (Bill) Tipping, chief of staff at the *Herald*. He had been educated at St Monica's Moonee Ponds and St Kevin's CBC where he was school captain in 1933, and at university where he was a member of the Campion and Newman Societies, and editor of the student newspaper *Farrago*. He served overseas with the RAAF during the war. In 1951 he was awarded a journalism fellowship to study at Harvard University. On return he wrote for many years a daily *Herald* news and gossip column 'In Black and White' which was widely read. The Brisbane poet and essayist Martin Haley wrote regular literary features for *The Advocate* in the post-war decades, while continuing to live in Brisbane. A traditionalist Catholic school teacher, Haley, born in 1905, was President of the Brisbane Catholic Readers and Writers Society, a small Queensland Catholic ginger group promoting the literary apostolate. This society included the writers Paul Grano, James Picot and Joseph O'Dwyer, all of whom by chance had started life in Victoria. Haley became one of *The Advocate's* best known and most prolific writers, filling one of the gaps left by the death of Patrick O'Leary. He also contributed to Catholic journals in Brisbane and Sydney, and to the periodical *Twentieth Century*, published by the Jesuit Institute of Social Order. The summer 1953

The Turning Year

By
JOSEPH O'DWYER

With wood-engravings by
ALLAN JORDAN

MELBOURNE
THE HAWTHORN PRESS
1944

32 Title page of a book of Joseph O'Dwyer's poetry, designed and printed by John Gartner at the Hawthorn Press. (MDHC)

issue of this journal included poems by James McAuley, Vincent Buckley and Joseph O'Dwyer.

While living in Brisbane Joseph O'Dwyer had poems published in early issues of *Meanjin* magazine, founded in Brisbane in 1940. O'Dwyer moved to Melbourne in the following year, living with his large family at Wonga Park, and later at Montrose on a property in the foothills of the Dandenongs owned by the English Catholic aristocrat Lord Clifford. O'Dywer was known foremost as a poet with two early volumes, *Poems* (1941) and *The Turning Year* (1944); the latter, decorated with woodcuts, was designed and printed in a handsome format by John Gartner at the Hawthorn Press. O'Dwyer best-known early poem 'The Trojan Doom' combined a T.S. Eliot style modernism with an interest in the classics. O'Dwyer had a wide ranging passion for culture and religion, which as an enthusiastic teacher from 1946 to 1963 he passed on to those Xavier students who were interested. To those who weren't O'Dwyer dedicated a poem 'A Teacher's Prayer that his Students Might Avoid their Inevitable Mediocrity'. O'Dwyer's later poems, published in his *Collected Poems 1930-1981,* were freer in style, and more relaxed and personal, although O'Dwyer himself became more a traditionalist. The foreword to this volume was written by his friend and fellow poet Phillip Martin. The O'Dwyer's eldest son Michael married Susan Burke, grand-daughter of T.M. Burke.

Power Without Glory

The publication in 1950 of Frank Hardy's novel *Power Without Glory*, with its depiction of alleged Catholic intrigue in politics, caused instant uproar. The controversy developed into a saga of miscalculation on both sides. Frank Hardy was a Catholic from Bacchus Marsh who on reaching early adulthood had transferred his redemptive hopes for the world from Catholicism to Communism. The Communist strategy at the time was to collect from its supporters as much dirt as they could find on both the Wren machine and the Movement, and then to get the party member, Frank Hardy, to put it all together in thinly veiled 'fictional' form as a novel. This they believed would discredit the Movement and the Catholic Church, their prime targets, by linking them with John Wren and his dubious business and political activities. The novel accused Wren of bankrolling the Movement, which revealed the Communists had badly (or deliberately) misunderstood the situation.

At the time a three-way clandestine struggle for the soul of the Victorian Labor Party was taking place between the Wren forces, the Movement and the pro-Communist left. Wren had operated as a background political manipulator for the past half century, but his influence was fading. His forces were being challenged by the two new kids on the block, the Movement and the Communists, both of whom were austere and highly ideological in contrast to the Wren forces, who were often bribe-grabbing time servers. So far from Wren backing the Movement, he was under siege from Movement forces who sought to replace him as old fashioned (he was in his seventies), and lacking ideological Catholic fervour. The Movement man Stan Keon strongly attacked Wren as soon as he got into the Victorian parliament. The Movement believed the ALP should be purged of both Wren hangers-on and secular leftists, and utilized for 'higher' Christian ends. Hardy could hardly attack the Movement for being ideological – the Communist pot calling the Movement kettle black – so the Movement had to be damned by associating it with the discredited Wren influence.

The 'novel' was also wrong about any strong Mannix-Wren connection. The plot has the Movement being financed and

33 John Wren, the central figure but not the target, of Frank Hardy's *Power Without Glory*. (MDHC)

supported by the Wren machine, with the Mannix figure portrayed as the sinister go-between and controller, thus tarnishing both the Movement and Mannix with the racketeer Wren connection. But Wren's intrigues had been essentially a political, not religious, operation, involving the ALP but not the Catholic Church. There were few if any documented occasions when Wren and Mannix met, though their homes were near each other. Niall Brennan quotes Mannix as saying: 'I have never visited Mr Wren's house'. Yet the novel has the two engaged in almost daily *tête-a-têtes*, as a tandem Machiavellian operation deciding over a drink who should be the next federal and state ALP leader, etc.

The book and Hardy's subsequent trial for criminal libel had the effect of putting Wren in the public spotlight, not the Movement, which was the Communist's real target. The Communists kept their heads down during the controversy, and the Movement forces could not respond as that would have blown their cover. So the Movement was not outed in 1950, though there was plenty on it in the novel, with the result that four years' later Evatt caused a sensation with his revelations. The Calwell-Kennelly group wondered which way to jump; as anti-Communists, but in the Scullin-Brennan tradition of putting party before religion in the political sphere, they did not back the Movement.

If the Communists had made a tactical blunder, so did the Wren faction by accepting legal advice to instigate a criminal libel action against Hardy. It meant the Wren forces were hit with the full force of bad publicity about Wren's past, admittedly sensational but a diversion from the main game. As a result the Wrens were diminished in the public mind rather than the Communists or the Movement. And anyway the novel came out too late. It was planned in the mid 1940s when the Communist stranglehold on key essential service unions was first being challenged by the Movement. But during the five years Hardy took to compile his book, the Communist hold had largely been broken, so the book's effect within the Labor movement was not as far-reaching as intended.[24]

One of Wren's advisors was the lawyer Jack Galbally who had just been elected as Labor member for Melbourne North in the Legislative Council; he was not aligned with the Movement. He came from a family of nine whose parents had struggled to make a living. The eldest child, Dr Kath Galbally, helped the others get a start in their careers. The family produced three doctors, two lawyers, and a headmaster. Jack Galbally became a Minster in the Cain government of 1952-5; during the split he was troubled and pulled both ways, but stayed in the ALP like his fellow Catholic Arthur Calwell. Both were subsequently made to feel unwelcome at their local parish churches, and by some pro-Movement Catholics.

The Alleged Takeover of the ALP

In the later 1940s many Catholic ALP members, like Calwell, were not happy to find their own party being shanghaied from a new quarter. Movement intrigues in the ALP now threatened their careers, just as earlier Communist tactics had. In 1948-9 Calwell and Kennelly in Melbourne, and Mulvihill and Ormonde in Sydney, were rolled from their state executive posts, a sign of strong Movement influence in both state branches. Calwell was now anti-Movement and so lost favour with Mannix, a personal setback to match his political one; Santamaria replaced him as Mannix's political advisor. Both Calwell and Simonds were now opposed to the Movement, which they considered was damaging church and party, but were unwilling to move against it by announcing its existence. Though opponents

---

[24] The definitive account of the novel's genesis and history is contained in Pauline Armstrong's biography *Frank Hardy and the Making of Power Without Glory*.

they too kept it secret, and as a result became incapacitated by their inaction. Calwell had attacked the 'anti-Communist obsession' of the Catholic right at the party's 1948 state conference, but that was in an internal forum and he didn't name the Movement. At the inauguration of Eris O'Brien as Archbishop of Canberra-Goulburn in January 1954 just before the split, Simonds similarly spoke out against those who 'involve the Church in underground political intrigue', rebuking 'her misguided children [who] seek to capture political power in her name', but only those few in the know picked up this oblique reference.

At this stage Calwell should have been bothering, not with the peripheral issue of Gilroy's Red Hat, but with handling the Movement's attempted takeover of the ALP. In the late 1940s he had a window of opportunity to explain to the public the problem: we called in Catholic Action to save the Labor movement from the pro-Communist left, but, that battle having been won, Catholic Action is now trying to take over us. The opponents of the Movement in the ALP needed to name and shame it publicly. In the vacuum caused by their failure to do so, Evatt seized the initiative a few years later, establishing his centre-left narrative as the dominant one. For the centre, led by Calwell, to fail to clearly state the problem, was fatal for church and state, not to mention his own career.[25]

In 1952 John Cain senior was again elected to government in Victoria, remarkably the first Labor government in the state to have a majority in its own right. However new complaints were emerging that the Movement was trying to take over non-Communist unions, and that it was trying to take over the ALP itself, indicating a major escalation from defensive action to power seeking. The Cain government was threatened by the increasing influence of Movement figures on its right, and left wing unions on its left. Groupers like Stan Keon and John Mullens had gained federal seats in 1949. The Groupers were close to control of the Victorian Labor Party. The

---

25 History is full of examples where in a civil war, one side calls in a powerful outsider in order to win an internal struggle, with the result that the outsider remains to dominate the situation, with no internal winners, for example the English called into Ireland in the 11th century, and the Russians called into Ukraine in the 17th century; neither left until the 20th century.

new factor was that the Movement was now changing its *modus operandi*. Previously it had the negative aim of defeating Communist infiltration. It now moved into its positive phase of trying to reform the Labor Movement along the lines of Catholic social principles. In December 1952 Santamaria wrote to his superior and confidant Dr Mannix:

> The Social Studies Movement should within a period of five or six years be able to completely transform the leadership of the Labor Movement, and to introduce into Federal and State spheres large numbers of members who possess a clear realisation of what Australia demands of them, and the will to carry it out.

In targeting institutions Santamaria used fuzzy terms like 'permeation' which blurred the distinction between influence and control.

This could at a stretch be deemed influence only, but a memorandum written by Santamaria on the day the Cain government took office in Victoria in the same month goes further. It lists 26 Cain supporters matched by 26 Bill Barry/Movement supporters in ALP parliamentary ranks, discusses the selection of the Cabinet and gives instructions about contacting wavering members, thus confirming that Movement parliamentarians and their supporters were organizing with Santamaria before party meetings.[26] This attempt to gain some form of control of the ALP led to a new series of objections to the Movement. The membership of any group in an organization can strive for control; this happens all the time. But an outside body, in this case the Catholic Church, should not have been financing a body which aimed to take over a political party, especially since church and state are separate entities in our polity. The church had encouraged Santamaria in his political ventures, but at the same giving him riding instructions (that he couldn't act in political parties) which effectively outlawed those activities.

The split was not just a political one between left and right, and a religious one between Catholics and others, it was a state-based one,

---

[26] B.A. Santamaria, *Your Most Obedient Servant* p. 75, and *Running the Show*, pp. 183-6.

with New South Wales pitted against Victoria. In the run up to the split, Panico's reshuffling of the hierarchy meant the wrong people were in the wrong places at the wrong time when the split erupted. In anti-Movement Sydney a pro-Movement Melbourne bishop (Lyons) was supervising the Movement there, whereas in pro-Movement Melbourne an anti-Movement Sydney bishop (Simonds) was second in charge. What a mess. After Lyons was replaced in Sydney in 1954 the new supervisor, Bishop Carroll, began to work effectively against the Movement. The split was caused not only by a sectarian attack by anti-Catholics led by Dr Evatt, but was partly instigated by one NSW faction. The Sydney Catholic Labor figure James Ormonde, outgunned in an internal ALP power struggle and encouraged by senior Sydney church figures, canvassed support from the Evatt pro-Left forces in the ALP, but found as a result of the split, his group was now captive to the Evatt forces they had invited in, a mirror image of the earlier Movement intrusion.

Preliminaries to the Split

The great split of 1954-5 was the most disruptive event in the history of the archdiocese as well as in the ALP, with reverberations down the decades. The couple of years before Evatt's bombshell of October 1954 exposing the Movement were full of barely subterranean rumblings in church and state. Rumours of a secret Catholic group were surfacing and finding their way to the press in garbled form. The Sydney Catholic journalist Alan Reid began publishing articles on what was going on behind the scenes. Official Catholic sources in Melbourne kept issuing qualified denials to muddy the waters. Fervent Movement-aligned Victorian ALP politicians (Keon, Mullens and Bourke federally, and Scully and Barry in Victoria) were now throwing their weight around. For example, Stan Keon in Federal parliament in March 1950 broadened the attack, arguing that the 'pinks' in the newspapers and universities who influenced public opinion were more dangerous than those in the unions. In October 1950 Mannix criticized those who objected to Catholic Action strategies, praising those Catholics who were fighting Communism in the unions.

In 1951 the federal executive of the ALP banned the magazine *News Weekly*, the mouthpiece of the Movement, which was accused of personally crusading against Labor leaders like Evatt and Calwell. This indicated the Evatt/left forces had control federally but not in Victoria. During the 1951 federal election campaign Calwell claimed in *The Advocate,* after Evatt had argued in the High Court against the Communist Party Dissolution Bill, that his leader and the ALP were not soft on Communism. Four letter writers disagreed, claiming that Calwell was being disingenuous about Evatt's leanings. Bernard Gaynor (Santamaria's solicitor) referred to 'the extremely watery support the A.L.P. Industrial Groups have received from Labour leaders of the seniority of Mr. Chifley, Dr. Evatt and Mr. Calwell himself'. This was a discreet outing of Calwell as a Movement opponent at this stage. Val Adami, one of the early Campions, was more blunt: 'In his [Evatt's] handpicked Department of External Affairs pinks were prominent. Catholics were almost non-existent'. These exchanges were part of continual skirmishes over the extent of Communist and Movement influence in the ALP. (*The Advocate*, 9 and 26 April 1951)

In August 1952 *The Advocate* published an editorial against Movement opponents in the church. Two anti-Movement *Catholic Worker* activists wrote to *The Advocate* (4 September 1952) turning its own editorial words against it:

> We feel that many of your editorials 'bring scandal and division upon the Catholic body by weakening the hands' of those engaged against reactionary forces in the political, cultural and industrial field.

The 'reactionary forces' referred to were the Santamaria operations in the unions and the ALP, but secrecy was maintained as they were not explicitly named. On a number of occasions in 1952 Mannix claimed that Catholics had halted Communism in its march: 'The first people in Australia to realize the menace of Communism were the Catholic body. They have been in the forefront of the fight against Communism. Were it not for the initiative and foresight of Catholics I think Australia would be in even a much worse position than it is today.' (*The Advocate*, 19 June 1952) This was a broad hint of the Movement's activities. In November 1953 the Victorian Labor Minister for Lands, R.W. Holt, dramatically ripped up his party's own bill allocating land for Santamaria's NCRM. In April 1953 the Presbyterian *Messenger* warned that the Industrial Groups were really Catholic Action spearheads.

The *Catholic Worker* group sent a private memorandum to the Australian bishops in 1953 outlining their objections to Movement activities, arguing that Movement tactics in union battles were improper, and Movement activities in the ALP were contrary to church rules. In September 1954 the bishops, alarmed at rumours about the Movement, separated it administratively from Catholic Action. Catholic Action was itself closed down rather than the Movement, which was causing all the trouble but had a momentum of its own, but the move came too late. At a grand reception in April 1953 at the Exhibition Building, Cardinal Agagianian, the Armenian Patriarch, and Cardinal Gracias of Bombay were guests-of-honour, along with Richard Casey, the Minister for External Affairs, the Governor Sir Dallas Brookes, Dr Evatt, Santamaria and Mannix. The latter three were soon to be protagonists in the split.

34 At a dinner in April 1953 to welcome overseas visitors: from left Archbishop Fernandes, Michael Chamberlin, Archbishop Mannix, Cardinal Agagianian, Sir Norman O'Bryan, Cardinal Gracias. (MDHC)

The Great Split

The public had not been aware of the gang warfare going on beneath the surface in both the Catholic Church and in the ALP. In the course of devising his election platform for the 1954 Federal election, Evatt took advice from Santamaria in order to secure Catholic and Victorian votes. He was expected to win the election, but after the defection of the Petrovs, lost narrowly. He blamed the Victorian branch of his party for not giving him full support. In October 1954 Evatt, weakened by his election loss, dramatically exposed and denounced the Movement as alien to the Labor Party in order to shore up his position. The fifteen months from the Evatt outburst in October to the next Federal election in December 1955, the period of the great split in the Labor Party, witnessed tumultuous changes.

Publicly the bishops and the Movement adopted a strategy of denial, evasion, vagueness and then limited admission after Evatt's exposure. Mannix, who was ninety at the time, issued a series of statements vigorously justifying organized Catholic activity in the unions, whereas Santamaria and *The Advocate* said very little. As a subterfuge Mannix and other Movement defenders spoke only of the ALP Industrial Groups, as though the Movement and Santamaria's activities did not exist. Mannix claimed that groups within the unions 'are not Catholic groups, they are industrial groups'. A similar line of argument was that because Movement cells contained some non-Catholics, they were not a Catholic organization. Both arguments were intended to cover up the reality. Soon after the Evatt revelation Mannix denied that the Catholic Church aimed to control the ALP through Catholic Action, though he had received a letter from Santamaria's saying they were doing this. There is evidence that some of Mannix's statements after the split were prepared by Santamaria. *The Advocate* editorial of 21 October, its only statement on the issue, did not mention the Movement, but claimed that 'the notion of a compulsive 'totalitarian' regimenting of Catholic votes or activities in favour of any Party or political ideology' was simply preposterous. Another argument, used by Mannix among others, was that the attack on the groups was a sectarian plot to embarrass Catholics. Santamaria issued a statement on 20 October replying to allegations that the groups, masterminded by him, sought to destroy the ALP. Santamaria admitted that for the past decade he was one among a number of people who successfully organized against the Communists in the unions. An incomplete reply, with no mention of the Movement, his leading role in it, nor of Catholic Church backing, all of which would be publicly revealed, and reluctantly admitted, in the months ahead. Mannix also said the Catholic bishops were united in favour of the Industrial Groups, implying incorrectly that all the bishops were happy with the present situation.

After Evatt's exposé in October, Santamaria decided to resist. At an executive meeting the Movement adopted the Santamaria position of boycotting what he called the Evatt Labor party, but Sydney delegates supported the 'stay in and fight' strategy. An internal split among the bishops, and among state ALPs, was beginning to be formalized, though this had not become public. The Sydney archdiocese gradually emerged with a decision that any Bishop could allow or disallow the Movement to operate in his diocese. This effectively spelt the end of the Movement as a cohesive Australia-wide operation.

The religious split was between the majority pro-Movement bishops led by Melbourne and traditionalist Catholics on one side versus the minority Sydney bishops, the *Catholic Worker* group and Catholic Labor identities who had remained with the ALP on the other. Calwell, his resolution weakened by the turmoil, lost a great chance when at a Caucus meeting he did not as deputy leader seek a spill motion against Evatt's severely weakened leadership, which would likely have succeeded. Both deputies in state and church, Calwell and Simonds, failed to press their case at this crucial juncture. But it was harder for Simonds, who operated in a quasi-monarchical system, to challenge the king than it was for Calwell in politics, where leadership challenges were par for the course.

In February 1955 the party's federal executive dismissed the pro-Grouper Victorian executive, replacing it with a left wing one. At the Hobart federal conference the pro-Evatt delegates had the numbers. The ALP split first formally occurred on 20 April 1955, when those members of the Victorian parliament who supported the old, pro-Grouper executive crossed the floor and brought down the Cain Labor government. (Like Curtin in his last years, Cain relinquished the agnosticism of his earlier radical days and became more sympathetic to religious attitudes, and was buried with Anglican rites.) The Groupers were expelled from the ALP and formed the party which became the DLP. In the Victorian state elections of May 1955, and the Federal election of December 1955, both won by the Liberals, all DLP-type members except Frank Scully in Victoria lost their seats, but the DLP gained enough federal votes to play a blocking role in the future. These events lead to the ALP being out of Federal Government for twenty-three years, and the state Labor party for twenty-seven years. The split of 1954-5 replicated in many ways events in the 1910s. In both Mannix was a central figure, in both there was an attempt by organized Catholics to penetrate the Labor Party in order to change its policies, in both cases the archdiocese was involved in a public controversy, in both cases the Labor Party split, and as a result in both cases the natural assimilation of Catholics into the wider community was retarded.[27]

---

[27] The account provided here is a simplified narrative of these complex, interconnected feuds; for a fuller version the reader is referred to the standard analyses of the period.

9

THE LATE 1950S:
THE VATICAN VERDICT

International and Internal Politics – Objections to the Movement –
The Vatican Decision – Fissures in the Church – Melbourne Catholic
Activity In Asia – Santamaria & Mannix – Late Mannix – The Height
of the Old Church Mentality

International and Internal Politics

The split had been caused by attitudes to Communism. On the international scene the Communist domination of Eastern Europe at this period was still a strong cause of local indignation. Anti-Communist Captive Nations groups, heavily Catholic in composition, were active in Melbourne. Speakers like Arnold Lunn came out on the anti-Communist circuit. The Hungarian revolution of 1956, the subsequent Soviet invasion, and Cardinal Mindszenty's fleeing to the US embassy, had a considerable impact in Catholic circles. In 1955 Pope Pius XII instituted the feast of St Joseph the Worker, to be celebrated on 1 May to counter Red May Day activities. In contrast to the creation of the feast of Christ the King, this revealed the church was now accepting egalitarian as well as monarchical systems. Communist advances in Asia added to the worries. In 1956 the foreign correspondent Denis Warner spoke at a Catholic gathering hosted by Mannix outlining this new danger threatening the region. A year later the first free election of a Communist government in the world occurred in Kerala, India. The Czech Jewish academic Dr Franta Knopfelmacher noticed when he arrived in Melbourne in the 1950s that:

> Australian Catholics play a key role in Australian politics...
> an important section of the Australian Catholic community
> awoke much earlier than other Australians from colonial
> slumber. While the others still slept, they were already

responding in an alert and intelligent manner to the political signals from a new and dangerous world…When I debated issues which interested me the people who were attuned to what I had to say, who were 'on the same wavelength', tended to be, more often than not, Catholics.[28]

Menzies defeated the Evatt-led ALP in 1955 and 1958. Calwell belatedly became ALP leader in 1960, but he inherited a party destabilized by Evatt and the split. Calwell, born in 1896, had been active in politics since 1917, a span of over four decades, and was showing his age. Menzies retained power with the help of DLP preferences. During the conscription controversy in 1917 Mannix had memorably said that Catholics did not vote in platoons, but now with the DLP they did. The Australian electorate was so evenly divided that the DLP Catholic vote could, by preference distribution to the Liberals, determine federal and Victorian election results. The DLP was an accidental party. No-one had wanted or designed it to come about; the expelled ALP members had been compelled to form a new party to preserve themselves as a political force. Some Catholics realized that a confessional Catholic party on European Christian Democratic lines was not acceptable in an Anglo-Saxon society. The DLP emerged out of a split in the ALP, and the National Civic Council (NCC) out of a split in the Catholic hierarchy. Santamaria viewed the DLP, which he did not join, simply as a tool to force the ALP to reform. But the DLP naturally saw itself as a party in its own right. Whatever the reality, Santamaria had to give the public appearance that he was running the DLP, and could determine its preference allocation.

Henry Bolte benefited in Victoria where the Liberal Party remained in office. Catholics were far from prominent in these Liberal ministries. The Victorian ALP branch, bereft of its large right-wing Catholic section, was now in the hands of extremists, led by Bill Hartley, a sectarian socialist left ideologue imported from Western Australia. This controlling ALP group was sympathetic to militant and Communist trade unionists, with which it devised 'unity tickets' to keep each other in power in the unions. Catholic

---

28 Frank Knopfelmacher, *Intellectuals and Politics*, p. vi.

Labor leaders like Calwell and Galbally had to watch all this impotently.

Victorian Catholics aspiring to political careers in this period were still sidelined, with their natural home until now, the ALP, out of favour with many of them. The Victorian ALP, reverting to its older, unsuccessful strategy of putting ideology before winning power, continued the branch's abysmal electoral record. Whitlam said disdainfully of it 'the pure are impotent'. In contrast the NSW ALP continued its dominant electoral record, remaining in power without a break from 1941 to 1965; during this twenty-four year period the Victorian party was in office for only four years. The NSW Premier during the split, the Catholic Joe Cahill, had adroitly managed, by negotiating with Gilroy, to keep the NSW party from splitting, with some Groupers holding their places in the unions and the ALP.

Objections to the Movement

In a Christmas broadcast in 1958 Simonds made his strongest public statement against the Movement:

> During the [1958] election campaign, the Church became involved in bitter political controversy, which is always a very regrettable circumstance. I am happy to say I was completely unconnected with it. Whenever the Church's ministry and spiritual mission becomes befogged with political issues the cause of religion always suffers.[29]

In these years Simonds' main task was an endless round of Confirmations on Sundays. Poor Simonds, the best twenty years of his life were wasted as coadjutor with no agreed role. With little to do, at one stage he decided to examine how the many religious orders in Melbourne were faring. When he reported to Mannix that all was well, Mannix replied that that came from leaving them alone. Mannix had a light administrative touch and a long perspective on events; he advised people who came to him with worries to let things sort themselves out, the knots would untie themselves. After the split the *Catholic Worker* issued a detailed exposé of the Movement. At a

---

[29] Rev. Walter Ebsworth, *Archbishop Mannix*, p. 417.

meeting of clergy after this was published, a priest asked Mannix if they were allowed to sell the *Catholic Worker* outside their churches, a test of Mannix's reputed tolerance of dissent. Mannix deftly replied that any priest who was so foolish as to support the *Catholic Worker* line was free to sell it. Mannix was tolerant within limits.

35 Fr Eric D'Arcy, left, and B.A. Santamaria, right, are awarded M.A. degrees at a University of Melbourne graduation ceremony in August 1959; between them is Dr Percy Jones, Vice Director of the university's Conservatorium of Music. (MDHC)

In May 1955 at the height of the split a letter from the Movement chaplain Fr Eric D'Arcy was leaked to the press. It invited 'carefully chosen Catholics in business and professional spheres' to a secret meeting to be addressed by the 'person best qualified to explain the present crisis' (obviously Santamaria). It alluded to 'the men working so stoutly to defend the Church in Australia'. This was a blunder as it clearly involved an influential priest crossing the line by becoming involved in politics. This incident severely held up D'Arcy's promising church career; it took another 26 years before he was made Bishop of Sale in 1981 and later Archbishop of Hobart in 1988. D'Arcy changed careers and took up a position at the

University of Melbourne in philosophy. He modified his stance on church-state relations to a more modern one, now writing in favour of tolerance in a pluralist society, a harbinger of things to come, as did Dr Max Charlesworth after he returned from his doctorate in Louvain to the university as a Senior Lecturer in Philosophy. Charlesworth became a *Catholic Worker* opponent of Santamaria, whereas Percy Jones and D'Arcy were supporters. Like Jones, D'Arcy came from a Geelong family. He had the Parkville parish and Jones the Carlton one, both conveniently situated close to the university, which meant they were not tied to presbytery life, and could move freely outside the restricted sphere of the church. D'Arcy was soon off to study for his doctorate at Oxford. Both later served on church commissions rewriting the liturgy. Every morning Mannix read the papers scanning them for material for his speeches. One day in 1960, on reading that Princess Margaret was engaged to a man named Jones, about whom little was known, he exclaimed: 'As long as it's not our Perce, I'm not interested', a dig at the worldly wise Jones' penchant for swanning around in higher social strata. As it was Jones himself who recounted this story, he understood, and enjoyed, its thrust.

Criticism of the Movement from other Christian churches was as difficult to handle as internal opposition. Methodist leaders issued a statement that it was better to combat the growth of Communism by ameliorating social evils than by opposing Communists in unions. They also claimed Catholics had acted like 'totalitarians of the right' in opposing those of the left. Some of the more unreconstructed Protestants had long believed Rome was fomenting sinister underground plots to take power in Anglo-Saxon realms, so when they discovered to their satisfaction this had been happening under their very noses, they understandably gave vent to unvarnished anti-Catholic prejudices. Who could gainsay them when their deepest fears seemed confirmed? Santamaria always claimed to be a victim of sectarianism, but precisely who begins any new round of sectarian skirmishing is always a chicken-and-egg question. Santamaria had been warned his activities were likely to have this result. In politics it's never a good idea to give your opponents a free kick. By his actions Santamaria was as much an initiator of sectarian tensions as he was a loser from them.

By the later 1950s, as the effects of the split widened, defenders of Catholic Action in the unions and ALP were under increasing pressure. Catholic spokesmen continued to deny the existence of the Movement, principally by their silence on the issue. Mannix spoke regularly against the Communist danger and defended the Groupers; Santamaria in contrast maintained a low profile, issuing statements only when under attack, making limited admissions when exposed, and adopting new justifications. He now admitted the Movement existed when challenged by Jean Daly of Sydney in the British *Tablet*.

The Vatican Decision

The bishops all signed a new pastoral letter 'The Menace of Communism', but their meeting in early 1956 confirmed a split in the hierarchy, and their inability to agree on a way forward. In October 1956 they decided to take the Movement debacle to the Vatican for a ruling on the vexed questions it had thrown up. The anti-Movement prelates Gilroy and Carroll from Sydney and O'Donnell from Brisbane travelled to Rome, the delegation Santamaria referred to derisively as the 'Italian pilgrimage'. The Melbourne side sent its case, which argued that its form of organization of Catholics should be allowed to flourish, a view to which the Apostolic delegate, Archbishop Romolo Carboni, was sympathetic. The Vatican's first ruling, issued in May 1957, stressed that the bishops should retain their authoritative role as pastoral leaders in these matters, but the laity were free to act in a responsible way. Organizations should be charged with the task of moral and social formation, but not of activity in trade unions or political parties; in addition the existence of a confessional party was discouraged. On 6 June *The Advocate* published a report of a speech by Gilroy making these points, without mentioning it was the outcome of a recent important Vatican anti-Movement decision, and with the article misleadingly headed by *The Advocate*: 'Lay Apostolate "Sorely Needed" in Public Affairs'. In the next edition of the paper Mannix interpreted

Gilroy's statement as 'an urgent call for action', when in fact it was a warning against unauthorised forms of action. Mannix now said there were two kinds of organizations: bodies like the YCW and the NCGM which were forms of Catholic Action approved by the church, and those like the Movement for which the church had no responsibility. No further explanation was offered of this starling new claim. People had assumed for decades that the Movement was church backed, which in fact it was, as the bishops had supported and funded it.

When Cardinal Gilroy discovered Melbourne was making use of its own interpretation of the new ruling, he requested clarification of certain points from the Vatican. A second Vatican ruling, issued in July 1957, was much more precise, confirming the Bishop's supervision in these matters, and explicitly ruling out direct or indirect action in unions or parties. Catholics could only act individually and not involve the church. This ruling effectively ruled the Movement as it had operated out of bounds. Archbishop Simonds' and Arthur Calwell's long-standing and impotent objections had, too late for them, been vindicated. In 1916-7 Mannix as coadjutor had disagreed with his aging superior Carr over the Easter Rising. Similarly Simonds as coadjutor had fallen out with the nonagenarian Mannix over another controversial political issue, the Movement, in the last decade of his reign. Both coadjutors had been proved right.

At a Movement meeting on 17 December 1957, Santamaria and his officials resigned en masse and formed a new organization, the National Civic Council (NCC), a private, secular body, with Santamaria as President. But for the rest of his life Santamaria considered that what had happened on that day was a necessary legal fiction, and that the NCC was not just a successor organization to the Movement, but the same body. In 1959 Cardinal Agagianian, head of the Vatican's Propagation of the Faith department, arrived in Melbourne to check on suspicions that its aging archbishop was under the thrall of Santamaria. Calwell claimed Agagianian said he came armed 'with the power to remove Dr Mannix from office if he thought it advisable'. But Calwell and the Cardinal agreed to do so would cause too great a contretemps. When Bishop O'Collins was asked by the bishops to demonstrate his supervision of the Movement had been truly independent his reply was drafted by Santamaria!

These crucial events – the split in the bishop's ranks, the petitions to Rome, the two Vatican rulings against the Movement, the Movement's dissolution, and the formation of the NCC – were barely reported, if at all, in *The Advocate* and *Tribune*. Not to fully disclose them and discuss their implications was a serious failure of the magazine's duty to its readers. It still backed Santamaria, reporting his many activities as though nothing had changed. Bishop Lyons continued to praise the 'heroic work' of the Movement (*The Advocate*, 8th August, 1957). The paper carried a rare mention of the *Catholic Worker* in 1959, but only to strongly criticize it. The Melbourne church was still in denial; it had not learnt the lesson from the Movement episode that cover-up and secrecy eventually make any problem much worse. (Clerical paedophilia was beginning at this time and was swept under the table in the same way, only to explode decades later in another dispiriting catastrophe.)

Fissures in the Church

Political explosions like the split happen from time to time in politics, but after the initial uproar they tend to be absorbed by a return to normality, as happened after the conscription controversy in 1917. But the 1954-5 split unaccountably kept having a multiplier effect, setting off detonations at regular intervals for years to come. Its aftermath was traumatic for Melbourne Catholics. In *A Portrait of the Artist as a Young Man* James Joyce memorably describes a Dublin Christmas dinner descending into acrimony as family members disagree about the sudden disgrace of Parnell, their lost leader. Melbourne Catholics repeated these scenes half a century later. Many families and individuals were ravaged by having members on both sides of the new divide. The split produced few winners and many losers.

The Melbourne Archdiocese was now seen as the problem, not the leader, of the Australian church. Catholics were once again on the outer in the general community, Mannix was seen as subversive, as in conscription days, the DLP was viewed unfavourably by others, and with social embarrassment by its own voters, who were loath to admit their voting intentions to pollsters. A longer term problem was that alignments formed in the split days were confusingly redeployed when Vatican II became an issue. The strong DLP vote disguised deep turmoil in the Catholic community. Vatican II produced its own adherents and opponents, who came to be known (unhelpfully) as liberal and traditional Catholics respectively, labels which did not accurately reflect the tensions swirling underneath. As the division over religion in the 1960s seemed to closely follow the political division of a decade earlier, the two controversies unfortunately intertwined, which meant the agony of the Split was prolonged.

The split and the formation of the DLP helped in one way to consolidate the former 'Catholics together' mentality, but at the same time it punctured the air of infallibility about church activities, and produced an embryonic political opposition within the church. This was not helpful in the long run, as a temporary political polarization later morphed into a permanent religious one, long after the political divisions which initiated it had abated. Catholics who were traditional ALP voters experienced a conflict of loyalties, which could fracture their previous allegiance to the church. Even those who had followed the bishops' line on politics felt their previous commitment to the church somewhat tarnished, as it had lowered itself in their eyes by getting involved in a political manoeuvre. The split caused the Catholic Church in Victoria to prematurely fissure a decade before the church at large did as a result of Vatican II from the later 1960s onwards. In Victoria the majority church establishment continued to back the Movement, whereas the minority *Catholic Worker*, Newman Society and YCW groups strongly opposed it, and then opposed the Church's continued backing of it. Melbourne had taken on a division along French lines. The French hierarchy had fallen out with the Jocist-inspired 'worker priest' movement as too leftist, accommodating to secular values and outside church control. In both cases radical Catholic groups were at odds with the hierarchy on a political issue.

Santamaria appeared not fazed by his great setback, as he kept up an extraordinary range of activities: the Movement (now called the NCC), the rural movement, *News Weekly*, the annual Social Justice statement, the annual Christian Social Week lectures at the university, the Movement in Asia, his weekly talk on the Catholic TV program, and the Institute of Social Order at Belloc House. All were heavily publicized and supported in the Catholic press (except the Movement in Asia which, like its local equivalent, was kept under wraps). Denys Jackson provided ideological ballast, remaining a key figure among traditionalist Catholics, with talks and articles, amounting to hundreds in all, in *The Advocate* as 'Sulla', in *News Weekly* as 'John Calhoun', and with a weekly radio commentary on the 'Catholic Hour'. He now gave a good impression of an absorbed, absent-minded thinker. Ronald Conway wrote that he had 'great erudition and [the] clarion call of conviction…He had many of the lovable social lapses and endearing failings' of his hero, Chesterton.

Melbourne Catholic Activity In Asia

The years after the split were spent by many trying to assess Santamaria, either positively or negatively. But from the moment the split erupted he set up, with astonishing daring, an even more extensive Movement in Asia. His Australian opponents were so intent on raking over the coals of his Australian intrigues that for decades they missed knowledge of his new undisclosed Asian venture. They were looking in the wrong place. The long post-split debate on the Movement had the effect of camouflaging his new schemes.

The Catholic Church in Australia originally saw itself as part of Oceania, facing the Pacific not Asia. Australia's imperial and church mission was to oversee New Guinea and the islands of the South Seas, with Catholic missionary activity strong there. But after the shock of the Japanese advance south Australia looked more to Asia. St Francis Xavier was one of our patron saints. As a European outpost our providential mission in God's plan was deemed to be the headquarters for Christianizing Asia. From the mid 1950s the danger from Communism was not, Santamaria believed, so much an internal one (many unions had been won over from them by then), but an external one. Following Mao's success in 1948, Communist parties were poised to take over countries in South East Asia, which would eventually threaten our security. The deteriorating situation in South East Asia demanded special attention. A good deal of Santamaria's energy from this time on was devoted to setting up a Movement-type operation in Asia. He had already organized an Asian students' conference in Melbourne in 1953. Rebuffed in 1954 in Australia, Santamaria now turned to the wider battle in Asia to combat increasing Communist designs there. He attended a Pacific Conference on Social Action in Manila in 1955. Vin D'Cruz, a Catholic journalist from Kerala, came to Australia to alert us to the depredations of the Communist government there, and eventually stayed to work for the NCC.

Santamaria had originally intended to work directly through the Catholic Church in Asian countries, principally through Cardinal Gracias of Bombay, but the Movement explosion damaged his reputation in those circles, so he secularized the church's missionary vision: we now had to save Asia from Communism. Santamaria proposed a far-reaching Pacific Confederation to co-ordinate defence, trade and foreign policy in the region. In the mid 1960s he set up his own body, the Pacific Institute, to help in the defence of South Vietnam and other countries threatened with Communist subversion. He coordinated anti-Communist strategies run by a number of organizations, including Catholic ones, whose operations in this field were often run by Jesuits trained at Bellamine College in Rome. In this work he was assisted by Brigadier Bill Serong of Melbourne, a counter insurgency expert, and Frank Mount, an NCC operative seconded to administer the circuit. Amazingly at the height of the crisis in South Vietnam Santamaria set up a DLP-type Catholic party there, utilizing Australian Catholic mission funds, to provide an electoral base for President Thieu. His key man in Jakarta, the Dutch Jesuit Fr Beek, warned of a coming Communist takeover in Indonesia in 1965, information which Santamaria passed on to Australian intelligence bodies. He tried to raise awareness of defence as an issue and to elevate it into a national priority, writing a book on the subject, *The Defence of Australia* (1970).[30]

---

[30] A short account of the Movement in Asia is found in *Your Most Obedient Servant* pp. 542-7, and a longer one in Frank Mount's book *Wrestling With Asia*.

36 The Melbourne doctor and women's activist Mary Glowrey in her early years; she was later noted for her contribution to women's health in India as a religious sister. (CWSG)

Two heroic Catholic women from Melbourne had worked in Asia long before Australia's post-war interest in it. Little known here as a missionary during her lifetime, but in retrospect significant, was Dr Mary Glowrey, a Melbourne doctor and a founder of the CWSG, who, after learning of the appalling infant mortality rate in India, moved in 1920 to work among the poor at Guntur, half way between Calcutta and Madras. She joined a religious order as Sister Mary of the Sacred Heart, building up her own hospital at Guntur almost from scratch, and was eventually joined by other helpers from Australia. They ran a pre-natal clinic and dispensary, and greatly reduced the incidence of child death and malnutrition, one of the greatest health problems in India, by setting up a network of Baby Health centres in outlying towns. Her success was in part due to the reluctance of Indian women to be examined by male doctors, and she trained local women in the services she was setting up. She established the Catholic Health Association of India and published articles on ancient Oriental systems of medicine. Dr Glowrey laboured at her task until she succumbed to illness in 1957. Her work was in some ways a forerunner of that of Mother Teresa of Calcutta. A biography of Mary Glowrey by Ursula Clinton of the CWSG, launched by Dr John Billings, who had visited her hospitals in India, was published in 1967.

Among those who joined Sister Glowrey was another Melbourne woman doctor turned nun. Ethel Pitt was the daughter of William Pitt, a brother of the two Pitts who had married into the Buxton family; she was therefore a cousin of Kathleen Fitzpatrick. Ethel Pitt was educated at Vaucluse Convent and completed a medical degree in 1922, specialising like Dr Glowrey in eye and ear problems. After working for some time in Queensland she obtained from Fr Boylan of *The Messenger* details of the order of religious sisters Mary Glowrey had joined. Ethel Pitt journeyed to India in 1932, taking the name Sister Veronica. Both she and Sister Glowrey had to get permission from Rome to work in a medical capacity. After learning from Sister Glowrey, she set up her own hospital and clinic at Bangalore. Sister Mary Glowrey spent the last months of her life in Sister Veronica's care. The Apostolic Internuncio in India Archbishop Knox (later in charge of the Melbourne Archdiocese) advised Sister Veronica on how to raise funds for her Indian work.

37 A rare photograph of B.A. Santamaria and Archbishop Mannix together. Between them is the Jesuit Provincial Fr Austin Kelly, with Mannix's friend and Movement chaplain, the Jesuit Fr William Hackett, far left, and Stan Keon third left. The gathering was an Asian students' conference in Melbourne in 1953. (SLV)

Santamaria and Mannix

In the conscription controversies around 1917 both sides have been thoroughly analysed by historians. But there is a serious imbalance in accounts on the Movement and the split. There exist over a dozen books on these events, almost all strongly anti-Santamaria, except for Robert Murray's *The Split* and Gerard Henderson's Santamaria biography, which give both sides, and Gavan Duffy's *Demons and Democrats*, which is pro-Movement but hardly known. So it was left to Santamaria to be a lonely defender of his own controversial activities, always an unsatisfactory situation, as people responded with the comment: 'he would say that, wouldn't he'. In addition, those who directed the Movement (like John Maynes, Gerald Mercer and others) might have left important accounts, but they fell out with Santamaria in an internal row in the early 1980s, and remained silent.

Santamaria had that most disagreeable trait – in his early career he had always won out. So when he finally came a cropper in 1954, the *schadenfreude* among his former colleagues knew no bounds. Because he was the most reviled figure in public life for the next two decades, it was open season on him. This created a bandwagon effect, as there existed a receptive market for anti-Santamaria material, with many former colleagues obliging, tempted in the new atmosphere to exaggerate their earlier opposition. Some Catholics undoubtedly did disagree with some of Santamaria's tactics, but his most vocal opponents, based originally on former Campion members, were in the main lawyers, academics and ex-priests. They were not people who had got down and dirty in union struggles, so their knowledge was limited. Moreover their first objection was not to Santamaria taking over political bodies, but to him trying to take over Catholic ones, like the Young Christian Workers and the Newman Society. Santamaria was accused of secrecy on multiple occasions, but his Catholic opponents themselves also kept the Movement operation secret until late in the piece, because in many ways they had agreed with it.

Understandable partisan arguments over the activities of Bob Santamaria diminished the fact that we were witnessing a profound tragedy which Australian public life did not have the resources to fully comprehend. Classical Greek dramatists defined tragedy as an irreconcilable division not between a right and a wrong, but between two rights, in this instance ridding Australian politics of Communist infiltration, and on the other hand keeping the ALP free from other forms of infiltration. There was a personal as well as institutional tragedy caught up in these events. In *Hamlet* Shakespeare defines the essence of tragedy as the fate of a human being with a collection of outstanding qualities, but with one he takes so far it threatens to ruin him and occludes the good in all the others. Bob Santamaria appeared on the Australian political stage with a dazzling array of qualities hitherto unseen, but an overwhelming drive for control ('some habit that too much o'erleavens the form of plausive manners') eventually brought him undone ('shall in the general censure take corruption from that particular fault'). We as spectators were too limited in our emotional range to open ourselves to experiencing the more exalted sensations – sublime, destructive, cathartic – on offer, instead reducing the episode to everyday personal recrimination and taking sides. We viewed it more as low politics than high tragedy.

Santamaria was like his mentor Mannix in some ways. Both were wonderful orators, but with contrasting styles: Mannix softly spoken, humorous and indirect, Santamaria full on, comprehensive and deadly serious. One left an enormous archive, the other practically none. After the split they had in common a failed aspiration to save their country at a critical juncture, which for a time derailed both their careers. Mannix privately confessed to Santamaria his regret over his 1920 anti-British speech in New York, which had wrecked his Irish mission, leaving him an exile in the south seas. Santamaria's likely takeover of the ALP led to his exposure in 1954, rendering him an exile from the Australian mainstream. Both felt let down by the church they had devoted their lives to. Mannix did not publicly criticize the church, whereas Santamaria increasingly did so. After the split Santamaria presented himself as a confident analyst of events, but at the same time as a strangely humble and deferential individual, perhaps his way of indirectly admitting past shortcomings. Each gave over five hundred recorded speeches, but despite all they said and others have written about then, their personalities retain an element of mystery. We saw in each case only the public persona, a small part of the important activity going on below the surface; neither ever revealed his full hand. Both were protean but elusive in their activities, so we never have their measure. It is best to approach any assessment of them as works in progress. We will never fully understand the real relationship between them. Who was running the show?

Late Mannix

Mannix had never been peripatetic; in his later decades he never travelled overseas, and his visits interstate were minimal. He spoke on average more than once a week until his last decade, thousands of speeches in all. They were on public affairs as they affected the church, not, with a few exceptions, directly on religion, as he claimed all his life to be speaking as a citizen not as a church hierarch, a distinction without a difference to his flock. He projected his personality through them. At home he prayed, meditated, studied (he was a seminary academic by profession) and ruminated, the fruits of which are evident in his addresses, which contain an alluring mixture of humour, knowledge, subtlety, putdowns of his foes, and encouragement to his hearers. His influence derived mostly from his speeches, his greatest achievement.

When people of my generation first knew Mannix he was well into his eighties, and seemed to be transitioning into another dimension than ours. All his life Mannix world-wearyingly took on the tasks of public leadership; he was part of events but also beyond them. In his chapter on Mannix in *Cutting Green Hay* Vincent Buckley perceptively noticed that Mannix's humour was 'based on an intense awareness of *vanitas vanitatum*, in which an unillusioned mockery of the world's ways coiled back in a self-mockery that added to rather than threatened his authority'. This helps to explains how Mannix held together in his character the drives to both support and undermine authority. The long final decades of Mannix's life added a further sense of removal from ordinary life, in which he retained authority by the aura which surrounded him. But there was, naturally, a downside to his longevity. Mannix was eighty-one at the end of the second war and too old to instigate the changes needed to keep up with the rapid expansion of his archdiocese in the post-war decades. The priests in charge of most activities at this late stage, Fox and Moran, did not have the authority to make reforms.

The structure Mannix had inherited over forty years ago in 1917 was an old-fashioned power vertical. The king appointed a second-in-command, through whom all decisions of the realm were communicated by personal contact, and who in turn reported personally to the chief. By 1960 the archdiocese was a large and complex corporation. In round figures it had grown from 80 parishes in 1917 when Mannix took over to 160, from 200 churches to 300, from 200 priests to 600, from 250 brothers and sisters to over 2000, from 90 schools to 250. But its administrative structure had not changed. Modern businesses had boards, line managers, devolved chains of responsibility, and charts laying out organizational responsibilities. But in the archdiocese a few priests who held the key positions had to supervise both ways the traffic dealing with finances, buildings, clergy, parishes, religious orders, education, welfare services, visiting overseas dignitaries, meetings, Catholic organizations and so on, not to mention the current issues and crises endemic to any large organization. Mons. Laurie Moran said of his regular meetings with Mannix, when he was grilled on all this: 'He terrifies me'. On the other hand Mons. Arthur Fox said Mannix was easy to get on with as he left you alone (which could be just as terrifying). The organism of the archdiocese was still alive and kicking, but its organizational structure was becoming rickety. A highly articulated operation was still being run as a personal fiefdom.

In Sydney Cardinal Gilroy surrounded himself with auxiliary bishops, plus legions of monsignori, some of whom, like the redoubtable Monsignor Tom Wallace of Darlinghurst, originally a CBC North Melbourne contemporary of Calwell, were baronial power brokers in their own right. In Melbourne the cupboard was bare. The only other bishop in Melbourne was Simonds, whose advice was not sought. Mannix was ninety when the split occurred, and needed an auxiliary freed from administrative burdens to help cope with ongoing crises in the wake of that disaster. So Mons.

Fox was relieved of his many positions as administration chief and promoted to Bishop in 1957; this was a further insult to the coadjutor Archbishop Simonds as Fox, his junior, was given the role of archdiocesan spokesman, a role for which, with his charmless personality, he was not suited. Bishop Lyons, a predecessor to Fox as second-in-command, had been head of Catholic Action in Sydney, but as a Santamaria ally he was not wanted there. In 1956 Lyons was removed from the fray by being appointed Bishop of Sale.

Fr Arthur Fox had been one on the first batch of priests ordained from the Werribee seminary. As Bishop he was outspoken in defence of the Catholic anti-Communist forces in the Labor movement, leading the apologias as Mannix aged. Did Fox ever say, as often alleged by his opponents, that it was a sin to vote for the ALP at the time because of its close ties to the pro-Communist left? Perhaps not, but he came close by asserting in June 1960 that 'no Catholic can with a good conscience vote for the ALP in the present circumstances', code in the Catholic mind for much the same thing. In 1957 Mons. Laurie Moran took over administrative duties from Fox, continuing Mannix's habit of concentrating authority in one deputy, as in the previous cases of Lonergan, Lyons and Fox; in addition Moran was appointed vicar general in 1961. He was promoted to monsignor and then bishop in the years after Mannix's death, but was by then, like Simonds himself, in failing health.

The Height of the Old Church Mentality

Before the war Catholic social services were provided by the Catholic Social Welfare Bureau (CSWB), and the Catholic Migration Committee which assisted refugees. After the war the Catholic Migration Office (CMO), which assisted immigrants, was opened in 1947 with Fr Michael Rafter as director. This function was assisted by the Caroline Chisholm Guild, headed by Fr Con Reis, which helped migrants to assimilate. The Catholic Social Welfare Bureau, with Fr Eric Perkins in charge, which had previously concentrated on children and wartime welfare needs, now expanded its functions to include the family as a whole. In 1954 one area of concern was hived off as the Catholic Marriage Guidance Centre, with Fr Maurice

Catarinich, son of Dr Catarinich, in charge, and in 1958 a Catholic Social Service Bureau was formed to concentrate on traditional welfare relief. In 1969 its name was changed to the Catholic Family Welfare Bureau, so it would not be confused with government social services. At the same time a Catholic Family Planning Centre was set up.

These changes reflected developments which the church faced in the emerging suburbia of the post-war world. Problems arising from upward social mobility, rising prosperity, and increased freedoms moved to the centre of the new agenda. The church in its social role now focused its attention on family breakdown leading to social breakdown, rather than on the issues thrown up in the depression years. It pressed governments for child endowment and welfare benefits for families, and assistance for its own charities. Some older friendly societies like the Hibernians lamented the coming of the welfare state which they thought diminished individual sacrifice and giving. The concerns for the church in its accustomed role as moral guardian were legion: drinking, sexual licence, adolescent delinquency, permissiveness, marriage breakdown, divorce, raunchy films and TV, contraception, pregnancies outside marriage, adoptions, and so on.

Much effort was spent on attempting to prevent these ills, but less on their underlying causes. Bishops issued regulations on such things as how many inches below the knee women's dresses had to be at Mass. New developments were condemned as secular or materialistic, every issue was treated as a dire problem, essentially a threat to faith, and in response the church's pre-ordained moral codes were imposed as blanket solutions – 'guard us when danger is nigh'. Guilt, moral scruples, and constant worry about sin were prevalent. This was too dark a view of human nature, one that did not allow itself to be surprised by joy. And it did not work, especially with the coming of the more relaxed attitudes of the sixties, where in matters of personal and sexual relations the church's advice was increasingly ignored. A breath of fresh air amidst all this gloom was Fr Ted Stormon's robust common sense on the 'Question Box' segment of the 'Catholic Hour' during the 1950s. In a time of fervid ideological extremes on all sides, his was a voice of calm and sanity. Women's dress fashions were, he pointed out, not a matter of morals but of taste, manners and context: women could turn up at Mass during the summer beach holiday season in more relaxed gear without being accused of indecency. Fr Stormon adroitly managed to ameliorate stick-in-the-mud Catholic and prejudiced Protestant enquiries without disagreeing with basic church beliefs. At this stage the 'Catholic Hour' was conducted by the Franciscan Fr Genesius Jones, and the Catholic TV program 'Sunday Magazine' by Fr Michael King.

In the 1950s all the statistics and key performance indicators were encouraging for the church: high allegiance, high participation rates, high number of vocations, high number of Catholic organizations. But all was not as satisfactory as it seemed. Under the surface a certain stasis and lack of new initiatives had set in. This period was the height of the old undisturbed Catholic way of life. Things we thought set in stone were soon to disappear: novenas, Confirmation by a bishop, altar rails, hatted women in church, regular individual Confession, kneeling for Communion, fasting from midnight, kissing a bishop's ring, indulgences, litanies known by heart, altar boys in frilly white, priests saying the Latin Mass facing away, nuns in very large numbers in distinctive medieval dress, and Holy Name men taking up the Sunday collection. It had all seemed as if it had gone on forever unchanged and therefore would never end. There was nothing wrong with these habits; communities of any kind need formal practices sanctioned by time to give them coherence. It was the suddenness of their going which was the problem, and the lack of replacement rituals.

The prevailing mentality was prolonging itself beyond its use-by date. In retrospect the appearance of energy can be likened to that of certain plant species which produce a final burst of efflorescence before decline. Fr John Brosnan noticed the years of the 1950s were:

> great ones for non-essentials in the Catholic Church. Every
> second week, it seemed, some priest or prominent layman
> would come back from overseas with a new devotion. If
> you weren't in the Third Order of Something or Other, the

38 One year's intake of Christian Brothers in Melbourne, 1960, the last period
of high numbers of vocations to the religious life. (MDHC)

Legion of This or That, or a participant in one of any number
of Novenas, you had no hope. The various lay leagues,
orders and sodalities were pushing their individual barrows,
and rosary 'crusades' were multiplying like chain letters.[31]

---

[31] Tom Prior, *Knockabout Priest*, p. 45.

	1950	1960
Parishes	121	162
Diocesan priests	239	337
Religious priests	230	286
Brothers	259	295
Nuns	1730	2023
Primary schools	163	207
Secondary schools	44	44
Primary School pupils	33,016	69,550
Secondary school pupils	13,082	23,730
Total Pupils	47,083	92,380

These figures show healthy expansion in most categories. The big jump was in school enrolments, as both primary and secondary pupil numbers doubled in the decade of the 1950s, without there being enough secondary schools to cope with the increase.

The church's unchanging regime was reinforced by the simultaneous reigns of Pope Pius XII and Mannix, and of Sir Robert Menzies and Sir Henry Bolte in the secular sphere. Melbourne Catholics born in the 1940s had by the early 1960s known few other rulers. In addition the appearance of the DLP had the effect of herding many Catholics back into their religious ghettoes. The Archdiocese's view of the future was faulty. This was illustrated by a new seminary, proposed in 1954 to be built on a prominent hill in Glen Waverley in the outer east. An up-to-date organization would have had financial projections, insight into current social trends, and other relevant data on which to base a decision; a look around would have revealed the proposed architectural style was badly out of place in its suburban setting. An enlarged version of the past was envisaged, a giant brick basilica to accommodate 200 students, including a chapel with 35 side altars, as though the untypical growth of the 1950s would continue forever. At the same time the Christian Brothers at Bundoora and the Blessed Sacrament Fathers at Lower Templestowe built replicas of Glen Waverley as their novitiates, with wide wings splaying out from a central chapel. This was the church in monumental mode. Each parish, already struggling under its own building program, was allotted a required sum to defray the costs of the Glen Waverley folly, redundant almost from the time it was occupied in 1959. A few years later the reforms of Vatican II, with its opening out to the world, made the forlorn new palace even more anachronistic, almost literally a white elephant.

Old church ways began to fade with Mannix.

10

THE EARLY 1960s:
THE DEATH OF DR MANNIX

Politics and State Aid – The Professions – Authors – Central Europeans – The Last Years of Mannix – New Ideas – Archbishop Simonds – Catholic Groups

Politics and State Aid

Both Calwell and Simonds reached the position of leader of their organization late in their careers, Calwell becoming leader of the Federal ALP in 1960 at the age of 64, and Simonds the Melbourne Catholic leader in 1963 at the age of 73, in both cases too late to enjoy the fruits of their decades of hard work and commitment. Calwell had his chance in 1961, the credit squeeze election, where Menzies scraped home by one seat. Once again Lady Luck had deserted him. It was a devastating setback, as he never again came close to being Prime Minister. Calwell looked too out of date to appeal to voters, with the DLP incubus still round his neck. Although in private a gracious and accomplished person, he seemed to undergo a personality change when mounting a political platform, ranting on in a hoarse voice. Before the 1963 election Calwell stated the ALP could not win unless it received the DLP vote, or unless 'certain other events' take place. When pressed to be more specific, Calwell mentioned the 'Angel of Death', an anticipation of Mannix's demise. Perhaps he was remembering his long wait for Dr Maloney's seat. Now Mannix's longevity was stifling his career, as well as Simonds', but this demeaning reference to his former close friend did him damage among Catholic voters. Calwell lost the 1963 election after being photographed forlornly waiting as party leader for a Federal executive decision by the '36 faceless men'. The ALP remained in the doldrums both federally and in Victoria. Jack Galbally was reduced to moving

215

private members bills during his long tenure (1955-1979) as Labor Legislative Council leader. By this stage three of the four federal Labor leaders (Calwell, Nick McKenna and Kennelly) were inner suburban Melbourne Catholics, remarkably as Catholic factional antics in the Victorian branch had wrecked the party. The fourth leader was Gough Whitlam.

The biggest complaint of Catholics in Victoria was that they were being deprived of government funds to run their extensive school system. Carr and Mannix had pursued the issue unsuccessfully throughout their long reigns. Objections had come initially from hard-line Protestant and secular pressure groups. Politicians had treated the issue with silence rather than denying it was an injustice. But from the 1950s onwards the issue was coming to a head. The number of students in Catholic schools in Victoria doubled in the 1950s; in addition there were almost 50,000 Catholic students who couldn't get a place in their own parochial schools. It was much cheaper for the state to subsidize these students in Catholic schools than to educate them in their own, as Catholic parents paid a share of the school fees. The Catholic schools themselves, with up to 80 students in a single classroom, were obviously not coping. The Parents and Friends Federation lobbied effectively in Victoria. Bishop Cullinane of Goulburn (and later of Melbourne) caused a crisis in July 1962 by closing all his schools for a short period to demonstrate that the state couldn't function without them. Archbishop Simonds used the Universal Declaration of Human Rights, which included a provision that parents had a right to choose the kind of education they wished for their children, to further press the issue.

The status quo was unacceptable to many in public life. Now that the DLP vote was vital at elections, other parties had to angle for its support, and State aid was the prime Catholic political demand. The DLP was naturally in total support, the Liberals were sympathetic but hesitant to bite the bullet. They had to cope with the bigots on their own side, but more important than the old sectarian argument was a new financial one. By the early 1960s the Catholics had over 250 schools in the archdiocese, whereas other denominations had only a few, mainly secondary, schools, and mainly in the capital, so everyone realized the Catholic system would get the lion's share of any new funding. The ALP was duplicitous, having until the last minute an ambiguous policy on the issue, because the left who controlled the party had no love of Catholics whom they blamed for the split. The upper house Labor leader Jack Galbally was expelled from his party for a time by the Victorian left for supporting State Aid.

The issue was settled by stages during the 1960s. Education was constitutionally a state matter, but Menzies intervened, promising science facilities to all schools during the 1963 election. In NSW the Catholic Church had always had good relations with the ALP, so Cardinal Gilroy was able to conduct amicable negotiations with the Catholic Premier Joseph Cahill. After State Aid had become accepted, a row broke out over who deserved the kudos for initiating the breakthrough, but that didn't matter once it had been achieved. In all the heat generated by the struggle, it was often forgotten that a separate boost of State aid was going into Catholic hospitals and welfare organizations at the same time, as governments increased their subsidies without unseemly political disputes.

The Professions

Under Mannix's encouragement Catholic secondary schools, and Newman College and St Mary's Hall at the university, had been producing matriculation and tertiary graduates in increasing numbers; this was most evident in medicine, law, business, engineering and education. Until it came under increased government supervision in the 1960s, St Vincent's Hospital had operated under the Sisters of Charity as pretty much a Catholic employment preserve, though the hospital's services were open to patients of all denominations. The pathologist Dr Andrew Brenan, son of the hospital's founding donors, acted as mentor for younger specialists; his son the dermatologist Dr John Brenan was one of them. Andrew Brenan's sister Jennie Brenan was a well-known dancer in J.C. Williamson's productions; with her sisters she set up the Jennie Brenan School of Dancing in Melbourne, and was a founder of the Royal Academy of Dancing in Australia.

39 Dr Andrew Brenan, a crucial link between the hospital's founding and the post Second World War years (St Vincent's)

Dr Brenan had the ear of successive mother rectresses, and in 1929, at a time of financial crisis for the hospital, set up the hospital's medical advisory board, whose secretary he became. Brenan was described by a fellow specialist Dr Tom King as 'a man who worked behind the scenes in the hospital at those times and was pretty powerful…his hobby was the hospital, he was ruthless for this hospital. He didn't care what happened to him[self], as long as it was for the hospital's good.' In 1944 he handed over his position as secretary of the advisory committee to Dr Frank Morgan[32], who also had a long tenure in the position. In the post war-years Drs Frank Morgan and Tom King took over Brenan's role as chief advisers; they were said to run the hospital, being 'in and out of the rectress's office like a fiddler's elbow'.[33] Medical specialists held honorary positions at the hospital where they treated public patients, as well as teaching university medical students and conducting their own private practices. In each area of medicine St Vincent's had after the war at least one specialist admired in the community: John Horan and John Billings (physicians), Eric Seal (psychiatry) Carl de Gruchy (haematology), John Hayden (Professor of Medicine at the university), Frank Hayden and John O'Donoghue (gynaecology), Frank Morgan and Keith Henderson (neurosurgery), Edward Ryan and Kevin O'Day (ophthalmology), John O'Sullivan (radiologist), John Clareborough (thoracic surgeon), Tom King (orthopaedic surgeon), Fred Colahan (general surgeon) and Kevin Rush (inpatient surgeon).

Mother Dorothea was in charge of the hospital, Mother Fabian of the maternity section, and Dr William Keane was the hospital's medical superintendent. Sir Norman O'Bryan, Sir Michael

---

[32] The author's father.

[33] Dr Bryan Egan, *Ways of a Hospital: St Vincent's Melbourne*, pp. 97, 152.

Chamberlin and Dame Rita Buxton (married into the real estate Buxton family) were key members of the hospital's management and fund raising committees. Drs John Horan and Hugh Ryan, who treated Simonds, were appointed papal knights in the years after the death of Mannix. Sir John Eccles, who had been a resident of St Vincent's, had gone on to a distinguished career in neurobiology overseas; in 1958 he was awarded the Nobel Prize for Medicine. He later published his life-long speculations on the mind-body problem, which later became the ground-breaking research area of neurophysiology. Dr John Cade, a resident at St Vincent's in 1935, held senior posts at the Mont Park and Royal Park Psychiatric Hospital. In the 1950s he discovered that taking doses of lithium compounds had a calming effect on patients, and so could be used for mental illness like depression. His discovery won international recognition, part of a move to chemical treatment rather than psychiatric therapies in this area. From the 1960s onwards increased government funding meant the Catholic nature of St Vincent's Hospital was diluted.

Sir Norman O'Bryan continued his leading role in the law after the Second World War. Promoted to the Supreme Court in 1939 he remained on the bench till 1966, two years before his death; like Cussen he became the senior judge in Victoria but not the Chief Justice. He presided over many important Catholic functions. An accomplished sportsman when young, in maturity he sat on the committee of the Melbourne Cricket Club. His two marriages produced a legal and medical dynasty. From his first to Elsa Duncan, he had a daughter Bernadette, who married the barrister Frank Galbally. After Elsa died in childbirth he married her sister Violet, with whom he had further five children. One son, Norman, became a Supreme Court judge like his father. Another son Richard, a doctor, married Julianna, a daughter of Judge Arthur Adams (an early Campion). A grandson, the barrister Stephen O'Bryan QC, was appointed the first head of the Independent Broad-based Anti-corruption Commission (IBAC).

The legal firm Galbally & O'Bryan exemplifies one of the many marriage connections which were a feature of Melbourne's Catholic professional families. Justice Norman O'Bryan's sister Beryl was married to Tom Buxton, son of the businessman John Buxton. Judge Adams' mother Lily came from the Billings family. Linking all these families were the pioneering Bourkes of Pakenham, whose family history was compiled by the Jesuit Fr John Bourke, a former rector of St Patrick's College. Judge Adams described his relative Fr Bourke as 'fanatically attached' to his cousinage network. The extended Bourke family included, as well as those mentioned above, the surgeon Fred Colahan, and Sir Murray Tyrrell, Secretary to the Governor General. In the present generation David Bourke became chairman of the Victoria Racing Club, and was instrumental in arranging for international champions, like the Irish stayer Vintage Crop, to compete in the Melbourne Cup.

Among other prominent Catholic members of the legal profession in the decades after the war were a number of Supreme Court judges. Sir Robert Monahan, a barrister with a commanding presence in court, had defended John Kerr during a sensational murder trial. Sir Gregory Gowans conducted an inquiry into land scandals. Sir Murray McInerney was a former Campion and critic of the Movement. Sir James Gobbo of the Supreme Court later became Governor of Victoria. Two Melbourne barristers were appointed to jurisdictions outside Victoria. Sir John Minogue had been a Lt Colonel during the New Guinea campaign; the Minister for Territories Paul Hasluck selected him for a position on the Supreme Court of Papua and New Guinea in 1962. Xavier Connor, an opponent of the Movement, was appointed to the Supreme Court of the ACT in 1972. Both Minogue and Connor returned to Melbourne to head Law Reform Commissions. Other Catholic judges included Edward Dunphy of the Industrial Court, Archibald Frazer and J.X. O'Driscoll of the Liquor Licensing Commission, and Hubert Frederico of the Family Court. Prominent barristers and solicitors included Tom Molomby, Gerard Heffey, Tom Butler, and Thomas Mornane, the Crown Solicitor. Many of these legal identities lived in the suburbs of Kew, Deepdene and Balwyn. The dining room of the Celtic Club during these years had a high table at which some of these figures were regularly seen at lunch; Arthur Calwell would sometimes drop in.

Authors

Some Catholic authors like George Walton and Martin Haley of *The Advocate* were of a pre-modernist, deeply traditionalist type. The first Melbourne Catholic modernist writer was Joseph O'Dywer. His friend Phillip Martin published four volumes of poetry in the 1970s and 1980s, specialising in miniatures, subtly managed pieces which explored their subject matter with great economy. As well as love poems, his dominant genre, Martin wrote an impressive series of poems on ancestral voices, people who could retrieve from the depths the spirit of their forbears. As an academic critic Martin also produced an original study of Shakespeare's sonnets.

The major Catholic poet of the period was Vincent Buckley. The title of his first book, *The World's Flesh,* reflected the centrality of the Incarnation to his thinking. The poetry of his middle period was influenced by contemporary political events, reflected in 'In Time of the Hungarian Martyrdom' and 'Eleven Political Poems'. He was also writing books of literary criticism, *Poetry and Morality* (1959) and *Poetry and the Sacred* (1968), on the connection between literature and religion. Later in life his interest in Ireland and Irish Australia, always strong, deepened with two books on Ireland, the poetry volume *The Pattern* (1979) and the reminiscence *Memory Ireland* (1985). Like Phillip Martin he wrote on the submerged heritage of the past, in poems such as 'Gaeltacht' and 'Two Lost Languages'. Writing on the Irishness in himself he reflected: 'I feel the stirring of that insight, whether memory or guess, that links me with psyches of long dead ancestors…Most of these things could not be brought to Australia. What remains is the ache of their absence'. His autobiographical memoir *Cutting Green Hay* (1983) covers a rural Irish Australian childhood in the Kilmore district, St Patrick's College, the universities of Melbourne and Cambridge, the Newman Society, and Mannix as a 'Prince Bishop'. His posthumous volume *Last Poems* (1981) meditates on his coming end in poems such as 'An Easy Death':

> Catholics, we were trained for it,
> The maze of words, the candles

> unrolled from years of tissue paper
> for this moment, the petite firm
> forward-leaning priestly movements,
> necessary as the dying itself;
> trained to compose the soul
> for all crises.

With his colleague Dinny O'Hearn Buckley led a revival of interest in Irish culture. The 84-year-old Irish poet Padraic Colum, composer of the legendary Irish folk song 'She Moved Through The Fair', spoke in Melbourne on Irish literature in 1965. Dinny O'Hearn wrote the history of the Melbourne Celtic Club *Erin Go Bragh* (1990).

Morris West, born in 1916, lived his early years in St Kilda and after being taught at St Kilda CBC, joined the Christian Brothers when he was fourteen. He was for a number of years a member of the order without taking final vows. He left the order in 1955, and moved overseas, becoming a successful popular novelist, similar to Thomas Keneally. His international best sellers *The Devil's Advocate* (1959) and *The Shoes of the Fisherman* (1963) have Vatican themes. The former focusses on an Eastern European cleric, Cardinal Lakota, who after many years under Communist rule is unexpectedly elected Pope, a remarkable prefiguring of the election of the Polish Cardinal Wojtyla as Pope John Paul II. In a sequel novel *The Clowns of God* (1981) a Pope resigns to live in seclusion, as Pope Benedict XVI later did. West remained a Catholic, though he had some differences with church teachings, and problems over his divorce and remarriage. He published his autobiography *A View From the Ridge* in 1996 and died in 1999.

In 1964 the talented Christian Brother Frank McCarthy was awarded a Doctorate in Philosophy from Cambridge University for his researches on 18th century literature and art. He was a wonderful teacher and counsellor, inspiring a generation of students, particularly those from CBC Parade. Mother Eymard Temby's terms as Principal of Star of the Sea College, Gardenvale, in the 1940s and 1950s made the school a leading educational institution. But the star pupil of Star of the Sea in the 1950s, Germaine Greer, found Eymard's attempt at a philosophical justification of Catholicism so confusing it put her off religious belief, but not Catholic habits, for the rest of her life. Mother Eymard was appointed the first principal of Christ Teachers College, Oakleigh, in 1967. Br John Saul, Principal of CBC North Melbourne and an outstanding science teacher, changed vocation in mid career, moving to the US to study for the priesthood; ordained in 1963 he returned to Melbourne to serve as a diocesan priest.

Barry Oakley, who like Morris West had some difficulties with the church, began as a novelist producing picaresque tales of luckless young males navigating life in post-war Melbourne, then a number of plays, including *The Feet of Daniel Mannix*. He later moved to Sydney and became a journalist and literary editor. The painter Paul Fitzgerald, who married Mary Parker, an actress and TV presenter, produced portraits of many prominent Melbourne personalities, including Sir Robert Menzies, Sir Henry Bolte and Sir Norman O'Bryan, as well as others from overseas, including Queen Elizabeth, the Duke of Edinburgh and Pope John XXIII. Paul Fitzgerald died in 2017. Mary Parker's brother, Lt Commander Michael Parker, was equerry to the Duke of Edinburgh. The soprano Eileen Hannan was the daughter of Senator Hannan, and the violinist Desmond Bradley the son of the pianist Eunice Garland. Kenneth Hince was a Xavier College teacher and music critic for *The Australian* and *The Age*, in addition to running a number of antiquarian bookshops.

Central Europeans

The outbreak of war in 1939 meant the Vienna Mozart Boys Choir was stranded in Melbourne. Mannix used the opportunity to establish a Boys' Choir at the cathedral based on these Austrian singers, with some additional boys from the nearby St Patrick's College and CBC Parade. However the director of the choir, Dr Georg Gruber, was denounced to the authorities as a Nazi sympathizer, interned at the Tatura camp and deported back to Austria in 1947, where he was cleared of the charge. Dr Percy Jones became choir director in 1942, a position he retained over the next three decades. One former choir member, Otto Nechwatal, taught singing lessons, set up a religious supplies business in Elizabeth St, then later ran an Austrian restaurant. The baritone Stefan Haag developed a career as an opera singer and was later director of the Elizabethan Theatre Trust. Another choir member, Hans Onger, became secretary of the Latrobe Valley Trades and Labor Council.

The great wave of post-war immigrants included a number of artists. Two sculptors from central Europe who worked in wood and metal flourished in their new homeland. The Bavarian sculptor Hans Knorr arrived in Australia on the *Dunera* refugee ship and spent the war at the Tatura internment camp. In Melbourne artistic circles he met and married the writer Hilda Dent, of Methodist background, who converted to her husband's Catholicism. Hans Knorr's sculptures were first exhibited at the Catholic Centenary Exhibition in 1948. The Knorrs lived for a time in the Dandenongs in a rented house on the farm of the Austrian lady who had come out as the female guardian of the Vienna Mozart Boys Choir. Hilda Knorr recalled in her memoir rumours circulating that their mysterious landlady had had a close relationship with Dr Gruber, or that it was she who had informed on him to the authorities, or both. Eventually the Knorrs set up their Emerald Gallery, one of the first private art galleries outside the city, which became a weekend meeting place where people from Melbourne cultural circles mixed with the locals.

By the 1960s Hans, having extended his range into bronze, ceramic and metal sculpture, was widely recognized, with a number of exhibitions and many commissions. St Bernard's Church in East Coburg, for example, has a Madonna, Stations of the Cross, baptismal font and statue of St Bernard at the front, all by Hans Knorr. The Knorrs formed an artistic partnership, with Hilda, the mother of their six children and gallery organizer, finding time to write two novels, a book of short stories, occasional journalism, a study of her husband's output *The Sculptures of Hans Knorr* (1976), and a memoir of her life with Hans *Journey With a Stranger* (1986). Together they wrote *Religious Art in Australia* (1967).

Leopoldine (Poldi) Deflorian grew up in the Austrian Tyrol near the Austrian-Italian border, and trained as a sculptor in Vienna and Hallstadt. Her first husband died on the Russian front. She then

40 'Jesus, Mary and Joseph', a bronze plaque by Hans Knorr. (MDHC)

met and married Leo Mimovich, a Serbian who was in a prisoner of war camp near Salzburg. They migrated to Victoria, and after a stint at Bonegilla migrant camp, settled in Melbourne where Poldi, known as Mrs Mimovich, worked commercially as a wood carver, then set up her own studio at home in Kew. Her sculptures in wood and metal casting reflected central European and Catholic themes, and like Hans Knorr, her style became more modernist, free flowing and impressionistic as time passed. Mrs Mimovich's work is often seen in Melbourne churches and Catholic homes. Our Lady of Good Counsel church in Deepdene had a Hans Knorr statue and Mimovich wood-carved Stations of the Cross. In 1977 Henry Rohr published *Sculpture of Leopoldine Mimovich.* Mrs Mimovich published a book of drawings tracing her life entitled *Memories Guide My Hand* (1985).

Miloslav Dismas Zika had received a Doctorate in Psychology and Fine Arts from the Charles University in Prague before the Second World War. In 1941 during the Nazi occupation of Czechoslovakia, he married and protected his Jewish fiancée Heda Schaefer, who had converted to Catholicism. In 1942 he was sentenced to forced labour in various camps in Czechoslovakia and Germany. After a Czech Communist government came to power in 1948, the family escaped to Austria, and arrived in Melbourne as refugees. Mila Zika was employed as a foundry worker and stained glass painter, and in the Victorian public service, before setting up his San Damiano Art Studio. He designed the modernist St Clare's Catholic Church in North Box Hill in the mid 1960s, one of the first to break away from the standard rectangular shape. It was semi- circular in order to involve the congregation more closely in the ritual of the Mass, in line with the reforms of Vatican II. Mila Zika inserted, following medieval tradition, the Latin text 'Dismas made this' into his art projects. From 1966 he lectured in Art History at RMIT and in 1969 was appointed Head of the Art Department at Christ College, Chadstone. Heda Zika taught Biology and German at the Box Hill Our Lady of Sion College, run by an order of religious sisters whose mission was reconciliation with Jews. One son, Paul, became an artist and a senior academic in Visual Arts at the University of Tasmania; in 1994 he returned to his ancestral haunts in Prague, producing a series of art works based on the monstrances of Prague's Loreto Convent. Another son, Charles, who was awarded the Daniel Mannix Scholarship in 1971, became a Professor of History at the University of Melbourne, specializing in late medieval European studies. Another medieval historian was Barry O'Dwyer, originally from Warrnambool, who studied in Melbourne, played football for Fitzroy, won a Rhodes Scholarship, and produced books on Italian and Irish monasticism; he taught at Macquarie University in Sydney.

Helga Girschik was the daughter of an Austrian Catholic father and German Protestant mother. The family fled Iran, where the father was working as an engineer on construction projects during the Second World War, and escaped to Australia on a refugee ship. They were interned at the Tatura camp, where they lived for rest of the war, after which they moved to Melbourne. Helga was enrolled as a boarder at the Academy Mercy Convent in Fitzroy in 1947. At Melbourne University she completed an Arts degree, and was a member of the Newman Society, but preferred the approach of Max Charlesworth. She married James Griffin, a *Catholic Worker* contributor, academic and author of a favourable biography of John Wren and an unsympathetic one of Daniel Mannix. Helga's life up to her marriage is recounted in her autobiography *Sing Me That Lovely Song Again...*, the title presumably referring to her husband's fine tenor voice.

The Last Years of Dr Mannix

One day two bishops (probably Stewart and O'Collins) were flattering the aged Mannix about what posterity would think of him. Finally one of them triumphantly declared: 'I say that Mannix dead will be more powerful than Mannix alive'. To this Mannix in his quiet voice replied: 'That's all very well for you, but what does it do for me?' The circulation of the many Mannix stories continue to make him powerful in death, and still a haunting presence today. As the flesh left his face, his high cheekbones, parchment skin, wispy hair and soft voice gave him the air of an ancient Chinese sage. Mannix's attitude to church figures and to himself emerges clearly in remarks he made in his last year to the young Fr Joe Broderick, son of Wally Broderick, on Cardinal Montini becoming Pope Paul VI in June 1963:

> I believe he [Montini] remembers me. I can't say I remem-
> ber him. But that's not surprising. After all, in Rome at the

> head of the Australian pilgrimage in the Holy Year [in 1925],
> I was the Archbishop of Melbourne, and he was just another
> monsignor around the place. (longish pause) Now he's come
> into his own. And I'm still here, sittin' on the shelf.[34]

A rare personal statement, with an uncharacteristic touch of the
maudlin about it. The world saw the aging Mannix as a great figure
and heaped plaudits on him, whereas he remembered himself as
missing out, as he had on his last visit to Ireland almost four decades
before. Lesser people had overtaken him. His humour derived from
detachment from worldly ambition and from self-deprecation. He
was never bitter, instead casting a cold and amused eye on the
passing parade, humour arising from the sadness of missing out. A
lady who knew Mannix understood this:

> He seemed rather cynical at times despite his loving heart.
> He saw life and public affairs as just a sport, played against
> a backdrop of the infinite. I am sure he thought of his own
> episcopacy, even the Church he loved, as no more than a
> wayside station on the long journey to the eternal. Like
> all mystics, too, he knew how to keep silent on the very
> deepest things while he made grand fun of ephemeral hap-
> penings.[35]

Fifty years ago the Melbourne Archdiocese prepared a great
celebration for the 100th birthday of its famous archbishop, a
celebration which the guest of honour, with his customary reticence
and sense of timing, narrowly managed to avoid. He died in
November 1963, three months short of his 100th birthday. A vault
in the floor of the cathedral's western transept had been opened up
to receive his coffin. At Mannix's burial the TV cameras showed
Bishop Fox grasping the new incumbent Simonds, who had limited
sight at this stage, firmly by his vestments as the two shuffled slowly
across the floor towards the vault, lest he fall in again. Simonds was
now Archbishop of Melbourne, 23 years after he might have had the
Sydney post on Archbishop Kelly's death.

Some important developments occurred around the time of

---

[34] Brenda Niall, *Mannix*, p. 362.
[35] Quoted in Ronald Conway, *Conway's Way*, p. 82.

Mannix's death that the census statistics did not reveal. The period of substantial Irish migration to Australian began in the 1860s. The Melbourne Irish had intermarried over subsequent decades to produce a dense Catholic Irish-Australian network, conscious and proud of its coherence. Marrying into one's own group was so natural that by 1960, a century after the migration began, many Catholic families were still almost exclusively Irish Australian, as marrying out was uncommon. But from the 1960s onwards, with changing social mores, increased immigration of other races, and increased chances of travel, the gene pool was widened. This was one factor contributing to the growth of a more open society from the 1960s onwards.

New Ideas

In 1960 two future archbishops of Melbourne, George Pell and Denis Hart, began their studies for the priesthood at the Werribee seminary. The world of the fifties, spent austerely recovering from the war years, was over. Change was on the agenda in Western societies, symbolized by the counter culture, hippy communes, London's Carnaby St and the Beatles. President Kennedy was a symbol of the new spirit of the age. Wide ranging changes had occurred between 1920 and 1970. There now existed no overarching view of society (for example, the British imperial view in politics, traditional Christianity in religion and respectability in social mores) which the citizenry as a whole accepted. This meant that people increasingly had to tolerate views they did not agree with. Authority was not now automatically accepted. On the contrary disagreement with established verities, which came to be known as the adversary culture, was increasingly

41 The achievements of senior student George Pell appear in a 1958 advertisement for St Patrick's College, Ballarat. (MDHC)

evident. These changes of attitude were accelerated by the rise of the 'permissive society'.

But all was not pleasure and plain sailing in the 1960s, since the Cold War was still being waged, as the Cuban missile crisis of 1962 revealed. Novelty and freedom were the slogans of the swinging sixties, a decade of increased wealth, openness, freedom and travel. Various liberation movements, long kept dormant by a succession of world wars and depressions, began to flourish. The former Star of the Sea pupil Germaine Greer was in the forefront of this international ferment. It was a time to let oneself go, to embrace modernity full blown, to throw off repression, or so the new mind-set claimed. Its radical innovations enlivened the spirit of the age, but constantly threatened to derail it. Change was called for, but the change we got was not necessarily the one needed. The epidemic of paedophilia by priests (and others) has been correlated with this shedding of sexual and other inhibitions. Previously an occasional priest formed a relationship with a mature woman, sometimes a parishioner, and left; this was viewed as understandable, if regrettable.

One important area of ferment was in the world of ideas. For Melbourne Catholics reflecting on the split, an influential text on relations between church and state at the time was the American's Jesuit Fr Courtney Murray's book *We Hold These Truths*. Murray argued citizens had three important rights: 'The limitation of government whereby an order of inviolable rights [of citizens] is constituted, the principle of consent, and the right of resistance to unjust rule'. The old confessional church which ruled the roost was no longer desirable or even possible. In a modern pluralist democracy the Catholic Church was only one player, and was therefore obliged to surrender its previous claims to pre-eminence in the public sphere. It had to extend to other entities the tolerance and freedoms it expected for itself. Fr Eric D'Arcy published *Conscience and Its Right to Freedom* (1961) and Max Charlesworth *Church, State and Conscience* (1973), where these questions were discussed in the light of the vexed question of freedom of conscience.

An exchange on such ideas occurred at the fourth Christian Social Week at the University of Melbourne in September 1959. Fr

D'Arcy rejected the idea that Catholics had the right to use civil power to favour their own religion and suppress others. The old argument that error had no rights was no longer viable. A citizen had a right to practice religion, and no other person nor the state itself could gainsay that right; the state could suppress only ideas which threatened the overall well-being of the community. Dr Charlesworth argued that liberty of conscience was important, but that Australians had historically been more interested in equality and prosperity than in freedom. He hoped that when in the future Australian Catholics comprised a third of the society, they would not be tempted to regress by challenging accepted pluralist norms. Nor must we, he argued, let the threat of Communism be used to jettison traditional democratic freedoms. The poet and convert James McAuley, admitting to a libertarian past, argued the real danger came from the new ideas of liberalism and permissiveness themselves. Freedom has consequences; it is not harmless but 'a fragile thing maintained only by effort and sacrifice...a benefit that cannot be taken for granted'. Permissiveness could lead to deviations from legal and social norms.

It was a time for a diversity of Catholic opinion and for critical self-assessment. All these questions had been thrown into stark light by the Movement's activities. Were its activities allowable in a pluralist society, or were they a throwback to the bad old days of Catholic attempts to dominate society? These questions were the focus of a much discussed symposium, *Catholics and the Free Society*, edited by Professor Henry Mayer, which appeared in 1961. In this book Santamaria provided for the first time a history of the Movement, and an apologia for his actions. The book's authors generally dispelled the notion that the Catholic Church was a totalitarian-like entity secretly trying to take over society. Though some contributions were critical, most agreed with the editor that the Catholic Church in Australia had contributed to freedom of expression and diversity here by 'advancing demands different from those normally prevailing' in society.

These arguments led to calls for increased tolerance and ecumenism, and to objections to anti-Semitism and the White Australia policy. Other debates on ideas at the time among Melbourne

Catholics revolved around the Dead Sea scrolls, evolution and psychology, all areas of interest which were now regarded as less threatening to Christian beliefs than previously. Higher education was expanding. Monash University was established in 1961, with Michael Chamberlin its inaugural Deputy Vice Chancellor; Mannix College was planned as a Catholic residence. Geoffrey Chapman, a Newman Society member in the early 1950s, had moved to London where he and his wife set up a Catholic publishing house (like the Australian Frank Sheed and his wife before them) to propagate the new ideas. In a reversal of that traffic the London Catholic bookshop Burns Oates and the Sydney religious publisher E.J. Dwyer joined to set up a Melbourne branch, while the *Tribune* newspaper took over the long-standing Linehan's bookshop.

Archbishop Simonds

The coadjutor Archbishop Simonds, who was attending the Vatican Council when Mannix died, returned to automatically succeed him. He was now leader of his organization, as Calwell was of his. Both had come into their inheritances too late, and both had to assume responsibility for organizations in trouble. Simonds had become a seminarian in 1906, so he was now in his 57th year in the church. When he finally came into possession of the Melbourne See in 1963, he was old, infirm and with poor sight, which occasioned the current witticism: 'Long time, no See'. A rundown archdiocese was handed to a man who was himself run down. Always an opponent of the Movement, one of his first moves as reigning archbishop was to discontinue Santamaria's weekly TV commentary on the Catholic TV program 'Sunday Magazine'. Santamaria retaliated by arranging with Sir Frank Packer to transfer his commentary segment, now called 'Point of View', to GTV-9, also shown on Sunday morning. 'Point of View' ran from 1963 to 1991. In his reign of four years Simonds formed twelve new parishes, badly needed after the outer suburban population explosion of the 1950s, and began a program of educational reform. But he did not have the time nor health to make the more substantial changes needed after an organizational hiatus stretching over decades. Simonds had the administrative head, Mons.

Moran, promoted to bishop in 1964. This had the effect of removing Bishop Fox as the archdiocesan spokesman. Moran became the de facto second-in-command, with the role of giving major speeches and presiding at functions at which Simonds was unable to attend. Fr Leo Clarke replaced Moran as Vicar General, and Dr Frank Little was appointed Administrator of the cathedral.

42 Archbishop Simonds meets the Belgian Cardinal Cardijn, founder of the world-wide Young Christian Workers movement, in Melbourne in 1966.
(MDHC)

Catholic Groups

Santamaria acted within the NCC like a mini-Prime Minister or CEO, covering all areas in order to produce a co-ordinated strategy. Like an academic he kept up his reading, and like a senior politician he was able to give the current version of his rolling speech at the drop of a hat. Though he sometimes praised the church's support of the principle of subsidiarity (the idea that decisions are best made and implemented at the grass roots), he applied the opposite principle to his own organization. There was little room for dissent, but there existed leeway to discuss day-to-day problems.

In the 1960s Santamaria reoriented his thinking. The Australian Communist Party, itself fragmenting, was no longer the main problem. The new enemy was in his mind the permissive culture of the swinging sixties, and the general influence of trendy progressives in the world of ideas, as reflected in the universities, media, in some government bureaucracies, and among opinion-forming groups. Increasingly Santamaria directed the NCC's energies and resources into combating this new perceived threat. His pamphlet *Philosophies in Collision* (1973), describes the struggle between the libertarian, totalitarian and Christian viewpoints. The Catholic Church was in Santamaria's view affected by these new ideas, as he explained in a 1986 letter: 'The front line is the struggle in the Church itself to prevent the whole base swinging over to the quasi-Marxist Left. If the base goes, where will the troops come from? The second line is the universities, the source of the dominant Marxist-nihilism of the age, which provides leaders for parties, unions, professions, bureaucracies – and the Church.'[36] The church on whose behalf he had run the Movement had now become for him part of the problem. For the rest of his life Santamaria adopted the role of Old Testament prophet in the wilderness, or secular archbishop instructing the faithful on faith and morals in the absence, as he saw it, of proper church leadership after Mannix. Melbourne Catholics might continue to vote DLP, but to accept a swinging attack on their own church was for many a bridge too far. They were not yet ready for their loyalty to be eroded; that came later, and from the opposite direction, with the birth control issue.

Whereas once there was only *The Advocate* and *The Tribune*, there now existed a range of magazines for Catholics to contribute to and read, reflecting a diversity of opinion. *News Weekly* catered for traditional Catholics who identified with the NCC worldview. *Twentieth Century* was founded by the Movement-aligned Institute of Social Order, but carried a wider range of cultural items. When the Sydney-based poet and convert James McAuley founded *Quadrant* magazine in 1956, some Melbourne Catholic contributors transferred to it, and *Twentieth Century* eventually went into decline.

---

[36] B. A. Santamaria, *Your Most Obedient Servant*, p. 421.

Quadrant at this stage was an unlikely combination of Melbourne Catholics and Sydney bohemian libertarians, as both groups had in common objections to totalitarian infringements on personal liberty.

The split had crystallized a Catholic opposition, the *Catholic Worker* group, with older Campions like Kevin Kelly, Gerard Heffey and Tom Butler still active, but now reinforced by a post-war influx including Paul Ormonde (son of the NSW Labor Senator Ormonde), John Ryan, Jim Griffin, Tony Harold, Max Charlesworth, Niall Brennan and Colin Thornton Smith. Their prime motivation was to expose Santamaria's Movement, and to embarrass those many church figures who had gone along with it. They took the Vatican decision against the Movement as vindication of their stance. The *Catholic Worker* exemplified upward mobility; one commentator suggested the magazine should be more fittingly entitled the *Catholic Solicitor* or the *Catholic Senior Lecturer* than the *Catholic Worker*. On any given issue its writers tended to automatically advance beliefs current in the secular and university milieux which put the church in a bad light; the contributors were in the processes of transferring their primary allegiance from one sphere to the other. The church's age-old warning, expressed in St Paul's Epistle to the Romans: 'You must not fall in with the manners of this world', was being sidelined. Their initial rebellion over the Movement gave them inner permission to later widen their disagreement with the old church on a range of social and political issues.

The *Catholic Worker* accused Santamaria and the Movement of being negative and obsessed with anti-Communism, but they in turn became negative and obsessed with their own anti-Movement campaign. Both groups utilized Vatican rulings when it suited them, and disdained them when they didn't. This is a hint that the two perspectives were more ideological impositions than accurate descriptions of reality. Just as the terms 'left' and 'right' are practically useless today, so are the terms 'liberal' and 'conservative' Catholic, which are themselves partisan designations, setting up neat but unrealistic polar oppositions. These are terms used by each crusading group to name, but really to belittle, their opponents. They confuse as much as they disclose. For example many DLP-voting

Catholics went along with Vatican II. Into which category did they fit? The terms begin to lose their meaning. Ordinary people inhabit the large space between extremes, making endless accommodations which they can privately reconcile. They do not trumpet their views, nor do they think in the either/or categories into which commentators with a vested interest try to shoehorn them.

The Newman Society at the University of Melbourne, led by its influential chaplain, Fr Jerry Golden, SJ, had avoided, with some difficulty, being taken over by Santamaria's Catholic Action, so it shared with the *Catholic Worker* group a pronounced anti-Movement strain, and an impatience with many of the habits of mind of traditional Catholics. But it differed from the *Catholic Worker* group in a number of ways. The Newman Society was less interested in politics, and more interested in new theological and social ideas. Its members saw themselves not as duelling with the church, but as a harbinger of new ways of being a Catholic, and so a forerunner of Vatican II. Its members favoured separation of church and state, and relative freedom of conscience; they accepted modernity and believed in winning the battle of ideas in open competition. Influenced by French/Belgian thinkers like Suhard and Mounier, they desired to be a natural part of their milieu rather than trying to penetrate it. They disdained clericalism, promoted the notion of lay initiative in the church, and opposed an exclusive emphasis on individual piety. As early as 1940 Fr John Kelly had asked himself in his diary: 'Why is it that there is that touch of Puritanism among so many Catholics in Australia, among nuns especially? Is it a heritage from the Irish?'[37] Up to the 1950s the habits of mind of Australian Catholicism had been otherworldly, overemphasizing the desire for instant personal transcendence, the yearning to escape the world by going straight to God the Father. This attitude derives from the Manichean or Jansenist heresy, with its premature emphasis on the Resurrection. Incarnational theology focussed on working through the materials of this world to bring it towards its completion; by joining with Christ's actions in this life Christians were ultimately moving towards the *parousia*. There is no disjunction in this view between the world and

---

[37] Robert Pascoe, *The Feasts and Seasons of John F. Kelly*, p. 101.

the transcending of it. The Newman Society's main publication was the book *The Incarnation and the University*, talks delivered at the 1954 UCFA conference. Its principal figure was Vincent Buckley, untypical of the Newman Society in that he was an anti-Communist who voted for a time for the DLP, though opposing the Movement. The Newman's Society's best known product was the geologist Prof. Jim Bowler, who discovered Mungo Man. *Prospect* was a short-lived magazine originating from the Newman Society, which took a more middle-of-the-road position than the *Catholic Worker*.

The Newman Society and *Catholic Worker* nexus, though small in numbers at the time, formed the basis of a more outgoing view of the church which prefigured Vatican II on both lay initiative, and on a more liberal critique of the church. Both groups were influenced by French models and thinkers, and by the French Catholic left's quasi-Marxist critique of capitalism. Both began to question whether there was (or indeed ever had been) a single monolithic church. Ronald Conway, *The Advocate's* film critic at the time, launched into the Newman Society as too removed from the facts, and too obscure in its formulations, for which he received a volley of long-winded rejoinders. The fissures such issues gave rise to were to become more pronounced in the decades ahead.

11

The Late 1960s:
The Second Vatican Council

International and Australian Politics – Changeover – The Backward Glance – Vatican II – Liturgy and Architecture – Further Reactions to the Council – Humanae Vitae *– Archbishop Knox – The New* Advocate

International and Australian Politics

The late 1960s was a disturbed period internationally, witnessing the 1968 Soviet invasion of Czechoslovakia, and North Vietnamese advances in Indochina. The Cultural Revolution in Maoist China, reported on favourably in *The Advocate* by Neil and Deidre Hunter, was a sign of things to come. The Western world was shaken by widespread student and race riots in 1968; some cities in the United States were in flames as a result. Opposition to the US intervention in Vietnam was growing. It ushered in a period of radical ideas which sprang from disdain for the present order, derisively termed the *status quo*. The Catholic Church was not immune from this turbulence; as the findings of Vatican II were successively released, they were interpreted as being in tune with the progressive spirit of the age.

Melbourne Catholicism had to weather a perfect storm in the later 1960s, caused by a conjunction of factors: the administrative vacuum after the death of Mannix, the decline of senior functionaries, the fissures caused by the split, the decisions of Vatican II, and the Papal outlawing of contraception in 1968. These developments resulted in a tug of war pushing Catholic allegiances first one way and then the other. The Movement-DLP had reaffirmed the traditionalist position, Vatican II moved Catholics towards a more modern position, and then the ruling against contraception moved allegiances in both directions. These sudden shifts caused widespread personal tension.

Calwell was awarded a papal knighthood in 1964. He was defeated for the second time by Menzies in 1963. After a long reign Menzies resigned in 1966 and was succeeded in fairly rapid succession by Harold Holt, John Gorton and William McMahon. Calwell lost to Gorton in the 1966 federal election which was largely fought on opposing views of the Vietnam war. Gorton had a background similar to Calwell's predecessor Dr Maloney, being the illegitimate son of a wealthy Protestant grazier and a young Catholic lady from Melbourne's inner suburbs, a background he revealed to gain sympathy when in political trouble. Philip Lynch, whose father was a fitter and turner at the Fairfield paper-mill, became the federal member for Flinders in 1966, Minister for the Army in 1969 in the Gorton Government, and the most prominent Catholic in the Liberal Party; his wife, originally Brigid O'Toole from Warrnambool, eventually emerged as Lady Leah Lynch.

Calwell, having survived an assassination attempt in June 1966, stepped down as federal ALP leader in February 1967 and was replaced by Whitlam. It was a sad end to a long and ultimately unfulfilled career. The DLP vote, which was crucial in keeping the Liberals in office in the state and federal houses, remained in double figures. Senator McManus' strong vote in the federal 1969 election was the high point for the DLP, but a last hurrah as Whitlam was now modernizing the ALP, making it more attractive as the antagonisms aroused by the split began to fade.

Changeover

It was changeover time in both the political and religious spheres. Mannix, Menzies and Calwell were off the scene after extended careers. The end of Mannix's long reign produced the short terms of Simonds and Knox. It is always hard to fill the shoes of a great leader. A masterly personality usually produces unimpressive underlings, who, growing up in the shadow of genius, settle for dogged loyalty rather than giving free reign to their own abilities. Churchill was followed by Sir Anthony Eden, and Menzies by Holt, Gorton and McMahon, all of whom wilted under the burden of high office. The same happened in the church with Mannix. Lonergan and Moran may be excused because of declining health, but Bishops Lyons, Fox and Little did not display conspicuous qualities of leadership. Simonds had formed a strong personality earlier and elsewhere; his problem was that he couldn't exercise it. The talented duo of Dr Percy Jones and Fr Eric D'Arcy were able to flourish as relatively free spirits by developing independent interests, as were later figures like Bishop Hilton Deakin. Mannix did not create a structure where you learnt the ropes as you gradually advanced.

The gap between Mannix, detached, inscrutable and famous, and his deputies, was profound. Personalities did not flourish under this dual strain of full freedom without instructions and then full accountability. A leadership vacuum was noticeable after Mannix's death. In 1967 Bishop Fox was sent to Sale as suffragan bishop there (a less prestigious post than Ballarat or Bendigo), a fate that awaited successive Movement-supporting bishops, Lyons, Fox and D'Arcy, now that the Movement was not flavour of the month in church circles. Bishop John Cullinane from NSW was appointed an assistant bishop in 1967 to boost a depleted leadership group by bringing in new blood from outside, but resigned in 1974. The workhorse Bishop Laurie Moran died in 1970 aged 62 after a long illness.

Many leading *Advocate* figures were reaching retirement age at the same time. The archdiocese was becoming rudderless, steadied only by its familiarity with prevailing winds, but susceptible to storms on the horizon. One leading cleric who did have leadership qualities, Fr Eric D'Arcy, had been sidelined for a long period. He wrote a significant document, published in Mannix's name, for the Vatican Council. The clean out was capped off by Simonds' own decline, after only three and a half years in charge after waiting for twenty. His last public appearance was in July 1966. He was out of action in the Mercy Hospital for most of the last eighteen months of his life, due to increasing blindness and physical decline. Simonds resigned his position in charge of the archdiocese in April 1967, and died six months later.

Calwell relinquished the leadership of the ALP in the same year, 1967, as Simonds relinquished his, a final parallel in their careers.

They were the last major victims of the split. Though both lived in the North Melbourne region from 1943 to 1967, in his memoir Calwell recalls almost nothing of any relationship they may have had. Simonds to his credit had stoically accepted his twenty-year cross without demur, but Calwell was overtaken in his last years by bitterness at the fate dealt him. The parliamentary reporter Alan Reid recalled that when Calwell was federal Opposition leader he had a *priedieu* installed in an anteroom attached to his office in Parliament House, to which he would repair, ostensibly to mediate, but actually to have little recrimination sessions against his enemies. In his memoir Calwell describes many of his fellow Catholics as 'fear-striken, communist-hating, money-making, social-climbing, status-seeking, brainwashed, ghetto-minded people'.[38] These were the supporters he was happy to have sustain his career over many decades. However Calwell and McManus became reconciled before the former's death.

The Backward Glance

Mannix's passing naturally prompted local Catholics to ponder their history, as a long and distinctive era had clearly ended. In the 1950s Manning Clark had reinterpreted Australian history as a contention between three ideologies: Catholicism, Protestantism and Enlightenment humanism. This insight sparked a great wave of historical writing, led by Patrick O'Farrell, on the role of religion in Australia. Frances O'Kane published *A Path Is Set* on the early days in 1976. Melbourne also had its academic practitioners who wrote theses, such Greg Tobin on the Australian Home Rule Movement and Fr Paul Duffy SJ on the Movement. The Victorian historian John Molony's *The Roman Mould of the Australian Catholic Church* was published in 1969.

Two stalwarts of *The Advocate* who together had filled the large shoes of Patrick O'Leary were coming to the end of their careers. The paper traditionally had a priest as Managing Editor, who supervised the paper while running a parish. A couple of assistant editors actually ran the paper. Fr James Murtagh, commissioned by

---

[38] Arthur Calwell, *Be Just and Fear Not,* p. 166.

Archbishop Knox to write a Mannix biography, conducted extensive researches during a year in Rome, Ireland and England in 1970, but died in 1971 at the age of 63 with the project incomplete. Fr Walter Ebsworth based his subsequent massive Mannix biography (1977) on Fr Murtagh's research notes. Fr Ebsworth had been a contemporary of Norman O'Bryan at CBC Parade, and was dux in 1910 and 1911. Ordained in 1918, he had a position for six years at St Patrick's Cathedral before his long tenure as Toorak parish priest began in 1929. But he had other occupations, as journalism ran in his veins; his father, Alfred Ebsworth, had been brought out to Melbourne in 1868 as publisher of *The Argus* and *The Australasian*. Fr Ebsworth's Mannix biography appeared just after his own death in 1977. It includes many documents relevant to Mannix's life linked by lengthy commentary, providing abundant raw material for understanding its subject's life. It seemed comprehensive, but didn't prevent further biographies of Mannix from appearing in the years ahead.

Frank Murphy was a contemporary of Fr Murtagh, and their careers intertwined, as Fr Moynihan had employed both at *The Advocate*. Over the decades Murphy wrote an enormous number of articles. A book he hoped to write on his special interest, Gilbert and Sullivan's operas, was never finished. Like Patrick O'Leary and Fr Murtagh, Murphy was consumed by the strain of weekly *Advocate* deadlines. All three died towards the end of their working lives, so they had no time in their retirement years to complete their pet projects. Murphy and Murtagh were tapering off during the changeover time of the later 1960s and died in the early 1970s. Thereafter *The Advocate* was edited from a different perspective, as the reforms inaugurated by Vatican II were being digested.

Florence Hagelthorne, a journalist on *The Advocate* in the 1960s, was a daughter of Frederick Hagelthorne, MLC in the Victorian Parliament from 1905 to 1920; he was also a founder of the CSIRO. Ms Hagelthorne had earlier written for the Brisbane *Catholic Leader*. She worked at the Maribyrnong munitions factory, a Catholic domain, during the war, and was later employed at Burns Oates booksellers. At *The Advocate* Frank Murphy arranged for her to present a weekly profile of an interesting personality for seven years from 1963 to 1970, over 300 articles in all. These profiles, which were widely read, are a valuable historical resource as they often provide more personal details than are usually found in formal obituaries, curriculum vitae and short biographies.

The Melbourne Diocesan Historical Commission (MDHC) was founded in May 1968 with Fr John Keaney as its first chair. A stimulus to this endeavour was the finding by Dean Frank Little of a previously unknown part of Archbishop Goold's diary, the major part of which had been loaned to Cardinal Moran for use in compiling his massive *History of the Catholic Church in Australasia* (1895). The MDHC, now based at the Cardinal Knox Centre in the cathedral grounds, continues to function; it current director (2018) is Rachel Naughton, and it has an archive, a museum and a journal, *Footprints,* begun in 1971 with Knox's backing. Fr T.J. Linnane of the Ballarat diocese compiled an index of all priests, secular and in orders, on the Australian mission before 1900, almost 1800 in all, of whom 69 became bishops, and Fr Kevin Hannan compiled an index of *The Advocate*, both invaluable research guides.

Vatican II

The Second Vatican Council's introduced substantial changes in Catholic attitudes and practices. It began its sessions in 1962; the pope who called the council, John XXIII, died in the next year, but the council continued until 1965. Its final documents and decisions were progressively (in two senses of the term) released, and took some time to be absorbed. In effect it repudiated the attitudes of the 'Syllabus of Errors' a century earlier by embracing the benefits of modernity, tolerance, and the separation of church and state. These reforms were summarized by the word *aggiorniamento*, meaning catching up with present times, which should have been done in the previous half century. The council moved the church away from its mistaken embrace of the conservative establishment in Europe, which had tainted it in the 1930s and 1940s. It gave a greater role to freedom of conscience and to the laity, by implicitly lessening the idea of the priesthood as a remote caste, and by repudiating notions such as 'no salvation outside the church'. It encouraged closer contact with other Christian churches, and with other religions, including Judaism; a Vatican secretariat for non-believers was established. As a latecomer to modernity, the danger for the church was of a too drastic swing of the pendulum to the other extreme; it had to judge just how comprehensive its embrace of modernity, which it was not familiar with, should be, and how discriminating.

When they came the changes were for some startling. One Melbourne Catholic remembered: 'one Friday you could be burnt in Hell for eating steak and the next week it was all right.' For another it was similarly a relief: 'I can remember the Redemptorist Fathers – it would be fire and brimstone from the pulpit. You were damned – you were going to Hell no matter what. That was a frightening, fearsome God. That has changed.'[39] The overall reaction in Melbourne was an acceptance of the changes, more so the attitudinal than the liturgical and musical ones. The new translations of sacred texts seemed clear, but lacking gravitas and lift. Some regret was expressed at the watering down of traditional church music. A Latin Mass society was formed in Melbourne to deplore these changes, or, as a compromise, to at least allow traditional forms to co-exist with the new ones, but this was not welcomed by church authorities for some decades. The tolerance which was supposed to be a hallmark of Vatican II was not always extended to traditional Catholicism.

Liturgy and Architecture

Melbourne had an outstanding guru on liturgical and musical matters, Dr Percy Jones, but the changes put him in a terrible bind. As a facilitator he was placed on key liturgy committees in Rome and in Australia; in Melbourne he was Episcopal Vicar for Ecumenical Affairs. Returning from the first session of the Council in November 1962 Jones referred in *The Advocate* of 15 November 1962, to the 'rising excitement' generated by it. Jones faithfully carried out his duties in superintending new translations and revising hymnals, but he was himself a deep traditionalist in the Benedictine mould. His whole career had been devoted to absorbing the musical and liturgical

---

[39] Janet McCalman, *Journeyings*, pp. 256, 257.

practices of the church, and to bringing them alive in Melbourne, which he had done successfully for a quarter of a century before Vatican II. In his biography, dictated in retirement, he disclosed some of the worries he had at the time. When he and his colleagues agreed to the first and last parts of the Mass being in English they never envisaged the central part, the Canon, would not remain in Latin. He thought the decision to produce 'lowest common denominator' translations produced some banal outcomes. He disliked the fact that only one vernacular translation was authorized for each language. He had adored the church's musical repertoire from Gregorian chant onwards, and now lamented its decline. He felt, like many others, that the newly devised religious services and ecumenical ceremonies were often not satisfying, being too domestic and earth bound, and not opening out to the transcendent.

The new emphasis was on concelebrated Masses, the 'sign of peace' handshake after the Consecration, and general absolution without individual confession, the latter withdrawn in most places after some controversy. Participation by women, and lay readings and lay distribution of Communion became the norm. All these changes took place gradually, and on a worldwide scale. After the reforms of Vatican II, dioceses instituted further renewal programs every decade or so. Individual piety was downplayed, being replaced by new small organizations with special missions, with names like Cursillo, Serra and Equipe, many deriving from the United States. Vatican II had not withdrawn the church's traditional support for practices of piety, but in the passion for reform they were silently sidelined. As decline in Mass attendance coincided with the decline of these habits, the two may be linked, leading to the conclusion that inner piety is a necessary prerequisite for a thriving community of the faithful.

Changes to the liturgy were one of the biggest issues to emerge from the Council, and in the end the most controversial. The Mass, now said in English to make it more understandable to the laity, became a dialogue in which the congregation took an active part. In keeping with these changes the altar was detached from the wall and moved forward. The priest now faced his congregation from behind a plain table-like altar set closer to the congregation. Altar rails, which had designated a separate sacred space occupied, as in Orthodox churches, only by the priest and his assistants, disappeared as did the more Baroque embellishments around the church. The hallowed music of the church was on the whole replaced, except on special occasions, by a mixture of popular hymns, modern music, folk songs and other styles depending, within limits, on the taste of any particular parish and its priest. These changes, including local languages and liturgies, emphasized the communal and inclusive aspects of the Mass. The previous otherworldly emphasis was downplayed, with the focus now as much on horizontal and social planes as on vertical and transcendent ones.

The 1950s was a transitional time in church architecture. Growing congregations at mass combined with shortages of building materials and finance meant converted army recreational huts and other cheap constructions were utilized. From the 1960s the design of new Catholic churches in the middle and outer suburbs began to give physical expression to the priorities announced by Vatican II. Plain lines and space rather than over-decoration and clutter now became the desirable norm. Side altars and pillars disappeared, giving a clearer line of sight to the altar, and natural light replaced the diffused light produced by stained glass windows and sombre interior decoration. The rectangular box shape was often discarded, and the church turned on its axis, with the long wall, not the short one, now becoming the focal point of the interior. This design often evolved into a form like a Roman amphitheatre, with banked seating splaying out sideways and backwards in a semicircle from the altar and the back wall. Developments in building materials played their part.

Internal steel roof girders and external roofing material of the colorbond type meant churches often featured irregularly shaped, pitched tent or umbrella-like roofs, which previous roof materials did not allow. A triangular tower at the front or middle of the church sometimes replaced the spire at the rear. St Bernard's Church in East Coburg in 1955 is an early example, as is Mila Zika's 1966 unique polychrome St Clare's North Box Hill. St Gregory's Doncaster, St

43 The post-Vatican II interior of St Francis Xavier Church, Prahran. (MDHC)

Peter's Clayton and St Agnes' Highett are other examples. Such churches were built in what was then the outer ring of suburbs. In the mid sixties, for example, Simonds had established new parishes in Seaford, Springvale, Boronia, Doncaster, Blackburn, Bundoora, Lalor and Altona.

Further Reactions to the Council

Melbourne Catholics faced Vatican II with a different profile from other dioceses. Here the split had consolidated a strong religio-political nexus, DLP Catholicism, which supported the hierarchy, and a small articulate dissenting minority. This post-split alignment did not fit in well with Vatican II's new orientation, causing a range of confusions to a flock seeking above all a rest period after the traumas of the past decade. Vatican II had extensive ramifications. The great majority of Catholics agreed with the changes, or at least passively accepted them, including traditional Catholics.

In the past when Catholics were told their church was 'catholic' in the sense of being all-encompassing and universal, proved by the fact that wherever they travelled in the world they would hear the same Mass in Latin, they agreed with this. Now when they were told the opposite, that a vernacular liturgy was proof of a church successfully inculturating itself in local societies, they also agreed. When Catholics were told for ages that the priest facing away from them at Mass and speaking mysteriously in Latin signified the sacred, transcendent aspects of the rite, they agreed, and when they were now told the priest facing the people without the barrier of altar rails and speaking in the vernacular signified the communal and inclusive aspects of the rite, they also agreed. These radical changes seemed momentous, but their swift acceptance revealed that the deeper undercurrent of belief denoted a loyalty to whatever the church prescribed, whether traditional or modern. This undercut the rhetoric that Vatican II was all about change, and allowed ordinary Catholics the freedom from more disruption they desired.

Both traditional and progressive Catholics used the new Council policies to continue their antagonisms from split days, but in doing so had to reverse their attitude to the church. The progressives, previously dissident, now agreed with the church, arguing that the Council's *aggiorniamento* proved the Santamaria stance was out of date, whereas Santamaria and his followers began to adopt a more dissident position. More relaxed, pro-laity and pro-modernity attitudes, foreshadowed by previously small ginger groups like the *Catholic Worker* and Newman Society, now became par for the course. This bouleversement was accentuated by the fact that pro-Vatican II progressives, more radical that the norm, became dominant in many church bureaucracies. Instead of representing the faithful, these bodies often tried to convert them to newchurch attitudes, sometimes emphasizing social justice over explicitly religious interests. Traditionalist Catholics found that many faith habits which had sustained the Catholic community for decades were now disparaged as personal piety, an incomplete description since they had formed an ensemble of communal worship practices. The new liberal consensus learned to criticize the church, and as a result to weaken allegiances already becoming more tenuous. At the same time traditional Catholics were to some extent made to feel uncomfortable. The church thus lost a good part of both groups. Any large institution which wishes to survive must renew itself constantly but gradually. Non-renewal leads to stagnation; quick attempts at radical change run the danger of alienating old adherents while not being able to hold on to new ones. This is the classic way a reforming organization hollows itself out.

Activist groups like the *Catholic Worker* and the Newman Society took Vatican II as a green light to widen the boundaries of what Catholicism meant, and in the process to widen their criticism of the church when it did not agree with them. They interpreted Vatican II as an admission that the conservative church of the past had been remiss in not engaging with the contemporary world and its problems. They took a generous view of Vatican II, selecting views which fitted their own interests, stretching the reforms in new directions. They attempted to reconcile this new outlook with their faith with varying degrees of success. A group of activist priests joined forces at this stage with the progressive lay Catholics to form a broader coalition.

The *Catholic Worker* group and the National Civic Council should not be seen as mirror opposites. The former had made their point that the Movement had breached Vatican guidelines and that they welcomed Vatican II. As they were not broadly based, and as they concentrated on socio-political issues rather than religious ones, their influence diminished, with the *Catholic Worker* ceasing publication in 1974. It is not clear whether liberal Catholicism was a new way into religion, as its proponents claimed, or a new way out. The Movement-NCC-DLP complex, having the achievement of rescuing Australian society from Communist and secular white-anting, represented a substantial slice of the Catholic sector, *News Weekly* continues to be published, and the NCC founded the journal *AD2000* to ventilate its continuing religious concerns. Strongly traditional Catholics, like the Latin Mass groups and others dubious about some aspects of Vatican II, now constituted a minority group, with the silent supporters of Vatican II now the majority. During the first two decades of the NCC's existence, Santamaria believed the Catholic Church was going through a period of worrying liberalization, as a result of a misinterpretation, in his view, of the teachings of Vatican II. He wrote in 1967:

> The true situation which confronts us is that the Second Vatican Council issued a series of documents quite masterly in their presentation of Catholic orthodoxy, while expressing that orthodoxy in terms more comprehensible to the 20th century. Our problem is that many of those who style themselves intellectuals speak of the "spirit of Vatican II" when what they ought to speak of is the statements, declarations and the decisions of Vatican II. The "spirit of Vatican II" is so delightfully vague and subjective that it can cover the wildest eccentricities.[40]

But as the years passed Santamaria went further: he thought the Catholic Church itself had been high-jacked by new heterodox trends. He contrived to lead opposition to some church policies. However things changed for him with the elections of Popes John Paul II and Benedict XVI. Both were youngish participants at Vatican II and supporters of it at the time, so the later view of them as hidebound conservatives like Cardinals Tardini and Ottaviani was misguided. The two future popes were part of a sizeable group of advisors who welcomed the changes inaugurated by the Council, but some of the more way-out interpretations of the council's decrees later caused them to be mugged by reality and to restore a mainstream consensus. The Melbourne Archbishop after 1996, George Pell, a seminary student at the time of the council, had an intellectual trajectory similar to the two popes.

Humanae Vitae

The papal commission on birth control reported in 1966; in the interim it was expected that some lenient ruling would be announced, in line with the reform expectations aroused by Vatican II. It was the issue on which progressive Catholics campaigned most strongly. But in 1968 Pope Paul VI announced in *Humanae Vitae* the continuation of the church's previous position of total abstinence on contraception, apparently overruling the advice of his own commission. A

---

[40] B.A. Santamaria, *Your Most Obedient Servant*, p. 244.

considerable number of ordinary practising Catholics for the first time silently acted against church teaching, while in other respects remaining loyal churchgoers. It is impossible to get accurate figures on such a private matter, but a strong hint came from a 'Suburban Doctor' who wrote a letter to *The Advocate* (4 November 1965) saying that from his observation Catholics who obeyed the church ruling on this matter were not as common as one might think. In his memoir the Melbourne author Barry Oakley wrote: 'After the birth of our sixth child Kieran in 1970, rather than spend the rest of our married lives worrying about the discordancies of the rhythm method, we had left the Catholic Church.'[41]

Many Catholics who ignored this ruling remained in the church. Figures in a later survey 'What do Mass attenders believe?' (2014) revealed that it was on sexual matters that Mass attendees has their strongest disagreement with church moral teachings.[42] On other basic church teachings (anti-abortion, the Eucharist, the resurrection, the Holy Trinity) belief ranged between 70% and 90%, whereas on sexual matters it was only 40% to 50%. The church in its wisdom did not strictly enforce its decision on contraception. Priests soon gave up on the issue, in the sense they didn't question parishioners about it and contemplate refusing them communion, as they did on some other issues. Thus a *modus vivendi* of sorts was established on both sides. But something more fundamental had occurred. The absolute command the church had had over its faithful had been breached, and absolute obedience jeopardized. This meant that over time ordinary Catholics could give themselves permission to disagree with other rulings of the church. The seepage and dissent caused by this controversy may have been a prelude to a later larger defection.

Those Melbourne Catholics expecting a progressive decision in line with their view of Vatican II were dismayed at the ruling against contraception. *Humanae Vitae* was seen by them as a backtracking on the hopes raised by the Council, but as a return to the sanity of the *status quo* by the traditionalists. This was a prime issue dissidents

---

[41] Barry Oakley, *Mug Shots: A Memoir*, p. 204.
[42] Robert Dixon, 'What do Mass attenders believe?', Pastoral Research Office, 2014, p. 13.

took up in their increasing disaffection with the church. They had supported a Vatican ruling against the Movement, but spoke against the Vatican ruling on contraception. The contraception issue raised the crucial question of the primacy of individual conscience, something the magisterium of the church could never fully accommodate.

44 The medical pioneers Drs Evelyn and John Billings. (*News Weekly*)

A Catholic Family Planning Bureau was set up in 1968 in response to the birth control and related issues. The Melbourne archdiocese made a contribution in world terms through the pioneering work on the female reproductive system by Dr John Billings, a physician at St Vincent's Hospital, and his wife Dr Evelyn Billings. Together they devised a method of family planning by determining the infertile days in a woman's menstrual cycle. This seemed a godsend for a church losing support on this issue everywhere. Dr John Billings published the first of many editions of his book *The Ovulation Method* in 1968, and his wife published her book *The Billings Method* in 1980. Their initial method was not failsafe, and was greeted with some scepticism by those who had tried it, as the phrases 'Roman roulette' and 'Billings babies' indicated. The Billings later devised an improved method. Birth control was only one of many pressures confronting the family at the time. It faced disintegrative forces at work in the society at large: relationship breakdowns, divorce, increased sexual freedoms, cohabitation, the diminution of the nuclear family and similar developments. This meant society's notion of the family profile was moving away from the Catholic Church's idea of it. In response the archdiocese sponsored pre-Cana conferences, and encouraged groups such as Marriage Encounter which arose to meet needs in this area.

The archdiocese was still in expansion mode, with growth in all categories.

	1960	1970
Parishes	162	195
Diocesan priests	337	418
Religious priests	286	374
Brothers	295	545
Nuns	2023	2356
Primary schools	207	228
Secondary schools	44	78
Primary School pupils	69,550	75,032
Secondary school pupils	23,730	34,552
Total Pupils	92,380	109,584

The Victorian Catholic population now passed the half million mark. But, though it could not be seen at the time, these figures represented a high point. The number of secondary schools almost doubled in the decade, catching up on the previous shortage. School figures generally and the number of Catholics and parishes continued to rise in the future, whereas Mass attendance and the number of religious began to plateau and then decline.

Archbishop Knox

Archbishop James Knox was appointed after Simonds resigned in April 1967 due to illness. Born in 1914 in Perth, Knox had applied unsuccessfully for entry to the priesthood. Perth's Archbishop Clune did not want an oversupply of priests whom he believed could later be a financial burden on his archdiocese, so entry was restricted. The young James Knox then applied to the seminary at the Benedictine New Norcia monastery, and was sent to Propaganda College in Rome in 1936, graduating as a secular priest. He continued his studies in Italy during the war, gaining doctorates in sacred theology and canon law. Ordained in 1941 he was appointed vice-rector of Propaganda College in 1945, a rapid promotion in an important institution after only four years as a priest. In 1948 he moved to work in the Vatican Secretariat of State (Foreign Ministry) under Monsignor Giovanni Montini, later Pope Paul VI. In 1950 he began a career as a papal diplomat in various posts, ending with that role on the Indian sub-continent, where he assisted the Australian nuns in India and Mother Teresa of Calcutta. He was then appointed to Melbourne, though he was little known in Australia, where he had not lived since 1936. It was a Vatican move more than an Australian appointment, and his first pastoral post. He was seen as a Vatican envoy sent to sort things out after the mess left by the split. His style was quiet, formal and reserved, self-effacing after the manner of a diplomat, rather than outgoing and pastoral, and as an outsider he was not taken to Catholic Melbourne's heart as the three earlier Irish archbishops had been. But that was not his mission. He had a job to do, and he did it.

His main activity in Melbourne was creating an administrative structure for the archdiocese, which had undergone minimal evolution under a leader who believed things worked well if you left them alone. Knox divided his sprawling domain into four parts, and in March 1969 set up administrative units each headed by an episcopal vicar, who acted like a cabinet minister with portfolio: education, finance, social welfare, pastoral formation, immigration, communications and mass media, tertiary education, lay apostolate, religious orders, and liturgy and sacred music. Knox implemented the reform program of Vatican II, supporting lay participation, ecumenism and liturgical reform. In 1972 the Victorian bishops sold off the large Glen Waverley seminary to the Victorian government to become a police academy, thereafter known locally as 'Coppers Christi'. With declining numbers its terminal date had come after

45 Archbishop Knox, formerly Apostolic Internuncio in India, greets Mother Teresa of Calcutta in Melbourne, 1972. (MDHC)

only a dozen years in operation. Seminarians were moved to a low, modest building adjacent to Monash University, where they could complete their secular studies.

The New *Advocate*

Knox had been sent to Melbourne in 1967 to act in line with current Vatican policies, whose general directions were clear, but whose ramifications still had to be worked out. Rome was in state of flux, just as the archdiocese was. Simonds had removed Santamaria's TV commentary on 'Sunday Magazine' as soon as he had assumed office, because he had always believed the church should not be pursuing political agendas. He wanted a more religious focus in his commentators, and a greater diversity of opinion on public issues. This was intended to restore debate to a more centrist position; Simonds was himself anti-Communist. But the progressive faction, energized by the perceived liberalism of Vatican II, read this limited anti-Santamaria move in a much wider context, that the archdiocese itself was moving in a more radical direction. The pendulum of *Advocate* editorial policy swung from traditionalist to radical, especially as Simonds became more incapacitated in the last years of his rule.

Previously the archdiocesan agenda had been set by the pronouncements of its bishops. Now in the authority vacuum after Mannix's death (lack of defined policies and lack of leadership) the formulator of church pronouncements partly became *The Advocate* itself. Within the paper the focus shifted from its editorial opinions to its features and to its much expanded the letters-to-the-editor pages. The views of the modernist faction, in particular of the *Catholic Worker* and dissenting priests, were giving prominent billing. Very heated controversies resulted, with priests firing shots at each other. The paper gave priority in its news reporting to the activities of the most daring experiments of overseas liberal Catholicism, exemplified by Fr Hans Kung and the Dutch Catholic radicals, who argued for the primacy of private conscience, obligatory attendance at Mass on any one day of the week, and preference for small local communities determining their own para-liturgies rather than formal parishes. In general this new social agenda, in common with the new liturgical agenda, emphasized caring and other social justice concerns over more traditional priorities – Mass was a communal meal writ large.

The figure who now made the running in *The Advocate* was its Assistant Editor, Fr Michael Costigan, who encouraged these policies, even if the paper's editorials were sometimes more circumspect.[43] Fr Costigan had been sent in 1963 to cover Vatican II for

---

[43] Michael Costigan's twin brother was Frank Costigan QC who chaired the Royal Commission into organized crime; their brother Peter Costigan was a well-known journalist who became Lord Mayor of Melbourne.

the paper. Fr Edmund Campion in his book *Australian Catholics* believed that 'in *The Advocate* Michael Costigan gave a more thorough day-to-day account of the Council than any other English-speaking diocesan weekly'. The paper claimed neutrality, but in fact promoted one side on all the main issues. In the early years of Knox's tenure of office the paper was simultaneously reporting on, and giving comfort to, four issues: pacifist opposition to the US involvement in Vietnam, support for dialogue with Communists, criticism of the Pope's encyclical on birth control *Humanae Vitae,* and support for various attempts around the world to take the spirit of Vatican II in new and unprecedented directions.

Those promoting dialogue with Communism saw it as an extension of the Council's ecumenical desire to reach out to others. They derided the traditional Catholic view that Communism was comprehensively evil. Arguing that as Communists were now ruling one third of the world's population and were a permanent part of the contemporary landscape, they had to be negotiated with. In fact Communism collapsed of its own internal contradictions just two decades later. Just as Catholics were liberalizing via Vatican II, so Communism, it was argued, was liberalizing with Krushchev's de-Stalinization and Dubcek's Communism with a human face. This reasoning was not helped by the 1968 Soviet invasion of Czechoslovakia, which occurred during these discussions, causing a major road block to the argument. The opponents of dialogue with Communists argued it was an asymmetrical debate. Those engaged in dialogue had to make the concession of talking to Communists who were at the same time persecuting their fellow Christians in Eastern Europe and Russia, yet it was not clear what equivalent concession the Communists were making. Communists here could influence Western opinion, but Christians in Communist lands were not given the freedom to do so there. 'Dialogue with Communism' was a passing phase which produced no results, fizzling out with Communism itself.

The Advocate was out of sympathy with many readers of long standing, whom it wished to enrol in the new radical agenda rather than to merely inform. The traditional readership of the paper expressed its displeasure in the letters columns. The paper had got too far ahead of the pack, as it had no brief to support policies not endorsed by the church through Vatican II. Caught up in the turbulence of the times and the passion to overthrow accepted ideas, it was now doing what many liberals had accused Santamaria of doing, using a Catholic organization to endorse political positions. Matters came to a head in early 1969. Knox had given an interview in which he stated that Communism was not a major issue, and that its solution was to be found in righting social ills. This statement was immediately used by progressive Catholics as a sign that Knox was adopting their anti-anti-Communist agenda. Niall Brennan of the *Catholic Worker*, speaking on the 'Labor Hour', inaccurately claimed that Knox had criticised the church for not doing its job properly in underdeveloped countries.

This was worse than a sin, it was a tactical mistake, as it forced Knox to take decisive action. First he clarified his original statement, now saying that Communism had been a problem, but had been defeated by resolute action (he didn't name whom he meant, but everyone knew), and it remained a potential threat both here and abroad, which demanded eternal vigilance. Knox deplored the way his words, intended as politically neutral, had been distorted for partisan political gain. He reiterated, like Simonds, that the church involved itself only when moral and religious issues were at stake. At the time Fr Costigan was publishing a series of articles on the Dutch Catholic reforms which he found 'enthralling'. Knox announced the Managing Editor of *The Advocate* Fr Denis Murphy was retiring, and that the new editor would be a lay professional journalist, Don Cunningham. At the same time Fr Costigan announced he was resigning both from the priesthood and from his editorial position on the paper, which forthwith took a middle-of-the-road position, ending its wild gyrations. A number of priests who had been prominent partisans of progressive causes in the paper left the priesthood around this time. Michael Costigan was later appointed Executive Secretary of the Bishop's Commission for Justice, Development and Peace.

In 1970 the two oldest institutions of Melbourne Catholicism ceased to exist: St Patrick's College, founded in 1854, was closed, and the last St Patrick's Day march, a feature of Melbourne life since 1843, took place. In the following year the Catholic newspaper *The Tribune*, which had first appeared in 1900, ceased publication.

46 The Cathedral block in 1929, showing St Patrick's without its spires. The Archbishop's palace and St Patrick's College behind the cathedral, and the three storey Catholic Ladies College in the street opposite the cathedral, were all demolished in the early 1970s. (MDHC)

12

EPILOGUE

Key Figures – Catholic Voting Patterns – Levelling Off and Decline
– Varieties of Belief – Culture Bearers

Key Figures

In 1973 Archbishop Knox was promoted to Cardinal by his former
mentor Pope Paul VI. This was seen by some as a posthumous
downgrading of Mannix's outstanding, if controversial, half
century in the post. But Knox's promotion was not connected with
his Melbourne position, but a necessary step for his forthcoming
posting. Less than a year after being promoted to Cardinal, Knox left
his only pastoral position to move back to Rome to head two Vatican
departments. Sydney as the 'mother see' was the natural home for
Australian red hats; it had already had two reigning Cardinals, Moran
and Gilroy, both promoted to that rank early in their reigns. In later
years the Sydney see was to boast three more cardinals, Freeman,
Clancy, and Pell (and the high Vatican official Cassidy) while Knox,
an outsider of short duration, remains Melbourne's solitary red hat.
Up to this stage Melbourne had had three Irish incumbents with
long reigns, and two non-Victorian Australians with short ones.
Archbishop Little's appointment in 1974 meant he was the first local
in the post after 127 years. With Knox, Little and Pell Melbourne
moved across to the Sydney Roman-trained pattern.

The three most famous figures to come out of the Melbourne
Archdiocese have been Saint Mary MacKillop, Archbishop Mannix
and Bob Santamaria. They have one remarkable thing in common: at
various times they all fell out in a serious way with Catholic higher
authorities. Mother MacKillop was excommunicated early in her
career by her bishop and only later reinstated. Archbishop Mannix
was offside with the Vatican during the conscription debates, with
the Vatican nuncio Archbishop Panico in the 1940s, and with the
Vatican's anti-Movement ruling of 1957. Santamaria was the

261

favourite son of the archdiocese from 1938 until the 1957 anti-Movement ruling, but after losing his church posts, he reciprocated in later life by criticizing the church. Dr Sister Mary Glowrey was formally declared a Servant of God by the bishop of Guntur in 2013, the first step on the path to possible canonization.

The research of Drs John and Evelyn Billings on the female reproductive cycle was recognized as original by medical scientists not in the applied field of family planning. Under Vatican sponsorship they took their method to many countries, particularly underdeveloped ones, with their method accepted by the World Health Organization and the Chinese government. The research by the Billings and others eventually led St Vincent's Hospital to move into the new field of bioethics. Both received papal knighthoods; Dr John Billings died in 2007 aged eighty-nine, and his wife Evelyn in 2013 aged ninety-five.

Sir Michael Chamberlin died in 1972 aged seventy nine, after a lifetime in the service of business and Catholic organizations. He had also been awarded a Papal knighthood for services to the church, and had come a long way since his first public activity as a committee member, with Arthur Calwell, of the radical Irish Ireland League of Victoria in 1919. Calwell died a year after Chamberlin, aged seventy seven; his daughter Mary Elizabeth has kept his memory alive through a number of publications defending his legacy. Poor lonely Simonds had no one to defend his reputation until Fr Max Vodola published his Simonds biography in 1997. Frank McManus died a decade after Calwell; both published valuable autobiographies after their retirement from public life.

Bob Santamaria died in 1998 and was granted a State funeral at St Patrick's Cathedral. One lesson of the Movement episode was the importance of keeping church and state apart. But the pendulum has swung so far that, anomalously, we now heavily privilege state over church, which has been to a large extent exiled from the public square. The poet and convert James McAuley was prescient in recognizing this problem as the split broke in 1954:

> Is the Labour Party to be regarded, as some of its members
> seem to imply, as a supreme and total moral authority

to which all other loyalties must bend or break? Does one have to check one's principles at the door, or is it permissible to take them into the party room? In particular, may Christians seek to develop the consequences of their Christian principles and persuade men to their views without being accused of tainting the pure milk of Australian Labourism with a Levantine ideology? (*Sydney Morning Herald*, 29 October 1954)

Dr Percy Jones retired from his many church posts in 1979 to live at Airey's Inlet, where he said Mass every morning in his house. He was not quite finished, as his achievement in 'retirement' was to persuade his friend from the world of music, Donald Cave, to tape-record his reminiscences, which are of considerable value as in them Jones reveals his private views, and because of the absence of similar priestly apologias. He was a close confidante of Mannix who sponsored his entire career. Dr Percy Jones died in 1992 aged seventy eight. Fr Eric D'Arcy was one of the few priests in Melbourne with leadership capacities in the post-Mannix era, but he had been sidelined. When he finally joined the Australian bishops' conference in 1981 as Bishop of Sale and later as Archbishop of Hobart, his clarity of mind enabled him to formulate and explain to the public the church's position, making him, late in life, an influential figure. Another victim of the split, he was probably the best qualified to lead the archdiocese after Knox.

Denys Jackson retired after almost fifty years of commentary on radio and in newspapers. In his swan song article in *The Advocate* of 29 May, 1980, he had regrets. He admitted he had been wrong about Mussolini and Hitler. He had however been correct, he believed, about the danger of Communism in post-war Europe, and in supporting our Vietnam commitment, but that venture had been ruined by hostile public opinion. He was worried about the outcome of Vatican II, especially current liturgical practices. His dream of an Australian Christian renaissance had been shattered, and he was disillusioned with the Australian Catholic Church which he considered had lost the plot and was without social impact. Overall he was pessimistic, believing we were living in a pagan and

47 A longevity and dedication to match Archbishop Mannix's – Fr Henry Johnston, SJ. (MDHC)

materialistic world, informed by humanism rather than by religious ideals. He disappeared from public life in his last years. His wife Rose died in 1977, and thereafter he was blind, lonely and suffered strokes. He died in 1986 aged eighty five.

Fr Henry Johnston SJ outlived by many years the Jesuits who came out with him from Ireland in the early 1920s. He had been around Melbourne seemingly forever when he died in 1986 at the age of almost ninety-eight. He began teaching at the Werribee seminary in 1925, and when his last stint ended there he was 82, having taught many of the priests in the archdiocese. A studious and reserved man, he was an all-rounder, proficient in moral and natural theology, scripture and biblical history. His persistence over six decades revealed him as driven, though his mild personality concealed this.

In the new millennium the last priests from the early years of Corpus Christi Werribee, were Fr Kevin Hannan, indexer of *The Advocate*, ordained in 1932, Fr Dan Conquest, the former Director of Catholic Education, ordained in 1934, and Bishop Alo Morgan, the former military chaplain-general, also ordained in 1934. Fr Conquest died in 2006 aged ninety-six. Both Hannan and Morgan had ambitions to live longer than Mannix, who had just failed to reach his century, but both also pulled up short, Fr Hannan dying in 2006 at the age of ninety nine, and Bishop Morgan in 2008, three months short of his 99th birthday. *The Advocate* ceased publication in 1990, a great loss as it contained within itself an invaluable institutional memory of the Archdiocese. A new journal, *Kairos*, replaced it in 1990; it ceased publication in 2016 and was replaced by the journal *Melbourne Catholic*, with a website to supplement the printed version.

Catholic Voting Patterns

In the 1950s and 1960s the two main parties ran neck and neck in Federal elections. By the early 1970s the effects of the split were wearing off. Menzies' dominance had gone, and Whitlam looked more in tune with the times than Calwell or McMahon. The DLP vote had weakened enough for Whitlam to win in 1972, and its vote collapsed in the 1974 elections. This meant in many ways the end of the political split, that is, the ability of the Catholic DLP vote to keep the ALP out of office. Talks to reconcile the ALP and DLP foundered on Calwell's opposition; an attempt to form a plausible County Party-DLP coalition of rural Protestant and city Catholic traditionalists likewise failed.

Thereafter the Victorian Catholic vote divided, and moved in opposite directions. At least half eventually moved back to Labor, with some right wing 'DLP' unions (including some former Santamaria operatives) rejoining the Melbourne Trades Hall in the early 1980s. This made it possible for John Cain junior to win the 1982 Victorian elections, ending twenty-seven years out of office for the Victorian Labor branch. The other portion of the Victorian Catholic vote moved to the conservative Liberal and National parties. But this had to be a two stage process, as it would have been too difficult for Catholics to suddenly in one move vote with their traditional class and religious opponents, the Protestant ascendency. The DLP provided a manageable two-stage phase, whereby they could first detach themselves from the ALP, but still vote for a party which called itself Labor. After having felt comfortable with this transition for some time, it was relatively easy to make the next step. This voting change also reflected Catholics assimilating as they became more upwardly socially mobile. Judge John Barry had noticed this trend as early as 1951: 'It is outmoded political thinking that Labour gets the whole Catholic vote; the Catholic middle class votes as does the middle class of any other denomination, and the RC middle class has increased greatly during the last 20 years.'[44] A similar transition was being made by

---

[44] Mark Finnane, *JV Barry: A Life*, p. 186. Janet McCalman documented signs of this development in her book *Journeyings*.

members of Melbourne's East European Jewish community, who had traditionally voted for socialist parties in their homelands, but, Labor supporters when they arrived, were now voting more heavily for the Liberals.

When Stan Keon lost his federal seat of Yarra to Dr Jim Cairns in 1955 the Cody family provided him with a position running one of their Austral Wine outlets. After the split some Labor identities on both side of the divide wished to retain personal relations in spite of their political differences. Organized by the journalist Ken Gott in 1958, they arranged to meet on neutral ground. One of the early meeting venues of the group was at Stan Keon's wine cellar off Little Bourke Street, so the group, which still exists, called itself the BookCellar club. By the mid 1970s a 'Catholic bloc vote' had ceased to exist, but as the Catholics were the largest religious group in the community, well organized and conscious of their influence, all major parties were for electoral reasons usually keen not to offend. By the time Bob Santamaria died in 1998, the split had faded as a live political issue, though some historical arguments over it persist, continuing the passions of the past and feeding into today's alignments. By 2014 the Governor General Peter Cosgrave was Catholic, as was the Prime Minister Tony Abbott, a product of the Santamaria stable who famously said the DLP was alive and well in the NSW Liberal Party. The Abbott Federal cabinet was almost half Catholic, revealing the historic deficit of Catholics on the non-Labor benches had been overcome. In Victoria the leaders of the three major parties, the Premier Denis Napthine, Peter Ryan and Daniel Andrews, plus the Chief Justice Marilyn Warren, were all Catholics.

In the past the Catholic Church in Melbourne, as in the rest of Australia, had seen continuing growth in all areas. By the 1970s it had hit its high-water mark in terms of crude statistics. In some areas, such as the number of clergy and Mass attendance, the figures plateaued for a time and then began to decline. In some other areas the figures increased roughly in line with population increases, so it was not all gloom.

Levelling Off and Decline

	1970	1980	1990	2000	2010
Parishes	195	219	233	232	220
Diocesan Priests	418	445	427	350	326
Religious Priests	374	359	344	294	269
Brothers	545	447	276	199	178
Nuns	2356	2395	1696	1323	1185
Primary Schools	228	239	259	256	253
Secondary Schools	78	88	85	69	62
Secondary School Pupils	34,552	48,568	60,784	58,862	64,036
Primary School Pupils	75,032	73,724	78,508	77,796	74,615
Total Pupils	109,584	122,492	139,292	136,658	138,641

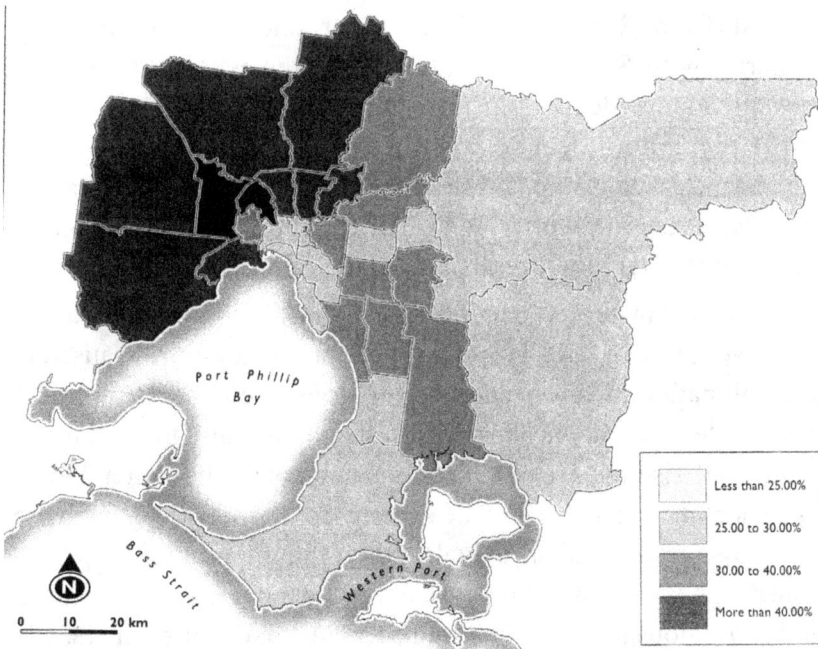

48 The distribution of Melbourne Catholics, from the 2001 census figures.
(*The Encyclopaedia of Melbourne*)

The Catholic population of Victoria doubled from 1970 to
2010, but has slightly declined in percentage terms. Allegiance

to the faith is less but still high. Anglicans had been the strongest religion in Australian with 38% of the population in 1911 compared with Catholics at about 22%. By 1991 Catholics in Australia were higher at 27% compared with Anglicans at 24%, because Catholics retained the beliefs and attendance of their flock better than other religions, and because of the large Catholic proportion among post-war immigrants. In 1991 the Catholic percentage of the population in both Melbourne and Sydney was around 31%, declining to about 27% a decade later.[45]

Comparing Catholics and Anglicans in Melbourne and Sydney (cities of roughly comparable size) early in the 20th century, more Catholics went to church in Melbourne than in Sydney, whereas more Anglicans went to church in Sydney than in Melbourne. So Melbourne was a Catholic stronghold. The number of 'census' Catholics has remained at a high level, as the 2001 map in a Melbourne encyclopaedia attests. In Melbourne Mass attendances declined from 225,000 in 1983 to around 147,000 in 2006, compared with Sydney's 100,000. Over the whole of Australia Mass attendance declined from 75% in the mid 1950s to 12% by 2011, a precipitous decline in absolute numbers, especially in the crucial 15-24 age group. It is estimated about 20,000 Australians each year cease to identify as Catholics, but church attendance is still in a healthier situation than in many other denominations.

The decline in the number of priests in the Melbourne Archdiocese in the two decades after 1990 was high, at about a third, caused by the combination of fewer entering the priesthood and some priests leaving. Clergy numbers had shown a steady rise until the mid fifties, then a brief rise until 1970, a last growth spurt, then after 1970 a steady decline. But there is some evidence of a small recent increase, caused by a traditionalist revival, and by the importation of priests. A third less priests was however not as striking a falling away as that for religious sisters, whose number halved, or for brothers, who declined by two thirds. Catholic women in general viewed Vatican II as a form of recognition for themselves. They now played a more

---

[45] Some of the figures quoted in this section relate to the Archdiocese rather than the Melbourne metropolitan area, but the difference is minimal.

prominent part in church organizations, as Mass servers and readers, and as conductors of para-liturgies. But some considered themselves still second-class citizens in the church, principally over the issue of women priests. Current feminist ideas were used to brand the Catholic church as patriarchal, with Celtic mythology replacing Mariology. Religious sisters, freed from a semi-enclosed life in convents, adopted normal dress and lived in community houses; some moved from being the most conservative and deferential to being the most radical.

In 1970 the number of pupils in primary schools was more than double that of secondary schools, but in four decades from 1970 to 2110 the number of primary schools pupils remained the same, while the number of pupils in secondary schools almost doubled, and was only 15% below that of the primary schools. This means most Catholic primary school students now go on to a Catholic high school, which fits in with increased retention rates across the board. The surprising decline in the number of secondary schools may be due to the formation of regional secondary schools, and the disappearance of some smaller inner schools, like St Patrick's East Melbourne. School pupil numbers increased with population from 1970 to 1990, then plateaued over next two decades even though the Catholic population was still rising. This in crude figures suggests a loss of Catholic allegiance of about a fifth, if school enrolment is a measure of the parents' Catholic faith. However many Catholics couldn't get their children enrolled into overcrowded Catholic schools in these decades, and others couldn't afford the school fees, or didn't wish to pay. So we have to be careful in extrapolating from school figures to Catholic allegiance rates.

In parishes there sometimes existed tension between a traditionalist parish priest who still had formal authority but a declining Mass attendance base, and on the other hand a parochial school with increased numbers, funding and prestige, where the teachers' ethos was progressive Catholicism; in this tussle ordinary Catholics were caught in between. Melbourne's new profile was part of a slow but continuing decline in religious belief, in numbers, and in credibility and self-confidence in all the countries of Western Christendom. Also important is the slow but continuous rise in the number of people self-describing as agnostic or of no religion.

Melbourne's particular problem was that the interregnum after Mannix's death overlapped with the beginnings of a general decline in attendance and belief. The retirement at the same time of many of its tired prime actors, both clerical and lay, disrupted institutional continuity and made it hard for the new leaders (until the advent of Archbishop Pell a quarter of a century later) to assert themselves with any conviction. Enormous attention has been focused on the drawbacks but the Archdiocese was strong enough, with its tradition of self-confident energy, to survive in reasonably good shape. The archdiocese remains a network of parishes, schools, religious orders and charitable institutions, each of substantial dimensions and continuing to perform. The charities sector (hospitals, orphanages, hostels, homes for the deaf and blind, shelters for the destitute, migrants, various welfare, support and accommodation services, homes for elderly, and so on) is much larger than most people realize. The heading 'Catholic Archdiocese of Melbourne' in the Melbourne phone directory extends to twenty columns of numbers, about 1300 phone numbers in all.

Whereas Catholic schools were once accused of being agents of social separation, they are now assimilated into the Australia mainstream, partly funded by governments, open to all, and with lay rather than religious staff. They are now themselves agents of integration, as the number of non-Catholics at Catholic schools grows, and as, on the other hand, a sizeable group of Catholic students now attend non-Catholic private and state schools. In recent decades smaller Catholic communities from Asia, South America and Africa have been added to the mix. Priests have been brought in from Poland, Nigeria and southern India to make up for the local shortfall. Melbourne therefore has become more truly catholic, in the sense that it now contains most elements of the universal church.

Varieties of Belief

Of a person who leaves the Faith, the Irish are not judgemental, saying, using a botanical metaphor: 'He was baptised but it didn't take'. Terms like lapsed or non-practising Catholic, or former priest, unhelpfully mask a wide range of affiliations. These black-and-white terms define individuals by what they have left, and do not disclose the past or present religious dispositions of those being described. It's more helpful to think of contemporary Catholicism as a spectrum. Many stay Catholic, whether strongly or vaguely, and are seen as such by others. Many remain Christian, some are believers, some are agnostic, most retain religious sensibilities to some degree. Few Catholics become atheist as distinct from agnostic, and anti-Catholics often remain religious believers. Moreover an individual's attitude to these matters is essentially a private matter, not to be second-guessed unless they themselves make it a public issue, which few do.

Some are still personally attached to the church, others feel let down by her; all, whatever their declared 'position', are indelibly marked by growing up in a strong Catholic culture, and so retain Catholic habits of mind. J.C.H. Aveling, an historian of Catholic England, has spelt this out: '[Catholics] had all grown up in a society where the Catholic religion was taken for granted as a natural fact of life, an inevitability like the soil and the weather...a communal inheritance in which all shared by birth. Individuals often sat light on religious practice: but they assumed they could no more escape God and the Church than they could jump out of their own skins.'[46] The US novelist Saul Bellow had a similar experience of being Jewish. Though himself a bohemian liberal and a non-observant Jew, from an early age Bellow acknowledged a basic and irremovable Jewishness, what he termed his 'first consciousness', as the ground of his being. In a moment of personal turmoil:

> I can do what I have done all my life: i.e. fall back instinctively on my first consciousness, which has always seemed to me to be most real and easily accessible. My own first consciousness has had a long unbroken history ... So in

[46] Quoted as an epigraph to Donald Cave, *Percy Jones*.

my first consciousness I was, among other things, a Jew. To turn away from those origins, however, has always seemed to me an utter impossibility. It would be treason to my first consciousness to un-Jew myself.[47]

Germaine Greer reflected similarly in the 1990s:

I am still a Catholic. I just don't believe in God. I am an atheist Catholic – there's a lot of them around. I don't want to escape from it. I'm very glad to be a Catholic. Very often, when Jehovah's Witnesses and all those people come around to make a nuisance of themselves, I open the door and say: 'This is a Catholic household.' Which it is. At least it was; at one time we were all lapsed Catholics in the house. One thing lapsed Catholics don't do is go in for an 'inferior' religion with less in the way of tradition and intellectual content.[48]

The beginning of the falling away from Catholicism, or at least from attendance at Mass, coincided with the ruling on contraception. Some left the church, others quietly practiced contraception while remaining Catholics. Barry Oakley felt directionless without the church and returned after the death of his father and the visit of Pope John Paul II in 1986:

The quiet nudgings that had urged me on now pushed me to the altar rails, to receive a pale circle of unleavened bread that at the consecration becomes, impossibly, the body of Christ. It feels uncomfortable to talk about this mystery – it's private in the way married love is private – but after one has taken the Host there's a stillness: being (ours) invaded by Being; love (our meagre portion) by Love...How can one believe we are headed for fullness and not nothingness, a state of purer being, a spirit-marriage with God? I did then and I do now, to the bemusement of our children and the mockery of friends.[49]

---

[47] Saul Bellow, *There Is Simply Too Much To Think About*, Viking, New York, 2015, pp. 256-7.
[48] J. Bennett and R. Forgan eds., *There's Something About A Convent Girl*, p. 93.
[49] Barry Oakley, *Mug Shots: A Memoir*, p. 206.

Figures show that religious commitment increases with age.

The deeper reasons for the decline of religious belief and practice, beyond the sociological or moral reasons usually advanced, are rarely admitted. In an article on the Spanish Civil War George Orwell, a non-religious person, suddenly out of the blue writes: 'The major problem of our time is the decay in the belief in personal immortality.' A couple of Australian ministers of religion from various denominations continued to preach in their churches after abandoning their beliefs in the Christian religion and in the existence of God. They were at least frank if conflicted, trapped in a profession in which they no longer believed. Depression and alcoholism among priests, or anyone for that matter, can be sign of an inability to face loss of personal religious faith. The realization, via writers like Sir James Frazer of *The Golden Bough,* that the Christ story fits the pattern of many tribal nature myths of death at mid-winter and rebirth, is for some the final nail in the coffin, for others a consolation that Christianity aligns itself with the basic belief systems of all cultures, even akin to the Aboriginal one, as Fr Worms found.

Most importantly, the foregoing spectrum analysis also applies to those who remain Catholics, for we all have to work things out for ourselves, as the poet and teacher Joseph O'Dwyer wrote in *The Advocate*, 15 October 1947: 'Even those of you who are "born" Catholics will have the necessity of becoming Catholics. We still have to undergo that conversion which changes us from nominal to real Catholics'. As he lay dying James McAuley juggled the competing claims of non-belief and belief in his final poem 'Explicit':

> Soon I'll understand it all,
> Or cease to wonder: so my small
> Spark will blaze intensely bright,
> Or go out in an endless night.
>
> Welcome now to bread and wine:
> Creature comfort, heavenly sign.
> Winter will grow dark and cold
> Before the wattle turns to gold.

We choose what we find essential from the 'vast moth-eaten musical brocade' (the poet Philip Hughes's phrase) which constitutes Christianity. By this we do not mean 'cafeteria Catholicism', a derogatory term used about those who choose only those beliefs which suit them and discard others. It is rather what one commentator has called 'refined religion', the process by which we each boil down and refine a coherent system of basic Christian beliefs into a personal myth we can live, and die, by.

Culture Bearers

In the newly settled European outpost of nineteenth century Australia, the churches and their schools were among the main culture-bearing and culture-transmitting organisms of society. Differences between the churches were not in the long run the crucial factor. Whether you attended Catholic, Anglican or Protestant schools or certain select high schools, you picked up a good idea of Greek and Roman times, the Dark and Medieval ages, and the Renaissance and Reformation, as much from religious practices and instruction as from formal history. What remained, after the fractious squabbles over the Reformation and other episodes had receded in importance, was that you had internalized the lineaments of European culture and beliefs.

At Easter and Christmas masses at St Patrick's Cathedral the combination of a High Mass, organ, incense, Latin liturgy, choral music, soaring architecture and a dense congregation gave one a brief experience, rare in Australia, of the atmosphere of a grave formal occasion such as occurs in Europe, a glimpse of a world long gone and far away. Non-Catholics sometimes attended these Masses for 'cultural' reasons. Learning languages like Latin and French, and participating in church music and liturgy, immeasurably deepened this immersion. It was a lasting deposit, as Josie Arnold remembered with gratitude:

> The panoply of the Church – its rich ecclesiastical language, dress and ceremonies – was a most wonderful hothouse for a young writer. It also taught me that ideas and philosophies existed and were part of the human experience – a lesson that is hard to come by in a world that becomes daily

more pragmatic...I loved the ecclesiastical Latin sung and chanted in church. Latin also gave a knowledge of root-words, which has been of immense practical use to me as a writer.[50]

The sacraments taught us more than their content. They gave us the experience of a formal ceremony where the words had dignity and gravitas, and the atmosphere transcended the immediate occasion. Shakespeare's Cleopatra declaims on behalf of us all: 'I have immortal longings in me'. Such longings are not satisfied by today's marriages and funerals conducted by fly-in celebrants lip-reading the family history. Secular society doesn't do ceremony well.

Irving Howe's book *The World of Our Fathers* is the record of his own New York Jewish community, like Melbourne's Irish Catholic one a tight religio-racial immigrant network which made its own distinctive contribution to the seaport metropolis in which it found its home. The present book could have been called 'The World of Our Parents'. It is written in gratitude to parents, families, teachers, religious and others who created, often at some cost to themselves, this deepening of the spirit which gave Melbourne Catholicism its distinctive atmosphere. It is an attempt to repay them by rescuing from oblivion some parts of the dense fabric they wove. In his autobiography the writer Barry Oakley, by no means a rusted-on Catholic, refers to this in his memory of his teachers:

> The notion of sacrifice in the Christian Brothers ideal is now virtually incomprehensible. It was a life of plain food and plain rooms and weekend loneliness. No wife, no family, just the constant classroom grind. It was as relentless for them as it was for us, but because we were force-fed with the learning and literature of the Western world, we were, paradoxically, set free. The fact that a couple of them broke under the pressure and preyed on the students they were supposed to be educating makes what the majority managed to achieve all the more impressive.[51]

It's true we were force-fed, but there was also an inherent love

[50] Josie Arnold, *Mother Superior Woman Inferior*, pp. 140, 143.
[51] Barry Oakley, op. cit, pp. 210-1.

of learning. We were taught, for example, that the Battle of Lepanto in the Eastern Mediterranean in 1571, in which a Christian flotilla repulsed the Turks, was one of the great turnings points of European history. Half a century later, with the recent Muslim resurgence in Europe, Lepanto is back in the history books again. However our Christian Brother teachers did get one battle wrong. In Roman history classes we were told the story of barbarian tribes trying to sack Rome in 390BC, and how the locals were alerted in the nick of time by squawking geese who gave the intruders away. We were barracking for the Romans of course, and breathed a sigh of relief as Rome was saved from destruction so it could fulfil its destiny as the Eternal City. My later reading told me that those who threatened Rome on this occasion were Celtic tribes, who were not barbarians as they possessed their own long-standing culture, which the Romans, just getting started on theirs, lacked at this stage.

The Celts had existed, I discovered, not just in the British Isles but all over Europe, from Galicia (the word means Gaul or Celt) in Spain to Galicia in southern Poland to Galatia in Asia Minor; St Paul's epistle to the Galatians may have been addressed to our fellow Celts. But in the centuries before and after Christ, the Celtic realms had been displaced by various upcoming races, including the Romans. The Catholic Church, centred in Rome, had absorbed the underlying value system of *Romanitas*. Its accumulated wisdom imposed itself on us as a powerful force, at once uplifting and overbearing. The Christian Brothers, though an Irish order founded as a protest against English penal laws in Ireland, had taken on board, through British culture and through the *Romanitas* of the church, the ideology of the imperial race which oppressed them. The Irish Catholic church uneasily contained within itself both Roman and native elements, so when the Easter Rising broke out in 1916, it didn't know which way to jump.

The Romans replaced the once widespread Celts in continental Europe. As we witness with today's Muslim insurgency, history is a panorama of dominant and suppressed cultures changing places over time, of empires congealing and then breaking up again. We all harbour in our own consciousness an imaginative understanding of these contrary experiences, as Mannix did. Downtrodden races live by their mythologies. In the longest perspective the rancorous outbreaks over conscription in 1917 and over the split in 1954, so special and particular to us, are just recent examples of ancestral voices propelling suppressed peoples to steal a march on their hereditary overlords in order to have their place in the sun.

ACKNOWLEDGEMENTS

This book is an unofficial history; it has not been commissioned by the Melbourne archdiocese. Its scope does not extend, except incidentally, to religious orders, parishes and schools. Sometimes dates can be imprecise; for example, the transfer of eight parishes in the Cranbourne-Pakenham area to the diocese of Sale was announced in 1958 and carried out in 1959. Citing such double dates has been avoided to prevent unnecessarily complicating the narrative. One big lack in assessing the half century from 1920 to 1970 is the relative absence of clerical voices. Bishops, the laity, and those in dispute with the church spoke out a lot, but we don't know much about what the ordinary suburban priest or religious sister thought on key issues. Dr Percy Jones, an untypical priest, left an invaluable dictated autobiographical reminiscence. In addition to Archbishop Mannix, Archbishop Simonds and Frs John Brosnan and John Kelly are the subject of biographies, but there are few extensive studies of other noteworthy clerics. In composing his own autobiography Arthur Calwell lamented the absence of similar efforts by his fellow politicians.

Thanks are gratefully made to indispensable sources such as the *Australian Dictionary of Biography*, the National Library of Australia's 'Trove' website, the Yarra Theological Union library at Box Hill, and the resources of the State Library of Victoria, including its Santamaria papers and microfilms of newspapers. The Melbourne Diocesan Historical Commission and its Chairman, Fr Max Vodola, and Archivist, Rachel Naughton, have provided much assistance. Professor Ian Waters, Douglas Kennedy and my wife Ann provided very helpful assessments of the text in manuscript form. Colin Jory's 1986 book on the Campion Society was invaluable in understanding the complex origins of Catholic Action and the Movement. Brenda Niall's biography of Mannix and Gerard Henderson's on Santamaria, both of which appeared during the writing of this book, have provided innumerable leads. It was a great help to have

279

the illustrations prepared for publication by Rachel Naughton and Ann Synan. For publishing early versions of material included in this book, thanks are extended to the editors of the *Journal of the Australian Catholic Historical Society*, the magazine *Tinteán,* the newspaper *The Australian*, and the book of essays *Daniel Mannix: His Legacy*. Help from Prof. Gabrielle McMullan, Dick and Julianna O'Bryan, Tom Buxton, Danny Cusack, Prof. James Franklin, and Dr Bob Turner of the Pastoral Research Office cleared up many problems. Permission for reproduction of illustrations, for which I am thankful, was obtained from the Melbourne Diocesan Historical Commission, St Vincent's Hospital's archive, *News Weekly*, the National Library of Australia, the Catholic Women's League of Victoria, and Cambridge University Press.

The events described in this book, unlike its predecessor, took place within living memory. My parents came from extensive Irish Catholic families; in the 1920s they attended the University of Melbourne, a small world in those days. My father went to school at CBC North Melbourne and spent his working life at St Vincent's Hospital; his three brothers were all priests. My mother's Brosnan family were related by marriage to James Scullin and Bishop Laurence Moran. For a combination of these factors our family knew many of the people who feature in this book. I grew up in North Essendon in the 1940s and 1950s; the proportion of Catholics in the outer north-west suburbs was then the highest in our history. I had no inkling of that at the time, as I assumed it was normal to be surrounded by fellow Catholics. Coming to the university in the early 1960s, I was fortunate in being in the first cohort not to have experienced the tremors of the split as an adult. I followed events closely in the 1960s, publishing an article on them 'Varieties of Political Catholicism' (*Quadrant*, Sept-Oct 1967), described by the conservative Martin Haley (*The Advocate*, 7 December, 1967) as a 'deplorable confusion of untruths'. Undeterred by this early setback, I have fifty years later ventured on an expanded version.

BIBLIOGRAPHY

Fr Bourke's bibliography in his *A History of the Catholic Church in Victoria* (1988) covers the period of this book, but is out of date. Robert Murray's *The Split* and Bruce Duncan's *Crusade or Conspiracy?* contain bibliographies on the Movement and the split. The most recent bibliography on Archbishop Mannix is in Brenda Niall's *Mannix,* and on B.A. Santamaria in Gerard Henderson's *Santamaria: A Most Unusual Man.*

Reference

Australian Dictionary of Biography, Melbourne University Press

Australasian Catholic Directory

The Advocate and *The Tribune,* microfilm, and the *Index to The Advocate*, State Library of Victoria

Brown-May, Andrew & Swain, Shurlee, eds., *The Encyclopedia of Melbourne*, Cambridge University Press, Port Melbourne, 2005

Jupp, James ed., *The Australian People*, Angus & Robertson, Sydney, 1988, repr. Cambridge University Press, Port Melbourne, 2001

Jupp, James, *The Encyclopedia of Religion in Australia,* Cambridge University Press, Melbourne, 2009

Strong, David, *The Australian Dictionary of Jesuit Biographies*, Halstead Press, Ruchcutters Bay, 1998

'Trove', National Library of Australia

Catholic History

The Catholic Church in Melbourne 1848-1948, The Advocate Press, Melbourne, 1948

Bourke, D.F., *A History of the Catholic Church in Victoria*, Catholic Bishops of Victoria, Melbourne, 1988

Carr, Hilary, *Believing in Australia*, Allen & Unwin, St Leonards, 1996

Ebsworth, Walter, *Pioneer Catholic Victoria*, The Polding Press, Melbourne, 1973

Hogan, Michael, *Australian Catholics: The Social Justice Tradition,* Collins Dove, North Blackburn, 1993

Hogan, Michael, *The Sectarianism Strand: Religion in Australian History,* Penguin, Melbourne, 1987

Johnston, H.A. SJ, *Plain Talks on the Catholic Religion*, Angus and Robertson, Sydney, 1936

Johnstone, Tom, *The Cross of Anzac*, Church Archivists' Press, Virginia Qld, 2001

Mackle, Francis, *Illustrated History of the Archdiocese*, The Advocate Press, Melbourne, 1948

Mackle, Francis, *The Footprints of Our Catholic Pioneers*, The Advocate Press, Melbourne, 1924

McConville, Chris, *Croppies, Celts and Catholics: The Irish in Australia*, Edward Arnold, Caulfield East, 1987

Matthews, Race, *Of Labour and Liberty: Distributism in Victoria*, Monash University Publishing, Clayton, 2017

Molony, John, *The Roman Mould of the Australian Catholic Church,* MUP, Carlton, 1969

Morgan, Patrick, *Melbourne Before Mannix: Catholics in Public Life 1880-1920*, Connor Court, Ballan, 2012

Murphy, J.M. & Moynihan F., *The National Eucharistic Congress*, The Advocate Press, Melbourne, 1936

Murtagh, James, *Australia: The Catholic Chapter*, Sheed & Ward, New York, 1946

Niall, Brenda et al., *Newman College: A History,1918-1018*, Newman College, Parkville, 2018

O'Farrell, Patrick, *The Catholic Church and Community,* New South Wales University Press, Kensington, 3rd rev. ed., 1992

Praetz, Helen ed., *The Church in Springtime: Remembering Catholic Action*, 1940-1965, Brighton, 2011

Turnbull, Jeffrey John, *Walter Burley Griffin: The Architecture of Newman College*, Vivid Publishing, 2018

Archbishop Mannix

Brennan, Niall, *Dr Mannix*, Rigby, Adelaide, 1964

Bryan, Cyril, *Archbishop Mannix – Champion of Democracy*, The Advocate Press, Melbourne, 1918

Ebsworth, Walter A.W., *Archbishop Mannix*, H.H. Stephenson, Armadale, 1977

Franklin, James et al. eds., *The Real Archbishop Mannix From The Sources,* Connor Court, Ballarat, 2015

Gilchrist, Michael, *Daniel Mannix: Priest & Patriot*, Dove Communications, Blackburn, 1982

Griffin, James, *Daniel Mannix: Beyond the Myths*, Garratt, Melbourne, 2012

Kiernan, Colm, *Daniel Mannix and Ireland*, Allela Books, Morwell, 1984

Mannix, Patrick, *The Belligerent Prelate*, Cambridge Scholars, Newcastle Upon Tyne, 2012

Murphy, Frank, *Daniel Mannix*, The Advocate Press, Melbourne, 1948

Niall, Brenda, *Mannix,* Text Publishing, Melbourne, 2015

Noone, Val & Naughton, Rachel eds., *Daniel Mannix: His Legacy*, MDHC, East Melboune, 2014

Santamaria, B.A., *Daniel Mannix*, Melbourne University Press, Carlton, 1984

_____ *Archbishop Mannix: His Contribution to the Art of Public Leadership In Australia,* MUP, Melbourne, 1978

The Movement, BA Santamaria and The Split

Aarons, Mark, *The Show: Another Side of Santamaria's Movement.* Scribe, Victoria, 2017

Costar, Brian et al., *The Great Labor Schism: A Retrospective*, Scribe Publications, Melbourne, 2005

Duffy, Gavan, *Demons and Democrats: 1950s Labor at the Crossroads*, Freedom Publishing, North Melbourne, 2002

Duncan, Bruce, *Crusade or Conspiracy?: Catholics and the Anti-Communist Struggle in Australia*, UNSW Press, Sydney, 2001

Fitzgerald, Ross & Holt, Stephen, *The Pope's Battalions: Santamaria, Catholicism and the Labor Split*, UNSW Press, Sydney, 2010

Henderson, Gerard, *Mr Santamaria and the Bishops,* Hale & Iremonger, Sydney, 1983

_____ *Santamaria: A Most Unusual Man*, The Miegunyah Press, Carlton, 2015

Mayer, Henry ed., *Catholics and the Free Society: An Australian Symposium,* Cheshire, Melbourne, 1961

Mount, Frank, *Wrestling With Asia,* Connor Court, Ballan, 2012

Murray, Robert, *The Split: Australian Labor in the Fifties*, Cheshire, Melbourne, 1970

_____ *Santamaria and Labor,* Australian Scholarly Publishing, Melbourne, 2017

Ormonde, Paul, *The Movement*, Nelson, Melbourne, 1972

Ormonde Paul ed., *Santamaria: The Politics of Fear*, Spectrum Publications, Richmond, 2000

Reid, Alan, *The Bandar Log: A Labor Story of the 1950s*, Connor Court, Ballarat, 2015

Santamaria, B.A., *The Earth Our Mother*, Araluen Publishing, Melbourne, 1945

_____*Your Most Obedient Servant*, Miegunyah Press, Carlton, 2007

_____*Running the Show*, Miegunyah Press, Carlton, 2008

_____*Against the Tide*, OUP, Melbourne, 1981

Politics

Colebatch, Hal, *Australia's Secret War*, Quadrant Books, Sydney, 2013

Calwell, Arthur, *Labor's Role in Modern Society*, Lansdowne Press, Melbourne, 1963

Cain, Frank, *The Origins of Political Surveillance in Australia*, Angus & Robertson, Sydney, 1983

Horner, David, *The Spy Catchers*, Allen & Unwin, Sydney, 2014

Murtagh, James, *Democracy in Australia*, Hawthorne Press, Melbourne, 1946

Noone, Val, *Disturbing the War: Melbourne Catholics and Vietnam*, Spectrum, Melbourne, 1993

O'Brien Patrick, *The Saviours: An Intellectual History of the Left in Australia*, Drummond, Richmond, 1977

Strangio, Paul, *Neither Power Nor Glory*, Melbourne University Press, Carlton, 2012

Orders, Schools & Institutions

Allen, Sister Maree, *The Labourers' Friend: Sisters of Mercy in Victoria and Tasmania,* Hargreen Publications, North Melbourne, 1989

Abrahams, Olga, *88 Nicholson Street: The Academy of Mary Immaculate*, The Academy of Mary Immaculate, Fitzroy, 2007

Boland T.P., *St Patrick's Cathedral: A Life*, The Polding Press, East Melbourne, 1997

Bygott, Ursula, *With Pen and Tongue: the Jesuits in Australia, 1865-1939*, MUP, Carlton, 1980

Clark, Mary Rhyllis, *Loreto in Australia*, UNSW Press, Sydney, 2007

Dening, Greg,, *Xavier: A Centenary Portrait*, Old Xavierians Association, Melbourne, 1978

Egan, Bryan, *Ways of a Hospital: St Vincent's Melbourne 1890s-1990s*, Allen & Unwin, St Leonards, 1993

Gott, Ken, *The Book Cellar*, 4th edition, 2009

Head, Michael & Healy, Gerard, *More Than a School: A History of St Patrick's College East Melbourne 1854-1968*, East Melbourne, Eldon Hogan Trust & Jesuit Publications, Richmond, 1999

Jory, Colin, *The Campion Society and Catholic Social Militancy in Australia 1929-1939*, Harpham, Sydney, 1986

Kane, Kathleen Dunlop, *The History of Christian Brothers College, East St Kilda,* Christian Brothers College, 1972

McConville, Chris, *St Kevin's College 1918-1993*, MUP, Carlton, 1993

O'Donoghue, K.K., *Brother PA Treacy and the Christian Brothers in Australia and New Zealand,* The Polding Press, Melbourne, 1983

O'Hearn, D.J., *Erin Go Bragh – Advance Australia Fair – a Hundred Years of Growing,* Celtic Club, Melbourne, 1990

Rule, Paul J., *To Learn and to Do: A History of St Bernard's College 1940-1990*, St Bernard's, West Essendon, 1990

Stewart, Ronald, *The Spirit of North, 1903-2000*, CBC North Melbourne, 2000

Biographies

Armstrong, Pauline, *Frank Hardy and the Making of* Power Without Glory, MUP, South Carlton, 2000

Barry, Bill, *Of Home Politics and World Trade*, Australian Scholarly Publishing, Melbourne, 2017

Buggy, Hugh, *The Real John Wren*, Widescope, Melbourne, 1977

Calwell, Mary Elizabeth, *I Am Bound To Be True: The Life and Legacy of Arthur A. Calwell 1897-1973,* Mosaic Press, Melbourne, 2012

Cave, Donald, *Percy Jones: Priest, Musician, Teacher*, MUP, Carlton, 1988

Clinton, Ursula, *Australian Medical Nun in India*, The Advocate Press, Melbourne, 1967

Coogan, Tim Pat, *De Valera: Long Fellow, Long Shadow*, Hutchinson, London, 1993

Finnane, Mark, *JW Barry: A Life*, UNSW Press, Sydney, 2007

Fitzhardinge, L.F., *The Little Digger: 1914-1952: A Political Biography of William Morris Hughes,* Vol II, Angus and Robertson, Sydney, 1979

Greer, Germaine, *Daddy We Hardly Knew You*, Hamish Hamilton, New York, 1989

Griffin, James, *John Wren – A Life Reconsidered*, Scribe, Carlton North, 2004

Kiernan, Colm, *Calwell: A Personal and Political Biography*, Melbourne, Nelson, 1978

Laffin, Josephine, *Mathew Beovich: A Biography*, Wakefield Press, Adelaide, 2008

Livingstone, Tess, *George Pell*, Duffy & Snellgrove, Sydney, 2002

Luttrell, John, *Norman Thomas Gilroy: An Obedient Life*, St Paul's Publications, Stratfield, 2017

McCarthy J., *James Patrick O'Collins*, Spectrum Publications, Richmond, 1996

Niall, Brenda, *The Riddle of Father Hackett: A Life in Ireland and Australia*, National Library of Australia, Canberra, 2009

Pascoe, Robert, *The Feasts and Seasons of John F. Kelly*, Allen & Unwin, St Leonards, 2006

Prior, Tom, *Knockabout Priest: The Story of Father John Brosnan,* Hargreen, North Melbourne, 1985

Robertson, John, *J.H. Scullin A Political Biography,* University of WA Press, Nedlands, 1974

Torney-Parlicki, Prue, *Behind the News: A Biography of Peter Russo,* University of WA Press, Crawley WA, 2005

Turley, Frank, *Big Ned: Edmond John Hogan Twice Premier of Victoria,* c.1999

Wilding, Bill, *Flaming Torch: Francis Irenaeus MacCarthy*, Howden, 2012

Vodola, Max, *Simonds: A Rewarding Life*, Catholic Education Office, Melbourne, 1997

Autobiographies and Memoirs

Arnold, Josie, *Mother Superior Woman Inferior,* Dove Communications, Blackburn, 1985

Bennett, Jackie & Forgan, Rosemary eds., *There's Something About A Convent Girl*, Virago, London, 1991.

Buckley, Vincent, *Cutting Green Hay*, Penguin, Melbourne, 1983

Calwell Arthur, *Be Just and Fear Not,* Lloyd O'Neil, Hawthorn, 1972

Conway, Ronald, *Conway's Way: Memories, Endeavours and Reflections*, Collins Dove, Blackburn, 1988

Fitzpatrick, Kathleen, *Solid Bluestone Foundations,* Macmillan, South Melbourne, 1983

Foster, Chrissie, *Hell on the Way to Heaven*, Random House, North Sydney, 2011

Galbally, Frank, *Galbally*, Viking, Ringwood, 1989

Griffin, Helga, *Sing Me That Lovely Song Again...*, Pandanus Books, Canberra, 2006

Gobbo, Sir James, *Something To Declare: A Memoir*, The Miegunyah Press, Carlton, 2010

Hanrahan, John, *From Eternity to Here: Memoirs of an Angry Priest*, Bystander Press, Northcote, 2002.

Hogan, E. J., *Memoirs of Hon. E.J. Hogan*, Renown Press, Carnegie, nd.

Knorr, Hilda, *Journey With A Stranger*, Collins Dove Adelaide, 1986

MacManus, Frank, *The Tumult and the Shouting*, Rigby, Adelaide, 1977

McInerney, Murray, 'Memoirs', unpublished

Mimovich, Leopoldine, *Memories Guide My Hands*, Spectrum Publications, Melbourne, 1985

Molony, John, *By Wendouree,* Connor Court, Ballan, 2010

Molony, John, *Luther's Pine: An Autobiography,* Pandanus Books, Canberra, 2004

Nelson, Kate & Nelson, Dominica, eds., *Sweet Mothers, Sweet Maids: Journeys from Catholic Childhoods,* Penguin, Ringwood, 1986

Niall, Brenda, *Life Class: The Education of a Biographer*, Melbourne University Press, Carlton, 2007

Oakley, Barry, *Mug Shots: A Memoir*, Wakefield Press, Kent Town, Adelaide, 2012

O'Brien, Anne, *God's Willing Workers*, UNSW Press, Sydney, 2005

O'Collins, Gerard SJ, *A Midlife Journey*, Connor Court, Ballan, 2012

Parer, Michael, *Dreamer by Day: A Priest Returns to Life*, Angus & Robertson, Sydney, 1971

Smith, Ernie, *Miracles Do Happen: A Priest Called Smith*, Collins Dove, North Blackburn, 1993

Tehan, James, *For the Land and Its People,* privately printed, 1991

West, Morris, *A View From the Ridge: The Testimony of a Pilgrim*, Harper Collins, Pymble, 1996

Culture

Boylan, Fr Eustace SJ, *The Heart of the School*: *An Australian School Story*, Roy Stevens, Melbourne, 1920

Buckley, Vincent, *Selected Poems*, Angus & Robertson, Sydney, 1981

Hardy, Frank, *Power Without Glory*, Melbourne, 1950

Jones, Fr Percy, *Australian Hymnal,* The Advocate Press, 1942

Knorr, Hilda ed., *The Sculpture of Hans Knorr*, Spectrum, Richmond, 1976

Knorr, Hans & Hilda, *Religious Art in Australia,* Longmans, Croydon, 1967

Martin, Phillip Voice, *Unaccompanied,* ANU Press, Canberra, 1970

_____*A Bone Flute*, ANU Press, Canberra, 1974

Oakley, Barry, *The Feet of Daniel Mannix*, Angus & Robertson, Sydney, 1975

O'Dwyer, Joseph, *Collected Poems 1930-1981*, Globe Press, 1987

O'Leary, P.I., *Bards in Bondage*, ed. Joseph Dwyer, The Hawthorn Press, Melbourne, 1954

Rohr, Henry ed., *The Sculpture of Leopoldine Mimovich*, Spectrum, Richmond, 1977.

West, Morris, *The Shoes of the Fisherman*, Heinemann, London, 1963

_____*The Clowns of God*, Coronet, Sevenoaks, 1982

General & Miscellaneous

Billings, Dr John, *The Ovulation Method*, Advocate Press, Melbourne, 1964

Buckley, Vincent ed., *The Incarnation and the University: Studies in the University Apostolate*, UCFA 1955, repr. Pax Romana & Geoffrey Chapman, 1957

Charlesworth, Max, *Church, State and Conscience*, University of Queensland Press, St Lucia, 1973

D'Arcy, Eric, *Conscience and Its Right to Freedom,* Sheed & Ward, New York, 1961

Foster, R.F., *Vivid Faces: The Revolutionary Generation in Ireland 1890-1923,* Allen Lane, London, 2014

Hogan, E.J., *What's Wrong with Australia?* , EJ Hogan, Melbourne, 1953

Kennedy, Sally, *Faith and Feminism: Catholic Women's Struggle for Self Expression*, Studies in the Christian Movement, Sydney, 1985

Kiernan, Colm, *Daniel Mannix and Ireland*, Allela Books, Morwell, 1984

McCalman, Janet, *Struggletown*, Penguin, Ringwood, 1984

McCalman, Janet, *Journeyings*, Melbourne University Press, Carlton, 1993

McGuire, Paul & Fitzsimons, Fr J., *Restoring All Things*, Sheed & Ward, London, 1939

Noone, Val et al. eds., *The Golden Years: Grounds For Hope,* Golden Project, Melbourne, 2008

O'Brien, Anne, *God's Willing Workers: Women and Religion in Australia*, UNSW Press, Sydney, 2005

O'Farrell, Patrick, *The Irish in Australia*, New South Wales University Press, Kensington, 1986

Worms, Ernest A. & Nekes, Herman, *Australian Languages*, ed. William B. McGregor, Mouton de Gruyter, Berlin & New York, 2006

Worms, E. Aildred & Neverman, Hans, *Australian Aboriginal Religions*, Spectrum Publications, Richmond, 1986

Articles & Pamphlets

Bourke, J., 'The Coming of the Bourke Family to Pakenham', privately published, 1965

Campion Society, 'Prelude to Catholic Action', ACTS, Melbourne, 1936

Clarke, Bishop Leo, 'Archbishop Mannix: What Was He Like?' & 'Archbishops Simonds and Knox: Some Personal Reminiscences', *Footprints* June 2003 and December 2004

Costigan, Michael, 'From News Weekly to the Catholic Worker: Sixty-two Years Writing for the Religious and Secular Media', *Journal of the Australian Catholic History Society*, vol. 30, 2009

Franklin, James, 'Memoirs by Australian Priests, Religious and Ex-Religious', *Journal of the Australian Catholic History Society,* vol 33, 2012.

Gleeson, D.J., 'The Origins of Melbourne's Catholic Services Bureau (Centacare)', *Footprints,* June, 2002

Hilliard, David, 'God in the Suburbs: the Religious Culture of the Australian Suburbs in the 1950s', *Australian Historical Studies*, no. 97, October 1991

Hogan, E.J., 'The Pro-Communist Split in the Labor Party', Melbourne, 1955

Johnstone, Henry, SJ, 'The Early Years of Corpus Christi', *Jesuit Life*, c.1974

Jackson, Denys, 'Australian Dream', ACTS, 1947 & 1948

Kiernan, Brian, 'Xavier Recalled', *Quadrant*, vol. XIII No. 1, Jan-Feb, 1969

Kneipp, Mary, 'Australian Catholics and the Spanish Civil War', *Journal of the Australian Catholic History Society,* vol. 19, 1998

Knopfelmacher, Frank, 'Catholics and Communists: A Tragi-Comedy of Errors', *Intellectuals and Politics*, Nelson, Melbourne, 1968, pp. 59-115.

Linnane, Fr T.J., 'The Melbourne Diocesan Historical Commission and the Origins of *Footprints*', *Journal of the Australian Catholic History Society*, vol 9, no 3, 1988

McMullen, Gabrielle L., 'Dr Sr Mary Glowrey JMJ Servant of God', *Footprints*, December, 2015

Morgan. Patrick, 'Varieties of Political Catholicism', *Quadrant*, Sept-Oct, 1967

O' Brien, Anne, 'A Church Full of Men', *Historical Studies of Australia*, vol. 25, no. 100, April 1993

Santamaria, B.A., 'The Movement' in Mayer, Henry ed. *Catholics and the Free Society: An Australian Symposium,* Cheshire, Melbourne, 1961

_____ 'The Italian Problem in Australia', *Australasian Catholic Record,* October, 1939

Warhurst, John, 'Catholics, Communism and the Australian Party system: a study of the Menzies years, *Politics,* vol.14, no. 2, November, 1979

Theses

Barnard, Jill, 'Expressions of Faith: 20th Century Roman Catholic Churches in Melbourne's Western Suburbs', MA, Monash Public History, 1990

Capelllo, Anthony, 'To be or not to be an Italian', PhD, Victoria University, 2009

Close, Cecily, 'The Organisation of the Catholic Laity in Victoria, 1911-1930', MA, University of Melbourne, 1972

Cusack, Danny, 'The Australian Catholic Worker Newspaper 1936-76: A Political and Intellectual History', MA, University of Melbourne, 1985

Duffy, Fr Paul SJ, 'Catholic Judgements on the Origin and Growth of the ALP Dispute 1954-61', Political Science Dept., University of Melbourne, 1967

Harris, Alana, 'Spirituality and Social Identity – The Children of Mary', BA Hons, History, University of Melbourne, 2002

Moore, D., 'Migration Pressure in Catholic schools', M.Ed., Melbourne University, 1981.

Moorhead, Mary, 'The Roman Catholic Archdiocese of Melbourne 1945-1965', MA, Humanities, LaTrobe University, c.1994

Wilson, Michael, 'Changing Society and Changing Church: the Second Vatican Council and the Liturgy", MA, Dept. of Religious Studies, LaTrobe University, 1987

Newspapers and Journals

Australasian Catholic Record

Catholic Worker

Footprints

Journal of the Australian Catholic History Society

News Weekly

The Advocate

The Tribune

Tinteán

INDEX

A Path Is Set 242

A View From the Ridge 222

Abyssinia 95-6, 112

Adami, Val 84, 185

Adams, Judge Arthur 84, 111, 113, 219

Adams, Edward 17

Adams, Lily 111

Advocate, see *The Advocate*

Agagianian, Cardinal Grigor

Aggiorniamento 186, 197

Anglican Church 23, 58

Anglo-Irish war and treaty 12, 14, 30

Anstey, Frank 63

Archbishop Mannix scholarships 161, 175, 206

Archdiocese of Melbourne xiv, 16, 37, 112-4, 207-8, 241, 256-7, 261-2

statistics 5-6, 57, 114-5, 165-6, 212, 254, 267-9

organizational structure 3, 15, 37, 90, 207-8, 240, 255-6

Architecture 115-7, 247-8

Arnold, Josie 25, 274

Around the Boree Log 56

Asia 169, 200-3

Association for the Propagation of the Faith 128, 161, 173, 197

Austral Light 16, 85, 89

Austral Wines & Spirits Agency 45

Australasian Catholic Directory 5

Australia: The Catholic Chapter 166

Australian Broadcasting Commission 94, 108, 133, 175

Australian Catholic Federation 6, 91, 127

Australian Catholic Truth Society 6

Australian Dream 104

Australian Dictionary of Biography 152

ALP Labor Party – Victorian branch 12, 57-9, 192-3

Australian National Secretariat for Catholic Action 102, 106, 150-1

Australian Natives Association 6, 46

Australian Security Intelligence Organization 123-4

Australia's Secret War 122

Aveling, J.C.H. 271

Balfour, Arthur 14

Ballarat 59

Ballarat Echo 63

Balmain 155

Barbara Halliday 56

Bards in Bondage 143

Barry, Bill 57

Barry, Bishop John 15, 30, 37

Barry, Judge John 71, 99

Beek, Fr Joseph SJ 201

Belgium 76-9, 158, 237

Bellamine College, Rome 201

Belloc, Hiliare 76

Belloc House 152, 158-9, 200

Bellow, Saul 271

Bendigo 59, 62

Benedictine order x, 94

Beovich, Archbishop Matthew 37, 86, 109, 129, 159, 245, 255

Billings, Drs Evelyn & John 203, 218, 254, 262

Blackburn, Maurice 60, 107

Blessed Sacrament Fathers xi, 24, 212

Bolte, Sir Henry 192, 212, 227

Bourke, Bill 154, 184

Bourke, Fr John SJ & the Bourke family 220

Bowler, Prof. James 227

Boyd, Robin 116

Boylan, Fr Eustace SJ 22, 41, 176, 203

Bradley, Desmond 223

Brenan, Dr Andrew 68, 217-8

Brenan, Alderman J.J. & Mrs 68

Brenan, Dr John 217

Brendáin, G. 89

Brennan, Anna 41, 62, 113

Brennan, Frank 7, 34, 45, 62-3, 74

Brennan, Niall 235, 259

Brennan, Thomas 36, 61-2, 161

Broderick, Fr Joseph 227

Broderick, Walter 175

Brookes, Sir Dallas 186

Brosnan, Fr John 91, 210

Bruce, Lord 60, 89

Bruce, Mary Grant 56

Buckley, Maurice 28-9

Buckley, Prof. Vincent 157, 161, 178, 206, 221-2, 237

Buckley & Nunn 21

Burke Hall 47

Burke, T.M. 34, 46-7, 61, 159, 174, 178

Burns Oates 232, 243

Businessmen 43-8, 174-6

Butler, Tom 220, 235

Buxton, John & family 44-5, 55, 220

Buxton, Dame Rita 219

Cabrini Sisters and Hospital xi, 112, 139

Cade, Dr John 219

Cain, John jnr 265

Cain, John snr 58, 60, 152-3, 182-3, 189

Callil family 8

Callinan, Sir Bernard 175

Calwell, Arthur 14-5, 17, 54, 57-9, 63-7, 133, 142, 149, 155, 165, 197, 242, 262

Calwell, Mary 262

Camberwell 4, 112, 115

Cameron, Clyde 158

Campion, Fr Edmund 258

Campion Society xiv, 40, 81-91, 106, 108, 158, 185, 235

Capitalism xiii, 44, 76, 80

Capuchin order xi, 173

Carboni, Archbishop Romolo 196

Cardijn, Cardinal Joseph 76, 78, 158, 233

Carey, Dean 15, 30

Caritas Christi Hospice 112

Carr, Archbishop Thomas x, 13, 17, 37, 90, 197, 216

Carroll, Archbishop James 184, 196

Casey, Lord 55, 186

Castles, Amy 43

Catarinich, Dr John & family 68-9

Cathedral Hall 132

Catholic Action 101-4, 106-7, 123, 125-7, 131, 133, 150-8, 166, 169, 182-7, 196-7, 208, 279

Catholic Action At Work 154

Catholic Central Library 7, 38, 40, 84

Catholic charities 112-4

Catholic Church international 51

Catholic Church Sydney x, xii, 108

Catholic education 8, 37-8, 47, 109, 191, 174, 176, 232

Catholic Evidence Guild 40, 78, 84-5, 173

Catholic Family Planning Centre 209, 253

Catholic Family Welfare Bureau 209

Catholic Guild for Social Studies 79

Catholic Health Association of India 202

'Catholic Hour' 39-40, 82, 84-5, 100, 107-8, 200, 208-10

Catholic Ladies College 3, 66, 260

Catholic Life Exhibition 177

Catholic Migration Committee 147, 208

Catholic Social Service Bureau 113, 147, 209

Catholic Social Welfare Bureau 208-9

Catholic Welfare Organization 114, 121, 147,

Catholic Worker 100-1, 185-6, 193-5, 198-9, 235-7, 249-50, 257-9

Catholic Workers Association 18, 127

Catholic Women's Guild of Victoria 41-2

Catholic War Veterans' Association 114

Catholic Young Men's Society 6-7, 13, 18, 37, 47-8, 62-3, 65, 84, 126

Catholics and the Free Society 231

Cattaneo, Archbishop Bartolomeo 231

Celtic Club 6, 20, 220, 222

Centenary Celebrations 92, 162-4

Central Catholic Peace Commission 104-5

Chain of Light 172

Chamberlin, Sir Michael 7, 17, 46-8, 84, 159, 174-5, 186, 219, 232, 262

Chapman, Geoffrey 232

Charlesworth, Prof. Max 161, 195, 227, 230-1, 235

Chesterton, G.K. 76-7, 79, 98, 200

Chifley, Benedict 143, 152, 169-70

Christian Brothers xi, 3, 5, 58, 158, 170-1, 211-2, 222, 276

CBC St Bernards 171

CBC St Josephs 4, 14, 47, 64, 109, 111, 158, 190-1, 207, 280

CBC St Kevins 4, 7, 142,175-7

CBC Parade 3-4, 47, 59, 224

CBC St Kilda 5, 222

Christian Democratic Party, Italy 76, 151

Church, State and Conscience 230

Church history 17, 81, 164-6

Cistercian order 175

Clareborough, Dr John 68, 121, 218

Clark, Colin 177

Clarke, Bishop Leo 233

Cluny Sisters xi, 159

Cody family 34, 45, 38

Coffey, Bishop Jeremiah xii

Colahan, Dr Fred 218, 220

Collected Poems 1930-1981 178

Collingwood 3, 59, 89, 158, 174

Collins, Michael 11, 35, 40

Collins, Fr W.M. 15, 18, 34

Colum, Padraig 222

Columban Missionary Society 128, 173

Commonwealth Investigation Service 123-4

Communism xii-xix, 52, 75, 77, 86, 97, 99-100, 107, 127, 150, 154-5, 169, 184, 186, 191, 196, 200-1, 231, 258-9

Communist Party of Australia 123, 151, 155, 169, 185, 234

Conditions of Economic Growth 177

Connelly, Sir Francis & Lady Lurline 160

Connor, Judge Xavier 221

Conscience and Its Right to Freedom 230

Conscription xii, 9, 12, 36, 42, 49, 63, 133, 192, 198, 204, 261, 277

Contraception xiv, 103, 210, 239, 251-4, 272

Conway, Ronald 172, 200, 228, 237

Cooney, Hubert 165

Coral Sea, Battle of 140

Corporatism 80

Corpus Christi College, Werribee 38-40, 47, 68, 164, 264

Costigan, Michael 257-9

Council for Civil Liberties 71

Country Party 60, 73, 75, 142, 153

Cremean, Bert 3, 57, 64, 105, 107, 125-7

Cullinane, Bishop John 216, 241

Cummings, Bart 175

Cunningham, Don 259

Curtin, John 58, 99, 121, 123-4, 127, 133, 139, 141-2, 152, 189

Cussen, Sir Leo & family 69-70

Cutting Green Hay 206

Daly, Jean 196

Daly, Dame Mary 140-1

Daly, Sister Mary Berchmans 66

D'Arcy, Archbishop Eric 194-5, 230-1, 241, 263

Davitt, Michael 20

Dawson, Christopher 76, 82

D'Cruz, Vin 201

Deakin, Bishop Hilton 241

Decline in religious observance 267-71

De Gaulle, General Charles 32, 89, 99

De Gruchy, Prof. Carl 218

De La Salle Brothers xi, 3-4

Democratic Labor Party 189, 192, 198-9, 201, 212, 215-6, 234-40, 248-9, 265-6

Demons and Democrats

Depression, Great 47-8, 62, 73-7, 85, 101, 113-4

De Valera, Eamon 10-11, 33-6, 42, 49, 64, 88, 91, 123, 163-5, 176

Develop Australia League 47, 61

Devine, Sir Hugh 66-7

Devine, Dr John 67

Dictators 52, 54, 85-8, 95

Distributism 80

Divini Redemptoris 97

Dixon, Sir Owen 70

Doyle, Dr Leo 68

Druid's Benefit Society 46, 68

Duffy, Gavan 204

Duffy, Fr Paul SJ 242

Dunphy, Judge Edward 220

Dunstan, Albert 61, 75, 104, 142

Easter Rebellion xii, 19, 31, 62, 162, 276

Ebsworth, Fr Walter 166, 243

Eccles, Sir John 68

Ecclesiastical suppliers 20-2

Egan, Fr Matthew SJ 7

E.J. Dwyer 232

Ellis, Fr Kevin 141

Erin Go Bragh 222

Essendon 4, 75, 141, 170-1

Eucharistic Congress 1934 91-3

Eureka rebellion 59

Evatt, Dr H.V. 133, 157, 170, 180-9

Fascism 54, 78, 81, 86, 99-100

Federated Ironworkers Association
    155

Fitzgerald, Dr Eileen 42

Fitzgerald, Paul 223

Fitzpatrick, Brian 71

Fitzpatrick, Kathleen 45, 55-6, 203

Flynn, Julia 41

Foley, Bishop Daniel 33

Footprints 244

Forde, Frank 142

Fox, Bishop Arthur 17, 37-8, 129,
    132, 208, 228, 233, 241

France xi-xii, 76, 83-4, 99, 150

Franco, General Francisco 97-8

Frazer, Judge Archibald 220

Frazer, Sir James 138, 273

Frederico, Judge Hubert 220

Freedom newspaper 126

French influence xi, 20, 76-9, 83, 116,
    199, 236-7

Galbally, Frank 59

Galbally, Dr Kath 181

Galbally, John 59

Gartner, John 143, 166-7, 178

Gasquet, Cardinal Francis 30

Gaunts jewellers 21

Gavan Duffy, Sir Frank 70

Gavan Duffy, George 70

Genazzano Convent 4

German Centre Party 76

Gilroy, Cardinal Norman x, 34, 129,
    134-5, 154, 162, 182, 193, 196-7,
    207, 217, 261

Girschik, Helga 227

Glen Waverley Seminary 212-3, 255

Glowrey, Dr Sr Mary 41, 202-3, 262

Gobbo, Sir James 220

Golden, Fr Jerry SJ 157, 236

Goold, Bishop James 163-4, 176, 244

Gorman, Sir Eugene 71, 121

Gott, Ken 266

Goulding, Caroline ('Catherine Kaye')
    110

Gowans, Sir Gregory 220

Gracias, Cardinal Valerian 180, 201

Grail, The 103, 113-4

Greer, Germaine 223, 230, 272

Grey Sisters 42, 112

Griffin, James 227, 235

Groupers 153-6, 182, 189, 193, 196

Gruber, Dr Georg 223-4

Gsell, Bishop F.X. 142

Guild of St Luke 112

Guild Socialism 80

Guntur, India 202, 262

Haag, Stefan 224

Hackett, Fr William SJ 7, 39-40, 51,
    83, 85, 90-1, 151, 176, 203

Hagelthorne, Florence 143, 243,

Hagelthorne, Frederick 242

Haley, Martin 143, 177, 221

Hannan family 164, 244, 264

Hannan, Mons. James 111, 129, 161-2

Hart, Archbishop Denis 229

Hawthorn 4

Hawthorn Press 143, 164, 166-7, 178

Hayden, Dr Frank 218

Hayden, Prof. John 218

Hayes, Bishop Romuald 128

Head, Archbishop Frederick 92

Heagney, Muriel 99

Heffey, Gerard 82, 220, 235

Heffey, Fr John 104

Henderson, Gerard 204, 235

Henderson, Dr Keith 218

Heinze, Sir Bernard & Lady Valerie 94, 109

Hennessy, Sir David 160

Hennessy, Dr Raymond 68

Hibernians 6-7, 17, 37, 44, 209

Hidden Ireland 11

Hince, Kenneth 223

History of the Catholic Church in Australasia 244

Hitler, Adolf 52, 76, 85-7, 95-6, 99-100, 104-5, 107, 121-2, 137, 263

Hogan, E.J. ('Ned') 34, 57-8, 60-1, 63, 73-5, 121, 153

Hogan, Eldon 175

Hogan, James (1) 16

Hogan James (2) 45-6, 175-6

Holt, Harold 169

Holt, R.W. 186

Horan, Dr John 218-9

Horner, David 124

Holy Name Society 114, 126, 210

Hospitals 6, 23, 112, 217, 270

Howe, Irving 275

Howells, Fr Ian SJ 42

Hughes, William 12, 14, 29, 51, 58, 60, 122, 124, 159

Humanae Vitae 25-3, 258

Humphries, Barry 4-5, 158

Hurley, Dr John Gavan 68

Immigration xii, 6, 8, 139, 147-50, 170, 229, 255

Industrial groups 152, 155, 185-8

Ingwersen, Dr Stan 98

Institute of Social Order 152-3, 177, 200, 234

Ireland ix, xii, 6, 9-12, 29-38, 43, 49-53, 83, 90-1, 135, 165, 221, 276

Irish Civil War 35-7

Irish Exiles in Australia 165

Irish Free Staters 10, 35

Irish Ireland League 6, 17, 33, 262

Irish Republicans 10, 35

Irish Review 37, 64, 149

Italian immigrants 8

Italian influence xi, 43, 53, 112, 116, 138-9

Ives, Burl 108-9

Jackson, Denys 18, 77-85, 87-8, 99-100, 104-5, 107, 134, 200, 263

Jackson, Commander Robert 178

Jageurs, Peter & Morgan 16, 21, 36

Jansenism xi

Japanese militarism 52

Jesuits xi, 3, 21-2, 37-41, 51, 58, 69-70, 139, 152, 176, 201, 203, 264

Jewish plight 87, 137, 148, 226

Johnston, Fr Henry SJ 18, 40, 85, 176, 264

Jones, Basil 94, 109, 165

Jones, Fr Genesius 210

Jones, Percy, snr. 18

Jones, Dr Percy 18, 43, 85, 93-4, 108-10, 163, 165, 167, 173, 194-5, 223, 241, 244, 263

Journey With A Stranger 224

Journeyings 54, 245, 265

Joyce, James 23, 198

Kairos 264

Keane, Dr William 218

Keating, Frank 106-7

Kelly, Archbishop Michael x, 83, 88, 131-2

Kelly, Fr John 99, 236

Kelly, Kevin 84, 93, 98, 100-2

Kennelly, Pat Senator 14, 23, 63, 153, 170, 180-1, 216

Kenny, Dr Leo 17, 67-8, 72, 91, 93, 104, 112, 114

Keon, Stan 126, 153-4, 175-6, 179, 182, 184, 203, 266

Kew 4, 45, 112, 115, 158-60, 220

Kiernan, Colm 165

Kiernan, Dr T.J. 81, 165

King, Fr Michael 210

King, Dr Tom 218-9

Knights of the Southern Cross 7, 47

Knopfelmacher, Dr Frank 191

Knorr, Hans & Hilda 224-6

Knowles, Marion Miller 15, 17, 20-1, 56, 110

Knox, Cardinal James 203, 240, 244, 254-9, 262

Knox, Mons. Ronald xii, 77, 79, 98

Koo Wee Rup 8

Kung, Fr Hans 257

Lalor, Peter 59

Last Poems 221

'La Verna' 159

League for an Undivided Ireland 37, 64, 165

League of St Thomas More 72

Lebanese immigrants 8

Legal profession 69-72, 219-220

Legge, Jack 98

Legion of Mary, The 103, 108, 114, 172-3

Lenin, Vladimir 85

Lepanto, Battle of 80, 276

Letters From Rome 96

Liberal Party xv, 59, 104, 148, 189, 192, 216, 240, 266

Linehan, William 17, 232

Linnane, Fr T.J. 244

Liston, J.J. 46, 69, 91

Little, Archbishop Frank 233, 244, 261

Liturgy 22, 40, 94, 100, 108, 117, 164, 195, 245-7, 255, 257, 263

Lloyd George, David 32, 128

Lombard, Fr Frank 157

Lonergan, Bishop J.J. 7, 37, 42, 111, 113, 129, 208, 240

Louvain 7, 78, 132, 195

Lovegrove, Dinny 125

Lunn, Arnold 98, 191

Lynch, Sir Phillip & Lady Leah 240

Lyons, Bishop Patrick 37, 129, 158-9, 171, 184, 198, 208, 241

Lyons, Dame Enid 113, 170

Lyons, Joseph 73-4, 85, 160

MacEwan, Fr Sydney 163

Macnab, Francis 273

MacRory, Cardinal 92-3

MacKillop, St Mother Mary 261

McAuley, James 178, 231, 234, 262, 273

McCalman, Janet 54, 245, 265

McCarthy, Br Frank 222

McCarthy, Fr Timothy 121, 140

McCullagh, Francis 52

McGuire, Paul & Frances 77-9, 93, 99, 102, 169-170

McHale, Jock 59, 174

McInerney, Sir Murray 81-2, 102, 220

McKenna, Senator Nick 15, 216, 265

McMahon, William (1) 17, 91

McMahon, William, (2) 240, 265

McManus, Senator Frank 64-5, 126-7, 134, 153, 158, 240, 242, 262

Mackle, Francis 16

Madden, Sir John 44, 69

Madden, Walter 44

Maher, Frank 61, 81, 84, 101

Malone, Fr J.J. 17, 91, 162

Maloney, Dr William

Malvern 4, 29, 12, 160

Mangan, Fr William 16, 36

Mannix, Archbishop Daniel ix, x, xii-xiv, 13, 27-8, 35-7, 58, 62, 77, 90-1, 114, 129, 132, 134-5, 142, 160-2, 179-80, 185, 187-9, 196-7, 213, 243

aristocrat 88-90

last years 206-8, 227-9

overseas trips 30-5, 49-51

privacy 51, 88, 206

relation to the Movement 123-5

relation to Santamaria 205-5

sadness & humour ix, 11,50-1, 206, 228

speeches 6,9-11, 150, 160, 206

strategist 127-8

tribal chieftain 9-12

Maritain, Jacques 77, 82, 157

Martin, Phillip 178, 221

Maryknoll settlement 104

Maurras, Charles 52-3

Mayer, Prof. Henry 231

Maynes, John 204

Maynooth Seminary x, 38, 88, 89

Meanjin 178

Medical profession 66-8, 217-9

Melbourne Before Mannix ix

Melbourne Catholic 265

Melbourne Cricket Club 70, 219

Melbourne Cricket Ground 46-7, 110, 172

Melbourne Diocesan Historical Commission 244

Melbourne Irish-Catholic community 8, 13, 36, 229

Melbourne & Metropolitan Board of Works 46

Memories Guide My Hand 226

Memory Ireland 222

Menzies, Sir Robert 55, 70, 74, 89-90, 104, 121, 123-4, 159, 169, 191-2, 215, 217, 223, 240, 265

Mercer, Gerald 204

Mercy Academy 3, 227

Mercy Private Hospital 241

Merlo, John 81

Merner, Fr Francis 44

Mexico 52-3

Midway, Battle of 140

Military Vicariate 12, 173

Mimovich, Mrs 224-6

Minogue, Dinny 166

Minogue, Sir John 220

Missionaries of the Sacred Heart 129

Modotti, Fr Ugo SJ 112, 139

Moffit, Constance 113

Molomby, Tom 220

Molony, Prof. John 242

Monahan, Sir Robert 220

Monash University 70, 174, 177, 232

Moran, Bishop Laurence 37, 207-8, 233, 240, 242

Moran, Cardinal Patrick x, 12, 78, 124, 244, 261

Morgan, Dr Frank 218

Morgan, Bishop J.A. ('Alo') 140, 158, 264

Mornane, Thomas 220

Morning Star Boys' Home 112

Morrison, Fr Ken 141

Morton, Dr Murray 66

Mother Dorothea 218

Mother Eymard Temby 222-3

Mother Fabian 218

Mother Teresa of Calcutta, St 204, 255-6

Mount, Frank 201

Mount St Evin's Hospital 66, 93

Movement, The xi,11, 42, 77-9, 104-8,131, 133-5, 144, 150-8, 161, 167, 170,179-189, 193-9, 204, 220, 231, 250, 253, 261-2, 279

Movement in Asia, The 200-1

Moynihan, Fr Francis 15, 36, 111, 144, 167-8, 243

Mullens, John 127, 154, 182, 184

Mulvaney, Prof. John 161

Murphy, Agnes 35, 42-3

Murphy, Delia 165

Murphy, Fr Denis 168, 259

Murphy, Frank 84, 110, 143, 164, 166, 243

Murphy, Fr Jeremiah SJ 39, 51, 61, 85, 93, 176

Murray, Fr Courtney SJ 230

Murray, Robert 152, 204

Murtagh, Fr James 243

Mussolini, Benito 53-4, 76, 80-1, 86-97

National Archives of Australia 124

National Catholic Girls Movement 103, 154

National Catholic Rural Movement 61, 81, 101

National Civic Council 90, 103, 107, 192, 198, 200-1, 233-4, 250

National Trustees, Executors & Agency Company 44, 48, 174

National University of Ireland 38-40

Nationalist Party 12, 14, 59,

Naughton, Rachel 244

Nazism 87, 99, 137, 223, 226

Nazi-Soviet Pact 105, 107, 121

Nechwatal, Otto 223

Neither Power Nor Glory 12

Nerney, Fr John SJ 72

Newman College 7, 8, 59, 68, 81, 84-5, 93, 104, 116, 161, 167, 174-6, 217

Newman, Cardinal Henry 50, 77, 98, 134-5

Newman Society 6, 36, 38-9, 41, 52, 157-8, 199, 204, 221, 227, 232, 236-7, 250

News Weekly 126, 185, 200, 234, 250

Niall, Brenda 42, 129, 159, 280

Niall, Dr Frank 159

Niemeyer, Sir Otto 74

'No Mean City' 162

North Melbourne 4, 23, 59, 75, 133, 158, 171-3, 242

Oakley, Barry 223. 252, 272, 275

O'Bryan, Sir Norman & family 70-1, 186, 218-9, 220, 223, 280

O'Connell, Maude 42

O'Day, Dr Gerald 99

O'Day, Dr Kevin 68

O'Donnell, Dr Nicholas 16, 63

O'Driscoll, Judge J.X. 4, 220

O'Dwyer, Barry 227

O'Dwyer, Joseph 144, 177-8, 273

O'Flanagan, Fr Michael 35-6

O'Hearn, Dinny 222

O'Kane, Frances 242

O'Keefe case 148

O'Kelly, Sean 35-6

O'Leary, Patrick 18-20, 54, 56, 87, 91, 98-9, 142-3, 166-8, 177, 242-3

O'Loughlin, Count Thomas 17

Onger, Hans 224

Ordinariate for Anglicans 172

Ormonde, Senator James 181, 184, 235

Orwell, George 86, 273

O'Sullivan, Dr John 68

Pacific Institute 201

Page, Percy 175

Pallottine order xi, 129,137-9, 159

Palmer, Vance & Nettie 19, 98, 143

Panico, Archbishop Giovanni 128-135, 139-40, 184, 261

Parer family 8-9, 113, 142, 159

Parker, Mary 223

Partito Popolare Italiano 53

Payne, Thomas 116, 167

Pell, Cardinal George 229, 251, 261, 270

Pelligrinis xi, 21, 24

Perkins, Bishop Eric 147

Peyton, Fr Patrick xii, 92, 172

Phelan, Bishop Patrick 35, 37, 90

Philosophies in Collision 234

Pierce, Fr John 121

Piety x, 22-5, 103, 117, 210, 236, 246, 249

Pioneer Catholic Victoria 166

Pitt, Sr Ethel 203

Pitt families 44-5, 203

Poems 178

Poetry and Morality 221

Poetry and the Sacred 221

'Point of View' 232

Pope Benedict XV 128

Pope Benedict XVI 251, 222

Pope John XXIII 244

Pope John Paul II 251, 272, 222-3

Pope Leo XIII xiii

Pope Paul VI 251, 255, 261, 227

Pope Pius XI 52, 97

Pope Pius XII 104, 191, 212

Population 4, 6, 148, 170-1, 232, 255, 258, 266-9

Power, Fr Albert SJ 38-9, 176

Power Without Glory 179-181

Prasko, Bishop Ivan 173

Prelude to Catholic Action 102

Premiers' Plan 74

Prendergast, George Michael 58, 60, 63

Presentation Convents x 1, 5

Professional Men's Sodality 72

Propaganda College, Rome 94, 109, 134, 161, 255

Protestant Churches 5, 12, 14, 36, 44, 54, 56, 158, 172, 195, 210, 216, 242, 265, 274

Publications 84, 164, 166-8, 237, 264

Quadragesimo Anno 76, 81, 83, 101

Quadrant 234-5

Raheen 37, 47, 51, 79, 88, 90, 112, 137, 158-9, 162,

Redemptorist order xi, 22, 159, 245

Reid, Alan 184, 242

Reis, Fr Con SJ 147, 208

Religious Art in Australia 224

Rerum Novarum xiii, 63, 76

Restoring All Things 102

Richmond 3, 46, 59, 99, 1339, 154, 175

Roman Catholic Trusts Corporation 174

Royal Australasian College of Surgeons 67

Rush family 68, 218

Russia 52

Russo, Dr Peter 99

Ryan, Dr Edward 68, 159, 218

Ryan, Fr Paddy 107, 126

Sacre Coeur Convent, Glen Iris xi, 4

Sacred Heart Church, Kew 4

Sacred Heart Hospital, Moreland

Sacred Heart parish, Carlton 22

St Aloysius Convent, North Melbourne 4, 170

St Augustine's Church, Melbourne 23

St Benedict's Hospital, Malvern 112

St Bernard's Church, East Coburg 224, 247

St Clare's Church, North Box Hill 247

St Columba's Convent, Essendon 4, 170

St Dominic's Church, Camberwell 4, 115

St Francis' Church, Melbourne 15, 22-5

St Francis Xavier's, Prahan 248

St George's Church, Carlton 22, 173, 195

St Gregory's Church, Doncaster 247

St Ignatius' Church, Richmond 3, 6, 139

St Joan's Alliance 113

St Mary's Church, West Melbourne 15, 116, 132, 158

St Mary's Hall, Parkville 7, 61

St Patrick's Cathedral 24-5, 31, 51, 72, 89, 109, 116, 141, 165, 167, 223, 228, 233, 243-4, 260, 262, 274

St Patrick's College, East Melbourne 3, 164, 269

St Patrick's Day march 26, 29, 55, 260

St Patrick's Society 6

St Peter's Anglican Church, East Melbourne 22-3

St Peter's Church, Highett 248

St Vincent de Paul Society xi, 37, 114

St Vincent's Hospital, Fitzroy xi, 15, 36, 66-8, 135-7, 171, 175, 218-9, 253, 262

Sale 194, 208, 241

Salesian Order xi, 92, 112

San Isidore settlement 104

Santa Maria Convent, Northcote 4, 170

Santamaria, B.A. 53-4, 77-81, 84, 90, 98, 134, 138, 156, 181-4, 195-6, 199-200, 232, 262

Saul, Fr John 223

Scalabrinian Fathers xi, 173

Schools Provident Fund 172

Schüller, Prof. Arthur & Margarete 135-7

Scullin, James 7, 17, 34, 46, 55-74, 180

Scully, Frank 185, 189

Sculpture of Leopoldine Mimovich 226

Seal, Dr Eric 218

Second Vatican Council, see Vatican II

Self Determination for Ireland League 20, 34

Serong, Brig. William 201

Sevenhill Wines 21, 45

Sharpley, Cecil 155

Sheed, Frank & Maisie Ward 78, 84-5, 232

Sheehan, Archbishop Michael 129

Sheen, Bishop Fulton xi, 163, 172

Shamrock and Wattle Bloom 56

Short, Laurie 155

Shorthill, Thomas 35-6

*Sing Me That Lovely Song Again...*227

Simonds, Archbishop Justin 36, 50, 78, 103, 106, 129-34, 140, 147, 151, 170, 181-4, 188, 193, 197, 207-8, 215, 217, 228, 232-3, 240-2, 248, 254, 256-7, 262

Sinn Fein 32, 49

Sisters of Charity 4, 66, 217

Sisters of Mercy 112

Socialism xiii, 79-80, 99, 123

Society of Jesus, see Jesuits

Solid Bluestone Foundations 45, 55-6

Solly, Robert 160

South Melbourne 5, 59, 112

Soviet Union 52, 97, 99, 105-7, 121-5, 169, 191, 239, 258

Spanish Civil War 53, 97-8, 182-9

Spanish immigration 8

Spellman, Cardinal Francis 163

Spender, Sir Percy 122

Split, The xiv, 132, 156-7, 192-200, 204-8, 217, 230, 235, 239-42, 248-9, 255, 262, 265-6, 277

Stalin, Joseph 20, 95, 105, 122

State Aid 7, 56, 62, 175, 216-7

Stewart, Bishop Bernard 4, 84, 139-40, 158-9, 277

Stormon, Fr E.J. SJ 156, 209-10

Stout, Vic 125-6

Strangio, Paul 12, 57-8

Studley Park 3, 112, 137, 158-9

Sturzo, Don 53-4, 76

Subsidiarity 80, 233

Sydney Catholicism 12-13, 83, 102, 126, 127-30, 133, 162, 184, 188, 196, 207, 235, 261, 268

'Syllabus of Errors' xiii, 244

Syme, Dr George 68

Talks About Poets and Poetry 162

Tehan family 104

The Advocate xiv, 15, 18, 32, 35, 61-2, 69, 73 ,79, 84, 87, 95-7, 110-1, 122-7, 154-5, 164-6, 187, 198, 243-4, 256-9

The Age 14, 85, 223

The Argus 26, 43, 243

The Australian Hymnal 108

The Billings Method 253

The Bulletin 19, 56, 78

The Clowns of God 222

The Defence of Australia 201

The Devil's Advocate 222

The Earth Our Mother 104

The Feet of Daniel Mannix 223

The Footprints of Our Catholic Pioneers 16

The Golden Bough 273

The Heart of the School 41

The Herald 177

The Incarnation and the University 237

The Irish Review 37, 64, 149

The Madonna 22, 41, 176

The Messenger of the Sacred Heart 22, 41, 176

The Old Munster Circuit 11

The Ovulation Method 253

The Purple East 162

The Rats of Tobruk 67

The Roman Mould of the Australian Catholic Church 242

The Sculptures of Hans Knorr 224

The Shoes of the Fisherman 222

The Southern Cross 78

The Split 204

The Tablet 196

The Thirteenth Greatest of Centuries 80

The Tribune 16-7, 22, 35-6, 64, 79, 88, 91, 94, 96, 127, 149, 167, 198, 232, 234, 260

The Turning Year 178

The World of Our Fathers 275

The World's Flesh 221

Theodore, Edward 73

Therry Society 108, 110

Tipping, E.W ('Bill') 177

Tobin Brothers 75

Tobin, Greg 242

Trades Hall Council 74-5, 125-6, 265

Triado, Ray 81, 104

Twentieth Century 152, 177, 234

Tyrrell, Sir Murray 220

Ukrainian Uniate Church, North Melbourne 173

United Australia Party 74

University of Melbourne 94, 97, 108, 161, 194, 226, 230, 236

Vatican xiii, xiv, 27, 30, 51, 53, 81, 86, 128-32, 135, 170, 222, 232, 248, 253, 255-6, 262-2

Vatican decision 196-8, 235, 268

Vatican II 17, 199, 213, 226, 236, 239, 243, 244-53, 255, 257-9, 268

Vesters, Bishop Gerard 142

Victoria x, 6, 16-18, 29, 55-6, 59-62, 69-70, 73, 84, 92, 143, 152, 166, 184, 187, 199, 216, 265

Victoria Cross 27-9

Victorian Cities 88

Victorian Football Association 46

Victorian Irish Association 64, 91

Victorian Socialist Party 12, 58-9, 152

Vienna Mozart Boys Choir 223-4

Vietnam War xiv, 105, 169, 201, 239-40, 258, 263

Villa Maria 113

Vodola, Fr Max 262

Wallace, Mons. Tom 207

Walsh, J.M. 19, 44

Walsh, T.P. 19, 35

Walton, George 110

Ward, Barbara 177

Wardell, William 116

Warner, Denis

We Hold These Truths 230

Welfare organizations 42, 113-4, 121, 147, 208-10, 270

West, Morris 222

What's Wrong With Australia? 75

'Whelan the Wrecker' family 75

White Australia policy 6, 103, 128, 147-8, 231

Wild-Briar and Wattle Bloom 162

Winter, Joseph 16, 168

Women's organizations 41-3

Worms, Fr Ernest 137-8, 273

Wren, John 3, 26, 29, 34, 45-7, 59-60, 154, 159, 174-5, 179-81, 227

Wrestling With Asia 201

Xavier College 4, 19, 40-1, 47, 160-1, 176-7, 223

Young Catholic Students 103

Young Christian Workers 77, 103, 147, 154, 157-8, 197-9, 205, 233

Zika, Mila & Heda and family 226

www.ingramcontent.com/pod-product-compliance
Lightning Source LLC
Chambersburg PA
CBHW051952270326
41929CB00015B/2624